# WEST OF IRELAND

## Connemara, Galway, & the Burren

DIRECT FROM
IRELAND

# WEST OF IRELAND

## Connemara, Galway, & the Burren

Trish Fitzpatrick and Tony Whilde

PASSPORT BOOKS
a division of *NTC Publishing Group*
Lincolnwood, Illinois USA

This edition was first published in 1995 by Passport Books, a division of
NTC Publishing Group, 4255 West Touhy Avenue, Lincolnwood (Chicago),
Illinois 60646–1975 U.S.A.

Originally published in Ireland by
Gill & Macmillan Ltd
Goldenbridge
Dublin 8
© text Trish Fitzpatrick and Tony Whilde 1995
© line artwork Pádraic Reaney 1992
© maps Gill & Macmillan 1992
Designed by Design Image, Dublin
Print origination by
Seton Music Graphics Ltd, Bantry, Co. Cork
Printed in Ireland by ColourBooks Ltd, Dublin

ISBN 0–8442–9712–7
Library of Congress Catalog Card Number 95–67860

Maps in this book are based on
the Ordnance Survey by permission
of the Government (Permit No. 5587).

# CONTENTS

# INTRODUCTION TO THE GUIDE

Each of the guide's sections has an introduction giving a brief history of the area, an ecotour, useful information, suggested excursions by car and by bicycle, activities for children, activities for rainy days, daytime and evening entertainments, where to eat, where to shop and where to stay.

The 'where to eat' sections are not good food guides. The information given is to assist visitors locate suitable or convenient places to eat. Similarly, the 'where to stay' sections are not evaluations of the accommodation. A list of hotels, rented accommodation, hostels and caravan parks is given for each area. The bed and breakfast establishments are not listed in detail as there are many homes offering this type of accommodation in the regions. Displayed outside a house offering bed and breakfast will be a sign indicating 'Bed and Breakfast', 'B/B', 'Guests', 'Room and Breakfast' or 'Accommodation'. In Gaeltacht areas the word 'Lóistín' is displayed.

The Irish Tourist Board, Bord Fáilte, advises visitors to stay only in those homes which are registered with the Board. Registered houses may display a shamrock or say 'I.T.B. approved' on their sign. Visitors can be confident that houses registered and approved by Bord Fáilte provide a high standard of comfort and hygiene. All registered homes may be contacted through the Tourist Office in Árus Fáilte, Victoria Place, Galway, and for a small fee your accommodation can be booked in advance by the Tourist Office.

Other homes not registered with Bord Fáilte may offer an equally good standard of accommodation. It may be that the owners have only just started offering hospitality and have not yet contacted the Board or that they prefer not to be affiliated.

Many guest-houses provide en-suite bathroom/shower facilities. Many will prepare an evening meal or direct guests to local restaurants. Most houses and hotels levy a surcharge on single guests using double rooms. Some will have single accommodation at single rates. Some homes have family rooms, with extra beds put in for children, at a moderate extra cost.

If travelling around without having made reservations during the high season (July and August) it is probably wiser to book into your accommodation by 6 p.m. or 7 p.m.

You may ask to look at the accommodation without obligation to stay, but once you have entered into a verbal agreement to stay you will be expected to take up the accommodation and pay the stated rate. Currently, this is between £12 and £15 for room and breakfast, although this is not a compulsory charge.

Usually you will be offered a traditional Irish breakfast of cereal, fried bacon/eggs/sausages, brown bread and toast. Some hostesses/hosts offer a menu. If you prefer a 'continental style' or vegetarian breakfast you should say so. If you want breakfast at an earlier time than stated, you should ask if this is possible. Your hostess/host will be anxious to make you feel at home. In some homes you will be offered a key if you intend to be out late. If you wish to prolong your stay in any one house tell your hostess/host at breakfast. Sometimes a cheaper rate can be agreed for longer stays.

The rate for self-catering accommodation is not given or indicated in this guide as it varies throughout the year. During the winter months the rates are modest, but they are, of course, high during June, July and August. Many of the cottages sleep up to nine people so they can be an economical way to stay in the region. Everything is provided in the rented cottages and homes down to the last little details like aluminium foil and paper towels. Visitors only have to provide their food. Only groups of purpose-built self-catering cottages or apartments have been listed. Bord Fáilte publishes a descriptive list of many registered houses, bungalows, apartments and cottages to let throughout the region. It is available from Bord Fáilte, Árus Fáilte, Victoria Place, Galway.

Hostels throughout the region charge a nightly rate of between £3 and £5 per person.

The rate charged by the hotels is indicated but visitors should always check when booking as seasonal variations and adjustments for inflation may occur.

The authors wish to state that every care was taken to ensure that the information given is accurate and up to date. They cannot, however, be held responsible for changes which may have occurred since they completed their research.

## Acknowledgments — Guide

I would like to acknowledge the research assistance of Ellie and Tom Fitzpatrick and the support and encouragement of Kevin Fitzpatrick. Thanks to Anne Kennedy for the use of her library, Jim Higgins for archaeological information, Tom Kenny for information about literary Galway, Michael Hernon of Hernon's Aran Tours for the tour of Inishmore and the owners and staff of Sheela-na-gig bookshop for information and advice. Thanks also to Shannon Development, County Clare and Bernadette Donnelly and Tom Mongan of Galway County Library. Finally, a special word of thanks to Marianne ten Cate for all her hours of unpaid proofreading.

Trish Fitzpatrick,
Moycullen.
March 1992.

## Introduction to the Ecotours

The purpose of the ecotours is to introduce you to nature in the west of Ireland by describing what can be seen at representative sites along several routes between Shannon in the south and Inishbofin in the north. It provides only a taste of what Connemara, Galway and west Clare have to offer, but I hope that it will be sufficient to evoke a sense of appreciation and caring in you, the reader. The Irish landscape and the plants and animals which bring it to life form an intricate web which, in places like Connemara and the Burren, can be easily broken. So it is my hope that you will enjoy what you experience but leave nature as you find it, for the sake of nature itself and for the people who follow.

To enhance your journey I recommend that you acquire the ½ inch to 1 mile Ordnance Survey maps 10, 11, 14 and 17 to which the grid references (e.g. Poulsallagh M088016) refer. In addition, Tim Robinson's maps of Connemara, Galway and the Burren are worthy companions and works of scholarship to be treasured long after your journey is over. Many other maps, books and leaflets about the region are available in shops and tourist offices. Some are mentioned in the text, but the large numbers of such items produced in recent years precludes us from mentioning them all.

English plant and animal names presented in the text have been listed in alphabetical order with their scientific names in the Glossary. A geological time scale is also presented (page 261) to put the names and ages of rocks referred to into context.

# A NOTE ON PLACENAMES AND ROAD NUMBERS

The placenames used in this guide are taken from the Irish Ordnance Survey ½ inch to 1 mile maps 10, 11, 14 and 17. However, you will find that placename spellings are different on some other maps and on some road signs. Unfortunately, it was not practicable for us to include all the alternative placename spellings in the text, but we do hope that you will not be too confused by the inconsistencies which you are bound to encounter.

Road numbers are taken from the Irish Ordnance Survey 1 inch to 4 miles 'Holiday map' number 2, 'Ireland west', which most closely matches the signs on the roads.

Both series of maps are readily obtainable from Tourist Offices, bookshops and some of the filling stations, supermarkets and souvenir shops in the region.

# ACKNOWLEDGMENTS —— ECOTOURS

I would like to thank Dr David Harper and Dr John Waddell for supplying geological and archaeological information respectively and for valuable discussions. Brendan Vaughan shared with me his knowledge of the history and folklore of the Cliffs of Moher and David Hogan kindly provided details of the natural history of Inishbofin.

The hospitality and help of Olwen and Michael Gill on Inishmore were very much appreciated. Island Ferries generously assisted our passages to and from Inishmore.

Trish and Pádraic were ideal companions in this co-operative effort which was initiated and skilfully guided to completion by Fergal Tobin.

Marianne ten Cate, always last but never least, typed the ecotour manuscript and helped in many other ways in the preparation of the ecotours. Thanks are not enough.

Tony Whilde,
Oughterard.
March 1992.

# THE WEATHER

The climate and weather of the West of Ireland have a profound influence on human activities, including touring, hill walking and nature study. In particular those venturing into the hills should have some knowledge and understanding of the conditions they are likely to meet.

The climate of western Ireland is largely the product of a westerly atmospheric circulation, and its proximity to the Atlantic Ocean. These two factors interact to give us westerly winds, mild damp weather and a narrow temperature range throughout the year.

Although the weather is highly variable there are a number of climatic features which appear to occur fairly regularly. During December and January there is a well-established low-pressure system over the Atlantic, spawning depressions which move rapidly eastwards bringing strong winds and abundant frontal rain. By late January, the cold anticyclonic weather centred over Europe may be extending westwards into Ireland, giving dry, cold spells, eminently suitable for outdoor activities. From February to June, the cold European anticyclones, reinforced sometimes by a southward extension of the Greenland anticyclone, tend to produce the driest period of the year. Towards late June or early July, pressure rises over the ocean and falls over the continent, initiating a westerly, water-laden airflow over Ireland. Cloud cover, humidity and rainfall increase and thunder becomes more prevalent, particularly during the warmer periods of August. Cold northerly air may bring active depressions in late August and September, but these can be interrupted by spells of anticyclonic weather. In October and November, rain-laden westerlies predominate, although an incursion of anticyclonic conditions can bring good daytime weather.

Prevailing winds are south-westerly and westerly, but, as noted earlier, winds from the north and east may occur in anticyclonic conditions. The winds are lightest from June to September, and strongest from November to March, with January producing some of the severest gales.

May tends to be the sunniest month with an average of 6–7 hours of bright sunshine per day. Surprisingly, however, July tends to be relatively dull, with less bright sunshine than June or August.

Snow is fairly uncommon in our mild maritime climate, occuring in brief spells usually in January and February, although it does occur on the higher mountains and in sheltered north-facing corries from November to April, and occasionally into May.

The Burren receives 1,250–1,500 mm (50–60 inches) of rain per annum, while in Galway City the average yearly rainfall since 1966 has been 1,150 mm (46 inches). In Connemara there can be 2,000–3,000 mm (80–120 inches) in the mountains, but much less on the coast. And on the offshore islands such as Inishmore the annual total is about the same as in Galway City.

Finally, if it is not already apparent that waterproofs are an essential item of equipment in the West of Ireland, there are on average 200 'wet days' in the Burren and 225 in Connemara annually, that is, days on which more than 1 mm of rain falls. However, the scene is not really as dismal as these figures suggest because rarely does it rain continuously for more than a few hours, and most days are blessed with dry periods.

# LIST OF PHOTOGRAPHS

# LIST OF LINE ILLUSTRATIONS

# MAPS

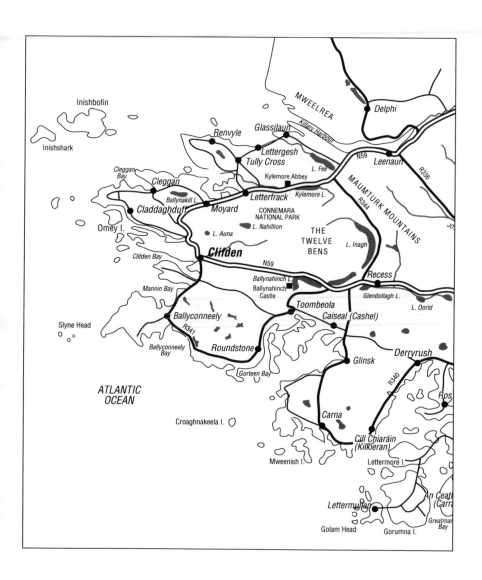

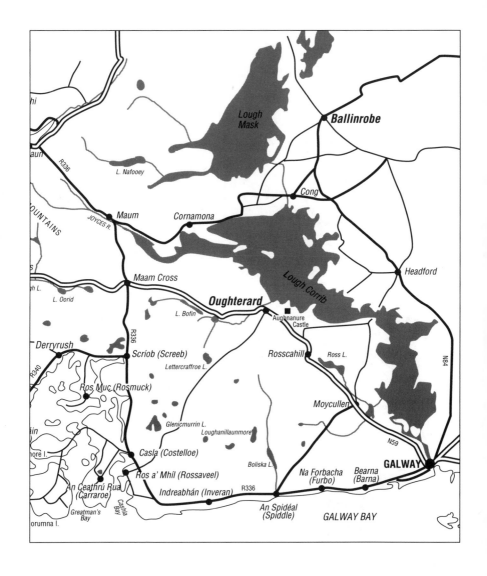

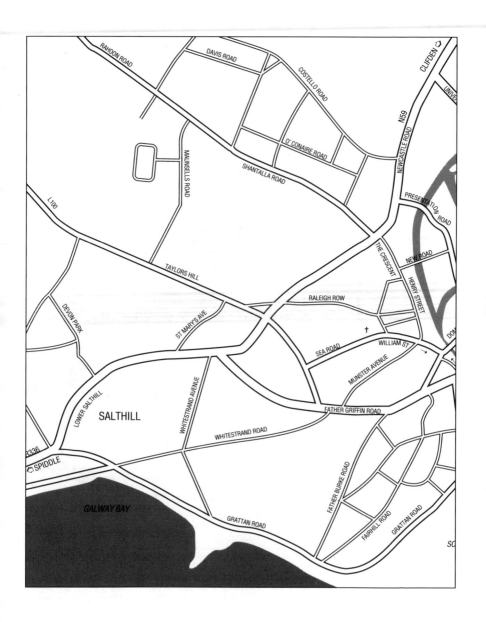

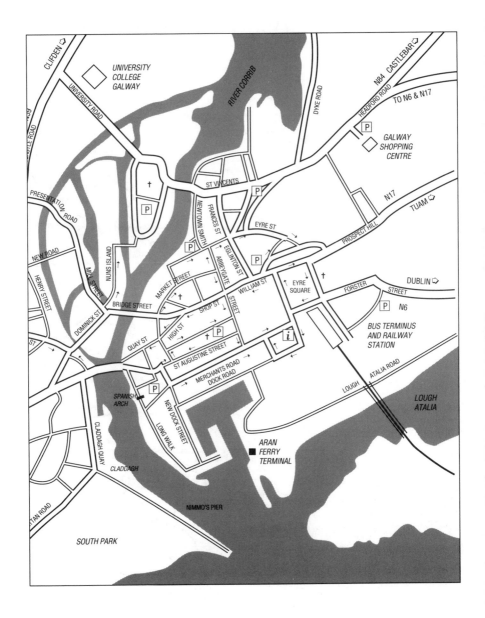

UNIVERSITY COLLEGE GALWAY

RIVER CORRIB

CLIFDEN

UNIVERSITY ROAD

N84 CASTLEBAR

DYKE ROAD

HEADFORD ROAD

TO N6 & N17

GALWAY SHOPPING CENTRE

ST VINCENTS

PRESENTATION ROAD

NEWTOWN SMITH

FRANCES ST

EYRE ST

N17

TUAM

NEW ROAD

EGLINTON ST

PROSPECT HILL

HENRY STREET

NUNS ISLAND

MILL STREET

MARKET STREET

ABBEYGATE STREET

WILLIAM ST

EYRE SQUARE

DUBLIN

BRIDGE STREET

DOMINICK ST

SHOP ST

FORSTER STREET

N6

BUS TERMINUS AND RAILWAY STATION

QUAY ST

HIGH ST

ST AUGUSTINE STREET

i

MERCHANTS ROAD

DOCK ROAD

LOUGH ATALIA ROAD

SPANISH ARCH

NEW DOCK STREET

LOUGH

LOUGH ATALIA

CLADDAGH QUAY

LONG WALK

ARAN FERRY TERMINAL

CLADDAGH

TTAN ROAD

NIMMO'S PIER

SOUTH PARK

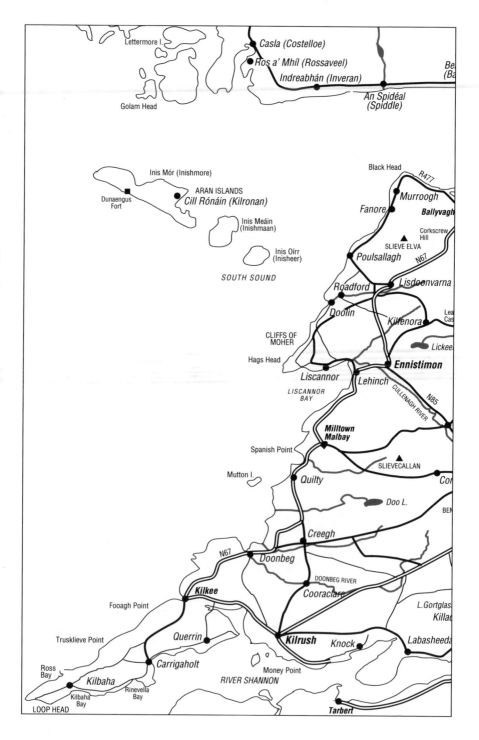

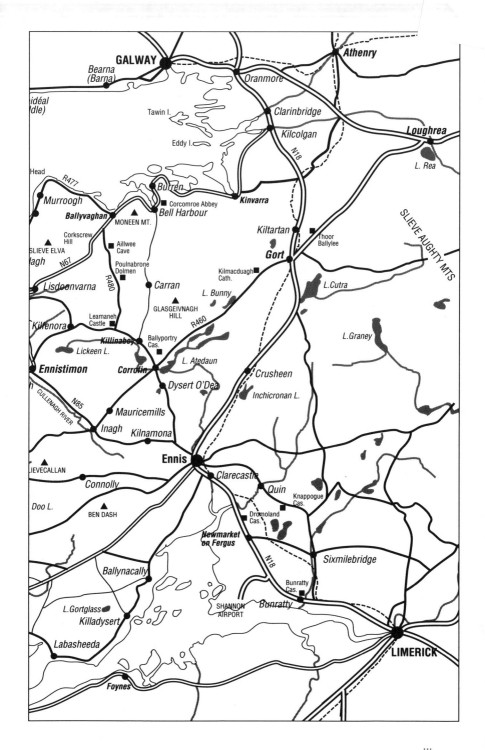

# CONNEMARA
## INTRODUCTION

The name Connemara comes from the tribe of Conmac, or Conmaicne, a warrior tribe which was sent into the area by the ancient Gaelic kings of Connacht to ensure their hegemony. The branch of the tribe which went to the coastal area became known as Conmaicnemara, or 'the tribe of Cormac by the sea'. This name was shortened to Connemara in the 18th century. Modern Connemara extends south from Killary Harbour almost to Galway City, and westwards from the west shore of Lough Corrib to the ocean.

During the 6th century, Christian mystics and hermits settled on Connemara's peninsulas and islands. Perhaps the most famous was St MacDara, an irascible churchman part of whose settlement on the island called after him still stands, although now ruinous. It was almost certainly a victim of Viking raids in the 9th and 10th centuries. As recently as 1947, shifting sand near Clifden revealed the fully clothed body of a young Viking warrior. He was on his back with his shield across his feet and his dagger, sword and spear beside him.

When the Normans arrived in the west, during the 13th century, the De Burgos gained Connemara, but they lost it shortly afterwards to the native O'Flaherty clan. Although regularly attacked, conspired against and subsequently divided into two branches, the O'Flaherty clan was never really defeated in Connemara until the mid-17th century, when they were dispossessed by Cromwellians after the defeat and sack of Galway City in 1652.

Once Galway was secure, Cromwell's men marched across Connemara and established a base on Inishbofin Island. The island was used to imprison Royalist soldiers together with scholars from Galway, 'popish priests' and other enemies of the new regime.

Cromwell forbade the people of Connemara to live within three miles of the sea. This was for security reasons, to forestall the danger of a fifth-column population welcoming a possible sea-borne invasion. But for a people whose life depended on the seashore for food and fertiliser, it was a harsh edict. In the meantime, Catholics whose land had been confiscated in other provinces were sent to Connemara to make their living where they could.

Even after the end of Cromwell's order and the Restoration of the Monarchy in England, the O'Flahertys did not regain their lands or position. Other landowners were granted or sold land in Connemara and a new order of land ownership was established. The first-born son in a family would inherit (providing he was a Protestant) and the land carried with it tenants who paid rents. There were no more elected chiefs; the old clan system was gone.

The Martins were a Catholic family from Galway who managed to buy their way into ownership of the largest slice of Connemara. They were good landlords, crafty and able, and spoke Irish with their tenants, but they gradually over-extended themselves financially. In particular, 'Humanity Dick' Martin (1754–1834) was a lavish spender, leaving debts that crippled the estate when the Great Famine came in the late 1840s. Connemara was hit particularly hard by the failure of the potato crop. The land was poor. Potatoes had grown well and were a nutritious staple food, but what could be grown to replace this crop, and who in 1845 could have realised that the potato blight would attack every year until 1848?

By the time the reality of the situation was understood, the peasants were either too weak or too dispirited to do very much about their situation. Some sought relief in the workhouse, others were given road building relief work, some managed to sell turf in Galway. Many starved to death or emigrated.

The Poor Law Extension Act of 1847 transferred famine relief from central government on to the local rates. Some landlords, like Hyacinth D'Arcy of Clifden, bankrupted themselves trying to take their responsibilities seriously. The workhouse in Clifden could not cope with the numbers needing help; public work schemes were stopped; emigration continued unabated. On many estates, when a tenant farmer improved his productivity, his rent was increased as landlords grasped in desperation for additional revenue. If this 'rack rent' could not be paid, the tenant was evicted. In practice that meant that the farmer and his family were put out of the house and thrown upon the hopelessly inadequate resources of the Poor Law. Mass emigration was the only alternative to mass starvation. The population of County Galway fell by 27 per cent between 1841 and 1851, victims to the grim alternatives of starvation and emigration.

The 1850s, 1860s and 1870s brought a gradual recovery from the trauma of the Famine, but the agricultural depression of the 1870s brought back memories of the earlier disaster. This time, however, tenants mobilised to protect their interest. The Land League, under its founder, Michael Davitt, was founded in the west of Ireland, but quickly spread to most of the country. It pressurised the British government into major reforms of the land tenure system and also led to the establishment of the Congested Districts Board in 1891. Some land was redistributed, harbours were improved, fishing fleets subsidised, and new industries like lace-making and herring-curing started. The railway line from Galway City to Clifden brought tourists, and a resulting interest in tweed-making.

During this time there was an upsurge of interest among Irish intellectuals in the Gaelic way of life and the Irish language, both of which were rapidly disappearing from even the more remote areas of Connemara. Irish had been the language of nearly all Irish people at one time, but during the 18th and 19th centuries its use declined: English was the language of politics, commerce and law; jobs in the civil service or railway companies depended on a knowledge of English; the new primary (or national) schools taught through English, and Irish was strongly discouraged both by teachers and by parents who wanted their children to get good jobs.

Dr Douglas Hyde founded the Gaelic League in 1893 to encourage interest in the Irish language and folklore. A summer college for pupils of Irish was started in Spiddle (An Spidéal) in 1909. With the establishment of the Irish Free State in 1922, the restoration of the old language became a major aspiration of the new state.

The areas where Irish was the first language of the community were identified. South Connemara was, and still is, the largest of these Gaeltachts. There are a number of summer colleges here where secondary school students spend three weeks on holiday speaking nothing but Irish. Scholars and language enthusiasts from other countries as well as Ireland come here to improve their Irish by speaking with native speakers.

In the Gaeltacht area, the signposts, the shop fronts, and the pub names are in Irish, but you will be understood if you speak English. Many Connemara people have spent years working in America or England, and English-language television with its popular programmes is very influential.

Land in Connemara is poor. Most farmers require another source of income to survive. Many have turned their homes into guest-houses; some work in factories or in hotels and restaurants; some make and sell crafts or run hotels, hostels or restaurants; some work in a wide variety of new light industries, others in older industries such as quarrying, seaweed processing or forestry.

There are still fishermen living in the coastal villages, but few can compete now with overseas factory ships which process the fish as it is caught. However, the growing interest in good food in Ireland and the establishment of some excellent restaurants in the region have increased the market for fresh fish and shellfish, and some fishermen are developing tourist-related activities like sightseeing trips or sea angling.

Radio na Gaeltachta, the lively Irish language radio station, is based in Connemara, where many writers, film makers, musicians and visual artists have made their homes.

Peat bogs are still the main source of fuel for Connemara homes. The turf (peat) is cut during the spring weather and laid out to dry. Later it is turned over, stacked to continue drying and finally brought home at the end of summer. At one time all the initial cutting was done with a special spade called a slane. Today many bogs are cut by machine, but the work of turning and stacking is still done by hand. During the dry summer weather whole families, including children and grandparents, work together in the bog, stacking, bagging or loading the dry turf, to get it home before the onset of winter.

Occasionally you will catch a glimpse of Connemara ponies as you travel around. Some authorities claim that these lively little ponies are descended from the Arabian horses which swam ashore when the Spanish Armada was wrecked off the Connemara coast in the 16th century. Many of them wander free until they are rounded up once a year for checking. Some are sold.

Donkeys were introduced into the region from Spain. A few were imported in the 17th century, but the majority of Connemara donkeys were introduced to replace the horses bought up by the English during the Napoleonic Wars. The donkey became extremely useful to the Connemara farmer; with its small feet it was more useful than the heavier horse in boggy ground. It was used to carry baskets filled with turf or fertiliser, or to pull small carts. Today the donkey's use has declined, but some are still kept here and there, often as companions to a horse or as a family pet.

All tourist regions like to pride themselves on their hospitality, but Connemara really does have something special in this regard. Tourism is a vital part of the Connemara economy, but hospitality is part of the Gaelic code, and like the Irish (Gaelic) language, it still persists here. Connemara has been entertaining visitors for years: first, the early Christians and their subsequent pilgrims; then Catholics dispossessed in other parts of Ireland who were driven into Connacht; writers, artists and nationalists who came looking for Celtic inspiration; the *émigrés* coming home on holidays from England or America; those looking for their ancestral roots; and of course the tourist who has been coming for over a hundred years to fish or to delight in the magnificent scenery. Connemara is used to visitors and is unself-conscious about making them relax.

Finally, there is the weather! What starts out as a wet day may end in a dry evening with a magnificent sunset. Conversely, magnificent summer weather can soon turn wet as rain-laden clouds are driven in off the Atlantic. Without the rain, however, the extraordinary quality of the light would be very different. Connemara weather may be mercurial; it is never boring.

Prolonged rain can be a problem for the holiday maker, however. You can put on waterproof clothes and decide to ignore it, or consult this guide for suggested rainy day activities, or settle down with a good book and sit it out indoors. And finally, if you tire of reading, don't be afraid to start a conversation; conversation, like hospitality, is still part of the way of life in Connemara.

# USEFUL TELEPHONE NUMBERS AND INFORMATION

Listed below are some useful telephone numbers and information in alphabetical order. The telephone number prefix is used only if you are telephoning from outside the prefix area.

## BANKS

**Carraroe:**
Allied Irish Banks sub office, telephone 091–95218. Open Mondays, Tuesdays, Thursdays and Fridays, 10 a.m.–3 p.m. Closed for lunch from 12.30–1.30 p.m.

**Clifden:**
Allied Irish Banks, telephone 095–21129. 10 a.m.–3 p.m. Closed for lunch from 12.30–1.30 p.m. Late night banking until 5 p.m. on Wednesdays. ATM machine for 23 hour cash dispensing. Bank of Ireland, telephone 095–21111. Mondays to Fridays, 10 a.m.–3 p.m., lunch hour 12.30–1.30 p.m. and late night banking until 5 p.m. on Wednesdays.

**Oughterard:**
Bank of Ireland, telephone 091–82123. 10 a.m.–3 p.m. Closed for lunch 12.30–1.30 p.m. and late night banking until 5 p.m. on Thursdays. Allied Irish Banks sub office, telephone 091–24466. Mondays and Fridays, 10 a.m.–12.30 p.m. and 1.30–3 p.m. The Bank of Ireland Travelling Bank covers the following places, full banking facilities available:

**Mondays:**
Moyard, 10–10.15 a.m.
Leenaun, 10.45–11.45 a.m.
Letterfrack, 1.30–3 p.m.
**Tuesdays:**
Rosmuck, 10.30–11.40 a.m.
Rosmuck Cross, 11.45 a.m.–12.30 p.m.
**Wednesdays:**
Carna, 1.30–4.30 p.m.
**Thursdays:**
Tully, 11–11.30 a.m.
Tully Cross, 11.35 a.m.–12.35 p.m.
Kylemore Abbey, 2.10–3 p.m.
**Fridays:**
Cashel, 10.30–10.45 a.m.
Roundstone IDA, 12–12.30 p.m.
Roundstone, 1.30–3 p.m.
Allied Irish Banks visit Roundstone on Wednesdays 2.30–3.30 p.m.

# BICYCLE HIRE AND REPAIR

**Clifden:** John Mannion, Railway View, telephone 095–21160 or 21155 after 8 p.m.
**Lettergesh**: King's, telephone 095–43414.
**Moycullen**: Garage Gear, telephone 091–85509.
**Oughterard:** Tommy Tuck, Main Street, telephone 091–82335 and from the shed at the start of Pier Road.
**Roundstone:** Michael Ferron, Main Street, telephone 095–35838.
**Renvyle**: Diamond's Bar and Grocery, telephone 095–43486/43548.

# BUREAUX DE CHANGE (many open seven days and until 11.00 p.m.)

**Carna:** Michael Geraghty, telephone 095–32239.
**Carraroe:** Post Office, telephone 091–95127.
**Cleggan:** telephone 095–44640.
**Clifden:** Clifden Bay Hotel, telephone 095–21167.
**Kylemore Abbey:** telephone 091–41113.
**Leenaun:** telephone 095–42266.
**Lettermore:** Post Office, telephone 091–81111.
**Maam Cross:** Peacock's, telephone 091–82306.

**Moyard:** The Cottage Handcrafts Shop, telephone 095–41029.
**Oughterard:** Keogh's shop, telephone 091–82222.
**Renvyle:** Renvyle House Hotel, telephone 095–43511.
**Roundstone:** Malachy Kearns in the IDA Park, telephone 095–35808.
**Spiddle:** Máirtín Standún, telephone 091–83102 and Forbairt Pobal Teo 091– 83480.

## CHURCH SERVICES

*Catholic Churches* are located throughout Connemara. Mass times are available locally.
*The Church of Ireland* in Clifden holds a Sunday service at 11.30 a.m. throughout the
year. During July and August, Holy Communion Service is at 8.30 a.m.
**Oughterard:** Church of Ireland Service every Sunday at 10 a.m.
**Moyard:** Church of Ireland Service, Sundays at noon.

## GARAGES OFFERING PUNCTURE REPAIRS AND BREAKDOWN SERVICE

**Clifden:**
Brian Walsh's Garage, 24 hour service, telephone 095–21037 and after hours
(6.00 p.m.–9.00 a.m.) 095–41075.
**Moycullen:**
Garage Gear, telephone 091–85509, from 9.00 a.m.–6.00 p.m.
**Oughterard:**
Welby's Garage, telephone 091–82452. Six days a week. After 6.00 until about
10.00 p.m., 091–82102.
Seán Conneely, Main Street. 24–hour repairs service, telephone 091–82299.

**Rosmuck:**
Colman Mannion, telephone 091–74207.
**Tully Cross, Renvyle:**
Western Auto Point, telephone 095–43439.

## GARDAÍ (POLICE)

**Oughterard:** telephone 091–82202. Superintendent: 091–82439.
**Clifden:** telephone 095–21021. Superintendent: 095–21022.
The following stations are manned during mornings only:
**Carraroe:** telephone 091–95102
**Inveran:** telephone 091–93102
**Leenaun:** telephone 095–42236
**Letterfrack:** telephone 095–41052
**Lettermore:** telephone 091–81122
**Maum:** telephone 091–71100
**Moycullen:** telephone 091–85122
**Recess:** telephone 095–34603
**Rosmuck:** telephone 091–74102
**Roundstone:** telephone 095–35835
**Spiddle:** telephone 091–83122.

## LAUNDERETTES/LAUNDRY

Launderettes are available in Clifden, Moycullen, and Oughterard, Mondays to Saturdays, day time only. Laundry service available in Tully Cross. Dry-cleaning available in Clifden and Oughterard.

## MEDICAL

**Clifden District Hospital:** telephone 095–21333
**Ambulance service:** Clifden, telephone 095–21333.

## PHARMACIES

**Oughterard:** telephone 091–82348
**Carraroe:** telephone 091–95168
**Moycullen:** telephone 091–85170
**Spiddle:** telephone 091–83201
**Clifden:** telephone 095–21273 and 095–21452.
General stores usually stock simple pain-killing remedies, antiseptic, indigestion cures, soap, toothpaste and shampoo.

## POST OFFICES (OIFIG AN PHOIST)

Open Mondays to Fridays, from 9 a.m.–5.30 p.m.
Closed for lunch 1–2 p.m. Open on Saturdays 9 a.m.–1 p.m.

## TAXIS

**Carraroe:** Peter Folan, telephone 091–72159.
**Clifden:** Colm McLoughlin, telephone 095–21466.
**Letterfrack:** Cummin's taxi service, telephone 095–41055, and Lydon Mini-Bus Service, telephone 095–41043.
**Oughterard:** T. Morley, telephone 091–82828 and 088–556070.
**Roundstone:** Joseph King, telephone 095–35897.
**Tully Cross:** Patrick James Conneely, telephone 095–43453.

## TOURIST OFFICES

*The Tourist Office* in Victoria Place, Galway, is open all year, Mondays to Fridays, 9 a.m.–5.45 p.m., and Saturday mornings. During July and August the office remains open until 7 p.m. every day including Sunday. Telephone 091–63081.
*Clifden.* New tourist office to open in 1995 in the old courthouse.

*Renvyle/Letterfrack* area tourist information office is in the Credit Union office in Tully Cross. Open Mondays to Fridays from 10 a.m.–1 p.m. and 2–6 p.m. Telephone 095–43950/43464.
*Spiddle tourist information* from Fobairt Pobal Teo, telephone 091–83480, which is adjacent to the Spiddle Village Hostel, open Mondays to Fridays from 8.30 a.m.– 5.30 p.m. They do not take bookings; they give information only. *Cósta Conamara* tourist office is in the village.

# FESTIVALS

This list of festivals in Connemara cannot give the exact dates as these will vary each year.

## May

*Bog Week.* Usually held the last week in May/first week in June. Centred around Letterfrack. Talks and discussions on the environment. Traditional music sessions and dances. Information: telephone 095–43443.
*Currach Festival, Spiddle.* Bank Holiday Weekend (unless weather too stormy). Currach races, pub music sessions.
*Joe Heanue weekend in Carna.* Held every Whit (Bank holiday) weekend. Two days are devoted to a celebration of sean nós singing. (For explanation of sean nós, see 'evening entertainment', page 25).

## June

*Sheep and Wool Festival, Leenaun.* Mid-June. A week of special events, shearing demonstrations, wool spinning. Dances. Information: telephone 095–42231/41017.

## July

*Environmental summer school on Inishbofin.* Information: telephone 095–43443.
*Queen of Connemara Festival in Oughterard.* Second week of July. Funfair, discos, street dancing, beauty contest.
*Féile Mhic Dara.* Three-day festival dedicated to St MacDara, the patron saint of South Connemara fishermen. They used to dip their sails three times when passing Oileán MhacDara (St MacDara's island). Mass is held on the island on 16 July. The saint's church is a tiny, rectangular, early Christian church built of large stones. Part of the original stone roof still exists.

## August

*The Connemara Pony Show in Clifden.* Connemara ponies are displayed, bought, sold and ridden in gymkhana events. Held on the third Thursday of the month.
*Féile an Dóilín in Carraroe.* Currach races, tug-of-war, dances, discos, music sessions.

## September

*Clifden Country Blues Festival.* Top blues and country singers entertain. Second week in September. Ask the Tourist Office for further information: telephone 095–21163.
*Clifden Community Arts Week.* Usually held during the last full week in September. Concerts, exhibitions, readings. Festival has earned the reputation of being a very relaxed and fun-filled week. Top literary and musical names usually attend.

## October

*Sea Week in Letterfrack.* Talks and events with an emphasis on maritime topics. Traditional music sessions and dances. Telephone 095–43443 for further information.

# CYCLE TOURS

Connemara is perfect cycling country; near the coast the roads wind between inlets of the sea and lakes, while in the mountainous areas the roads tend to follow the valley floor. Cycles may be hired in Clifden, Oughterard, Moycullen, Spiddle, Renvyle and Roundstone. (See Introduction, page 6, for names and telephone numbers.)

**CLIFDEN TOURS.**
**Clifden to Roundstone.** A round trip of approximately 32 miles/51 km. This is a wonderful coastal and inland round trip which takes in a cycle across the famous Roundstone Bog.

Follow the R341 towards Ballyconneely and turn first left on the unmarked road across Roundstone Bog. This area was the focus of a lot of recent controversy when planning permission to build an airport was sought by a consortium of local business people.

4 miles/6 km along the unmarked road, on your left you will pass the site of the 'Halfway House', an early 19th century drinking house whose owners used to murder and rob their victims. When a few victims' bodies surfaced in the lake, the murderers were caught and taken to Galway where they were convicted and hanged.

Turn right at the T-junction back on the R341 towards Roundstone. This village was founded by Alexander Nimmo in the early 19th century. Nimmo was recruited to survey the roads and harbours of Connemara and to oversee the building of new ones. He bought land around the harbour he had planned, and took advantage of the government grants available to encourage people to settle in the village and build two-storey houses.

Beyond the village you approach Gorteen Bay and Dog's Bay. Ecotour Stop L 691386, page 74, refers. Continue on the R341 to Clifden.

**Clifden to Cleggan via the coast.** A round trip of approximately 32 miles/51 km. This takes you through some spectacular coastal scenery.

Take the north road to Cleggan for 3.12 miles/5 km and turn left at the T-junction for Claddaghduff. Keep cycling westwards towards the sea. As you cycle overlooking Streamstown Bay, you may like to reflect that in the 18th century this area was one of the most prosperous areas of Connemara because the bay was a perfect smuggling cove. On your left you will pass the ivy-covered gable of a ruined 17th century house which was built on the site of a 15th century O'Flaherty castle. Between the castle and the road is a 19th century limekiln. As you pass the Garden Centre you may like to stop to see the collection of salt air tolerant flowers and shrubs or have refreshments in the coffee shop.

Follow the coast around Aughrusbeg Lough. Out to sea you will have a good view of Inishbofin island and the smaller Inishark island at its side. Take the left turn for Cleggan. Return to Clifden via the main Cleggan/Clifden road.

**Clifden to Letterfrack.** A round trip of approximately 24 miles/38 km. To Letterfrack via Cleggan is a round trip of 33 miles/53 km. This tour will take you to the heart of the Connemara National Park. A return route via the beautiful Inagh Valley is a distance of approximately 50 miles/80 km.

Take the N59 east to Letterfrack. If cycling via Cleggan, take the direct route, then around by the shore and Ballynakill Lake to Letterfrack. If stopping here, see 'Connemara National Park and Letterfrack', page 45.

For the longer return route continue on past Kylemore Abbey (see 'Kylemore Abbey', page 34) and turn right on to the R344 through the magnificent scenery of the Inagh Valley. Turn right on to the N59 back to Clifden.

**Clifden to the Renvyle peninsula.** A round trip of approximately 32 miles/51 km. This will take you through the Connemara National Park and around the coast with views across to Inishturk island, Clare Island and the coast of County Mayo.

Cycle on to Letterfrack. Take the unmarked road towards Tully Cross for 2.5 miles/4 km. Turn left to Derryinver Bay. The coast road ends further on, so turn right just past the quay. Take a left at the next junction and left again. You will pass a ruined medieval chapel dedicated to the Seven Daughters. A holy well dedicated to these mysterious Seven Daughters is a little further on. Follow the road around to the right. The ruined castle by the shore was built in the 14th century by the Joyces then taken over by the O'Flahertys. During the 17th century Colonel Edmund O'Flaherty lived here. He supported the Royalist case in 1641 and was subsequently hanged in 1653 in Galway by Cromwellians.

Follow the road around to the right and back to Tully Cross, and across the Dawros River and into Letterfrack.

**Clifden to Salrock and Little Killary.** A round trip of approximately 48 miles/77 km which takes you along the coast past beautiful Lettergesh and Glassilaun beaches.

Cycle to Letterfrack, then Tully Cross. At Tully Cross take the road to the right and follow the coast around. Saint Roc is allegedly buried at Salrock. It was an old custom in Salrock to place the tobacco pipes smoked at the wake on the grave of the deceased.

**Clifden to Killary Harbour and Leenaun.** A round trip of approximately 56 miles/90 km. This is a direct and well signposted route through Letterfrack and past Kylemore Abbey. The village of Leenaun was used for the location of the film 'The Field'. The screenplay was based on the play of the same name by John B. Keane. The film was made in 1989 and it starred Richard Harris and John Hurt. Ecotour stop L833620, page 77, refers.

**OUGHTERARD TOURS.**

**Hill of Doon.** Round trip of approximately 18 miles/28 km. A short tour through some spectacular scenery.

Take the unmarked road to Glann and follow Lough Corrib around to the car park above the lake. Retrace your route to the first fork in the road and take the road to your right. This takes you via the scenic route back into Oughterard. (See Oughterard, page 26.)

*Near Letterfrack*

**Oughterard to Costelloe and return**. Approximately 40 miles/64 km. A cycle through a scenic valley to the Connemara coast with its lakes and sea inlets.

Take the unmarked road from Oughterard to Costelloe (Casla) signposted to the left near the church. Turn right at the R336 and follow this road around to the right, back to Maam Cross. Turn right on the N59 back to Oughterard.

**Oughterard to Recess**. Approximately 17 miles/27 km. A wonderfully scenic cycle by lakeshore and bog with the Twelve Bens range dominating the horizon.

Follow the N59 through Maam Cross and stop at the car park overlooking Glendollagh Lake which is just beyond Recess village. The name Recess seems to derive from a farm by that name which was leased by a Dublin Alderman, William Andrews, from the Martins in 1846. By 1853 his farm became a hotel and was renamed the Railway Hotel in 1894. It had its own railway platform opposite. It was burned by the IRA in 1922 to prevent it being occupied by Free State troops. The site of it is now occupied by Joyces. The marble factory was opened in 1820 on behalf of the Martin family.

**Oughterard to Spiddle (An Spidéal) and back**. Approximately 40 miles/64 km. Follow the unmarked road to Costelloe (Casla) and turn left along the R336 coast road to Spiddle village. A short distance from the village is the strand, the Ceardlann (Craft Village) and Ceol na Mara, the thatched restaurant and entertainment centre.

Return to the centre of the village and turn right at the cross roads for the road to Moycullen (Maigh Cuilinn). The view of Galway Bay from this road is spectacular on a clear day. As you descend to Moycullen the vista of the Corrib opens up before you. Turn left in Moycullen on the N59 for the return to Oughterard.

### SPIDDLE TOURS.

**Spiddle to Oughterard and back.** Round trip of approximately 40 miles/64 km. This route takes you inland by Ross Lake and Lough Corrib and back via the coast road.

Take the unmarked road to Moycullen village (8 miles/12 km) and turn left on the N59 to Oughterard.

2.5 miles/4 km along the road on your right you will see Ross Castle by the side of Ross Lake. (See page 32.) The entrance is just before Kinneavy's pub another 2.5 miles/4 km further on.

Aughnanure Castle is signposted approximately 4.5 miles/7 km further on. (See Aughnanure, page 28.)

In Oughterard you may take the short cycle tour to the Hill of Doon (see page 11) or continue through the village and turn left on the unmarked road for Casla (Costelloe). Turn left on the R336 to Spiddle.

**Spiddle to The Islands and back.** A trip of from 40 miles/64 km to 52 miles/83 km along the flat coast road and on to a series of islands linked by narrow bridges and causeways.

Take the R336 towards Casla (Costelloe). Just after Casla the road branches into three. The left road to An Ceathrú Rua (Carraroe), the right to Oughterard. Take the middle, unmarked road. Once you reach the islands you may turn back at any time, or explore the quays and beaches. If you have any Irish this is a good place to try out at least a greeting. Fishing, smuggling and poitín-making were important occupations here at one time. Fishing is still important. Return the way you came. Ecotour Stop L896274, page 66, and L882238, page 67, refers.

**Spiddle to Carraroe and back.** Round trip of 30 miles/48 km.

Take the R336 westwards to Inveran and the lakes beyond. Continue on to Costelloe (Casla), where the road forks. Take the left fork (R343) which hugs Casla Bay and into the village of Carraroe (An Ceathrú Rua). See Carraroe Sculpture Park page 31, also beach guide, below, for directions to 'coral strand'.

# DAYTIME ACTIVITIES

## BEACH GUIDE

### (Na Forbacha) Furbo. 8 miles/13 km west of Galway City.

Sandy beach. Safe bathing. Clear, clean water. Lifeguard in attendance during season. No public toilets. Car park. Wheelchair access to left of car park. Shop selling ice-cream on other side of road, a few metres back towards Galway. Drinks and light snacks available at pub overlooking the beach. Picnic tables.

**How to get there.**
Take the R336 from Galway City. Shortly after the church on the right-hand side the strand and car park can be seen on the left. Buses to Spiddle (An Spidéal) and Carraroe (An Ceathrú Rua) stop here. Check times with Bus Éireann office at the Galway railway station.

### An Spidéal (Spiddle). 10 miles/16 km west of Galway City.
Good stretch of sand. Grassy area for sitting on above beach. Access to strand for wheelchairs difficult. Safe swimming. Picnic tables and seats provided above end of beach nearest to the village. Toilets on beach side of road nearer to village. Parking on road. Craft village opposite provides good car park for its visitors. Other sandy beaches are located at the end of the short lane beside the church and by the pier.
**How to get there.**
Take the R336 out of Galway. The strand is visible before you reach the village. There is a regular year-round bus service between Galway City and An Spidéal. Check times with Bus Éireann office at the Galway railway station.

### Indreabhán (Inveran). 14 miles/23 km west of Galway City.
Sandy bay. Safe swimming. car park, toilets (open from mid-June to end of August) and picnic tables and seats on grass near car park.
**How to get there.**
Take the R336, drive through Spiddle (An Spidéal) and look out for the access road to the beach on the left just after passing Tigh Culainn. Check buses at Galway railway station Bus Éireann office.

### An Ceathrú Rua (Carraroe). 16 miles/25 km west of Galway City.
This beach is known as the 'coral strand'; although real coral is of animal origin the fragments on this beach are of calcified seaweed. Most of the 'coral' has been broken down by human traffic into a gritty white sand which can be hard on bare feet. Good dune walk for those interested in wild flowers. Safe bathing. Clear, clean water. Popular with snorkellers. Car park above beach. Wheelchair access difficult but not impossible. No amenities.
**How to get there.**
Take R336 out of Galway City until Costelloe (Casla) and turn on to the R343 for Carraroe (An Ceathrú Rua). Follow road past the church and keep straight on. If you need to ask the way, ask locals for Trá an Dóilín — pronounced 'Trar an doaleen'. Signpost indicates An Trá Choiréalach. Check bus times at Galway railway station Bus Éireann office.

### Kilkieran (Cill Chiaráin). Approximately 26 miles/42 km south-east of Clifden, 40 miles/65 km west of Galway City.
Sheltered beach of soft white sand. Access for wheelchair. No amenities. Car park.
**How to get there.**
Kilkieran lies on the R340, off the N59 from Clifden, or the R336 from Galway. Midway between Carna and Kilkieran look out for the signpost to Trá. Narrow access road ends in small tarmac area and the beach.

### Roundstone (Gorteen Bay). Approximately 50 miles/80 km from Galway City, or a pleasant 4 miles/6 km coastal drive from Clifden.

### Gorteen Bay.
Soft white sand. Dunes. Safe bathing in clear, clean water. (Can be cold for swimming when the wind is directly off the land.) Beautiful location with Errisbeg Mountain forming a spectacular backdrop. No public toilets. Small shop at entrance to nearby caravan park sells snacks and ice-cream. Wheelchair access difficult as descent to beach is down fairly steep cliff path. Good sitting area on grass beside car park above the strand.
**How to get there.**
Take the N59 from Galway City and turn left on to the R341 for Roundstone. Go through Roundstone for approximately 2 miles/4 km and watch out for narrow road to Gorteen Bay on the left. Ecotour Stop L691386, page 74, refers.

**Mannin Bay. 63 miles/102 km from Galway City, 8.75 miles/14 km from Roundstone, 6 miles/9.5 km from Clifden.**
This bay is fringed with sandy beaches and yellow 'coral strands'. Parking provided on the left-hand side of the main road about a mile beyond the village of Ballyconneely. No public toilets. Access for wheelchairs down stony ramp. Picnic food and snacks available in Ballyconneely. Hotel nearby is open to non-residents. Ecotour Stop L 628455, page 75, refers.
The derelict castle on the headland was started by Richard Geoghegan in 1838. To the south-west of the ruined castle is a derelict coast-watching post in use from 1939 to 45. This post was built on the site of a folly which Richard Geoghegan built in 1780 to commemorate the winning of free trade by Grattan's Volunteers.
**How to get there.**
From Galway or Oughterard, follow directions to Gorteen but continue on R341 for another 7 miles/11 km. From Clifden, take the R341 south for 4 miles/6.4 km approximately.

## Clifden.
A small stretch of soft sand sheltered by the cliff and jutting out into Clifden Bay along a sand spit. Toilets (closed in winter). Grassy area for sitting or playing. Park-bench type seats on the tarred path leading to the strand. Good parking in front of the Clifden Sailing Club.
**How to get there.**
The beach road is signposted off the town 'square'. The beach lies approximately 1 km at the end of this road.
There are other beautiful strands within 10 km of Clifden, but these beaches do not have car parks or amenities. Take the Sky Road out of Clifden, keep to the left fork and you will see the strands ahead of you at Eyrephort and further along on Kingstown Bay.

## Omey Island. Approximately 19 miles/31 km from Clifden.
Beautiful stretches of soft white sand. Access to the island is across a wide strand when the tide is out. During summer the approach strand is rarely covered. No amenities. Connemara pony races take place on the strand during August.
**How to get there.**
Access to Omey Island across the strand near Claddaghduff, 8 miles/13 km from Clifden. Take the Westport road out of Clifden and turn left at the T-junction.

## Inishbofin.
There are beautiful strands on this island which can be reached only by boat from Cleggan. Food and accommodation available for those who wish to stay overnight. See 'Inishbofin', page 39, and accommodation guide, page 52.
**How to get there.**
Cleggan lies approximately 11 miles/18 km north-west of Clifden. Take the N59 towards Letterfrack and watch out for signpost.

## Lettergesh, Glassilaun, Renvyle. Approximately 46 miles/75 km from Galway City, 15 miles/24 km from Clifden.
Sandy beaches in beautiful location looking across towards County Mayo. Safe swimming. Good parking. No amenities.
**How to get there.**
Drive to Letterfrack on the N59 and take the road signposted to Tully Cross. For Lettergesh, turn right in Tully Cross and follow the road as it hugs the hillside above the bay. Turn sharp left immediately after crossing small stone bridge. Glassilaun is three miles further on around the bay. For Rinvyle, return to Tully Cross, drive towards Tully village and drive through the village for approximately 0.5 km. First turn on the right leads to small caravan park. The second road on the right leads to small car park above a sandy beach. Return to the road and continue along it for approximately 4 km for a longer strand. A ruined O'Flaherty castle stands near the shore. The sand is gritty here

but the location is magnificent. This is a good beach for anyone wanting to practise stone skimming.

## ANGLING, FRESH WATER FISHING, GAME FISHING

Anglers must obtain a licence before attempting to fish. People under 18 and over 65 are exempt. Licences are available from the Western Regional Fisheries office at the Weir Lodge, Earl's Island, Galway (near the Cathedral), telephone 091–63118, or from tackle shops and hotels throughout the region. There are short-season, as well as annual licences available. Fishing for trout and salmon is permitted from February until the end of September or mid-October. Exact dates vary locally. If you have never fished before, the fishing school at Spiddle (see below) will get you started, as will the angling school at Oughterard (see below), or you could go out on the Corrib from Oughterard with an experienced gillie. Some waters are designated free. Others are privately owned and you will be required to pay a fee to fish these waters. A rough guide to waters is given here, but seek the advice of the Western Regional Fisheries Officers or local information through the tackle supply shop or licence distributor. Privately owned waters are indicated. Map references to OS maps 14 and 10 are given where it is thought they will help.

**When walking on or through farm land, please remember to close any gates you have opened, put stones back if you have knocked them off walls, and please take your litter home or to the nearest litter bin.**

### Clifden.

Brown trout in Glenbrickeen Lough (L660532), Shanakeever Lough (L670525) and Lough Auna (L685532). Season from 15 February until 12 October. The Clifden Anglers' Association control fishing on the Owenglin River which flows through the town, and 19 lakes in the area. Contact them through Noel Kirby, telephone 095–41054.
The Ballinaboy River flows into Ardbear Bay at Ballinaboy bridge and drains a number of loughs which provide good fishing for brown trout. Contact the Clifden Anglers' Association for permits, and for boat hire contact Col. A. Morris, Ballinaboy House, Clifden, telephone 095–21298. Part of this system is privately owned and is not available.
Mannin Bay has two small rivers flowing into it from a number of loughs, particularly Lough Emlaghnabehy (L640462) and Lough Nacorrussaun (L645448). Both rivers and the lakes are brown trout fisheries. West of Ballyconneely there are a number of brown trout loughs. Contact the Clifden Anglers' Association for permits and boat hire.

### Renvyle/Kylemore/Letterfrack Area.

Licences and permits from Mrs Aspell, Kylemore (opposite gates to the Abbey) for fishing in the Dawros River above the bridge. For fishing the Dawros River below the bridge, contact Renvyle House Hotel, telephone 095–43434/43444.
Fishing rights on Pollacapul Lough (L750583), Middle Lough (L758580) and Kylemore Lough (L770583) are owned jointly by Kylemore House and Kylemore Abbey. Only fly fishing is allowed on these lakes.
For fishing and boat hire on the Culfin system — that is, the Culfin River, Lough Muck (L773625) and Lough Fee (L790610) — contact one of the following people and you will be informed which person has the rights to the place you want to fish:
Mrs Willoughby, Salrock, Renvyle, telephone 095–43498;
Mr Owen King, Lettergesh Post Office, telephone 095–43414;
The Lady Abbess, Kylemore Abbey, telephone 095–41127.

### Leenaun/Killary Harbour.

The Erriff Fishery (the Erriff River and Lough Tawnyard plus numerous small loughs and tributaries) is one of the major salmon fisheries in Ireland. There are 45 pools divided into nine beats on the river alone and three beats on Lough Tawnyard. Information from the Manager, Erriff Fishery, Leenaun, County Galway, telephone 095–42252.

## Roundstone.

Six miles to the west of Roundstone are a number of lakes — Barrowen Lough (L652432), Emlaghkeeragh Lough (L660430), Maumeen Lough (L650413), and a tidal pool at Callow Bridge (L648450). Fishing is mainly for brown trout and sea trout, but occasionally salmon enter these waters. Best trout fishing is from July to October and salmon are often caught in the tidal pool during April. Fly fishing only on these loughs. Roundstone Anglers' Association (contact them through your hotel or guest-house) will advise on fishing in a number of small brown trout lakes in the Roundstone area. Ballynahinch Castle Fishery provides first-class salmon and trout fishing. The salmon fishing is best from mid-June until end of the season on 30 September. The river is divided into seven salmon beats and four sea trout pools each accommodating two rods each day. Boats available. Permits from Ballynahinch Castle Hotel, Ballinafad, County Galway, telephone 095–31006.

No fishing allowed from the top of Ballynahinch Lake nor the section of the river to the canal bridge on the N59.

## Toombeola Loughs.

Permits are available from the Anglers' Return, Toombeola, Ballinafad, County Galway, telephone 095–31091.

## Cashel Area.

The Zetland Hotel, Cashel, has the letting of a number of brown and sea trout lakes in this area and the letting of the Gowla system which consists of the Gowla River and 18 good fishing loughs. Brown trout run in all and salmon and sea trout run in some. There are four beats on the river and eight boats for hire.

Permits for the Gowlabeg River system are given by The Cashel House Hotel and Mr Martin Moylett, Carna, County Galway; there is no telephone number for Mr Moylett. Although the river is small, it has some good holding pools. All the interconnected lakes have brown trout in them and there is a run of sea trout from July.

## Carna Area.

There are a number of lakes in the Carna area. All the loughs hold brown trout and sea trout enter from around the middle of June, but are best caught during August and September. An occasional salmon has been spotted in this system. Permits from the Carna Anglers' Association and from Mr Martin Moylett, Carna, County Galway.

## Kilkieran.

The Invermore system drains into the sea at Kilkieran Bay. Sea trout run through this system from about the middle of June. Salmon can sometimes start earlier and continue to the end of September. Permits from the Fishery Manager at the Zetland Hotel in Cashel or from Mr T. Ryan, Cong, County Mayo, telephone 092–46035.

## Lough Inagh.

Spring salmon, grilse and trout. Eight boats for hire. Permits and information from the Fishery Manager, Lough Inagh Fishery, Recess, County Galway, (no telephone number).

## Recess/Maam Cross.

Permits for fishing in waters near here from Mrs Joyce, Tullaboy House, Maam Cross, County Galway, telephone 091–82305.

## Rosmuck.

*Lough Aroolagh (L925382).* The lake is alongside the Screeb/Carna road close to Pearse's Cottage. Good stocks of brown trout. Fishing can be good from April onwards. Permits for fishing on the Screeb system are controlled by Screeb Estates Ltd, Camus, County Galway, telephone 091–74110. Ten boats for hire.

*Lough Ahalia (L965400)* is divided into three sections, all tidal. The upper section is known as Screeb Lough and is noted for good runs of salmon and sea trout from late June/early July. The head of the spring tide reaches up the inflowing river at the

*Near Ballinahinch*

northern end of Screeb Lough. This part of the river is known as 'The Pool'. It is let as a separate beat. Screeb Lough is the most fished section of Lough Ahalia. The other two sections of the lough are fished for salmon and sea trout.

*Knockaunawaddy Lough (L972393)* is located to the east of the R336 Screeb/Maam Cross road about 1 mile/.5 km from Screeb Lodge. Holds sea trout from late July until end of season on 12 October.

*Lough Down (L982425)* is east of the R336 Screeb/Maam Cross road from a point 1 mile/.5 km upstream from the waterfall. Fishing from the shore only. Brown trout stocks and occasionally sea trout.

*Lough Nahillion (Illony Lough) (L990425)* is to the east of the R336 Screeb/Maam Cross road. Salmon and sea trout in July and August. Good stock of brown trout. Access can be difficult.

*Loughaunfree (Cornaree Lough) (L966430)* is close to the road on the west side. Although shallow, fish can be caught in all parts of it. Salmon and sea trout from July.

*Lough Nahasleam (Ashleam Lough) (L970440)* is crossed at its narrowest point by the road. Salmon and sea trout from July to end of season.

*Lough Shindilla Upper (L960460).* Sea trout and salmon from July. Rights jointly administered by Screeb Estates and Mr Hodgson, Currarevagh House, Oughterard, County Galway, telephone 091–82313. (Mr Hodgson has the rights on two other lakes, Lough Shindilla Lower and Lurgan Lough, both near Maam Cross.)

*The Loughanultera Lakes* which drain into Camus Bay are brown trout lakes. They are managed by Screeb Estates, Screeb Lodge, Maam Cross, County Galway.

## Gorumna Island.

These lakes are managed by Comlucht Forbartha, Turaseoireachta na n-Oileáin, Tír an Fhia, Leitir Móir, Co. na Gaillimhe. There are seven main lakes on the 'island' which is linked to Lettermore 'Island' by a bridge/causeway, which in turn is linked to the mainland at Bealadangan. Brown trout fishing.

## Carraroe (An Ceathrú Rua).

Contact the Carraroe Anglers' Association for boats and information. This association has no contact phone number. Ask in Carraroe Hotel or Ostán an Dóilín for information.

## Costelloe (Casla) Area.

Fishing rights administered by Costelloe and Formoyle Fisheries, Costelloe, County Galway, telephone 091–72196. Mr Peter Walsh, Glenicmurrin Lodge, Glenicmurrin, Costelloe (no phone number), owns some of the rights on this system. Either he or the Manager at the Costelloe and Formoyle Fisheries will advise.

*The Casla (Costelloe) River* is fished from the bank. From May the grilse run this river, but it is for sea trout that most anglers fish the river from early June until the end of the season in early October.

*Glenicmurrin Lough (L999310)* is divided into four beats. A boat is available for each beat and access to the boat piers is along bog roads. Sea trout runs from the middle of June and sometimes grilse.

*Lough Cloonadoon* is upstream from Glenicmurrin and holds mainly brown trout. September is the best month here.

*Cloondola Lough* is a short distance downstream from Formoyle Lough (M022330) and access is by boat which can be hired. Sea trout from end of July to the end of the season.

*Lough Formoyle* is close to the Costelloe/Oughterard road. Sea trout enter towards end of July. Boat available for hire. *Muckanagh Lough* (M000333) and *Muckanaghkillew Lough* (M001332) are quite large lakes joined by a narrow stream. Access is off the R336 Costelloe/Screeb road near the schoolhouse at Kinvarra. Boats for hire. Sea trout from middle of July until end of season.

*Dereen Lough* is a large pool on the river upstream from Lough Formoyle. Fishing

stands provided. Good for salmon and sea trout.
*Lough Carrickillawallia (Carrick Lough) (M030350)* is upstream from Lough Formoyle. Access is across the bog for less than 1 mile from Costelloe/Oughterard road. Fishing is best from end of August to end of September. Boat available for hire.
*Lough Aclogher (M040370)* is upstream from Carrick Lough (M030350) and access is by forestry road which is about 6 miles/2.5 km from Oughterard, and approximately 8 miles/3 km from Costelloe. Fishing for sea trout best during August and September. Salmon occasionally. Boat for hire.
*Shannawona Lough (M370398)* is 2 miles/1 km upstream from Lough Aclogher. No boats for hire. Sea trout from September, early October.
In addition there are a number of small lakes holding stocks of brown trout in the area about which the Fishery Manager will advise you.

### Indreabhán (Inveran).
Permits and boat hire for loughs in the area from Mr M. Bolustrim, Ballynahown, Inveran, County Galway (no phone number). Brown trout and some sea trout in these lakes.
*Lough Nagravin*, also known as Ballynahown Lough (L990211), is close to the junction of the Ballynahown/Rossaveel crossroads.
*Tully Lough* is on the north side of the R336 Spiddle/Costelloe road, a short distance from the Ballynahown crossroads. *Crumlin River* and associated lakes are managed from Crumlin Lodge, Inveran, Spiddle, telephone 091–93105.
*The Owenriff River* (also known as Knock River) and connecting lakes (Lough More, Lough Bealcooan (M080280)) may be fished from 15 February. The river is worth fishing in spate conditions.

### Spiddle.
*The Owenboliska River* from the sea to the weir is owned by Spiddle House, telephone 091–83395 and Thomas McDonagh, Merchant's Road, Galway, telephone 091–66111.
*Boliska Lough* (M120260) is located a few miles from Spiddle, off the Shannagurran road. It is fished for brown trout and some sea trout, and an occasional salmon has been caught when the water is high.
*The Upper Boliska River*, from Boliska Lough upstream, has sea trout in July and August if the water is high.
Spiddle Angling school and tours offers courses for beginners and improvers. Rods and tackle for hire plus tuition on casting techniques, telephone 091–83510. They will also advise and arrange fishing trips for the more experienced.

### Na Forbacha (Furbo).
*Knock River* has only a few holding pools and has an occasional sea trout from July. Free fishing, but contact the Western Regional Fisheries Officer at 091–85267 for advice and information.
*Knocka Lough* (M160279) has a good stock of brown trout. Access is via a bog road which runs off the Spiddle/Moycullen road.
*Lough Inch (M220250)* is about 2 miles/1 km from Barna village, west of the Barna/Moycullen road. Walk across the bog from the road. Small brown trout only.

### Moycullen.
As Moycullen is close to Lough Corrib you can arrange to go fishing for salmon or trout on that internationally renowned lake. Other brown trout lakes can be reached via the Derryherk road which leads from the Loughwell crossroads off the Spiddle/Moycullen road.
*Lough Naweelan (M130330)* is part of the Owenboliska system and lies in the hills behind the N59. It may be reached through the townland of Letter, off the N59 towards Oughterard, near Killanin. Take the path which leads through the forest near

Letter Lodge. *Lough Fadda* (M135330) is close by. No permit needed, but contact the Western Regional Fisheries Officer at 091–85267 for advice and information.

## Oughterard.

This village is probably the largest, most important centre for fishing on Lough Corrib. There are a number of tackle supply outlets (see below), and the hoteliers and bar proprietors are also a fund of angling knowledge. A large, easily read map indicating good fishing areas on Lough Corrib and surrounding district stands on the village street. A map of the Corrib with slipways, piers and fishing advice is available from the Regional Fisheries Office in Galway or from the fishing tackle outlets in Oughterard. The brown trout season is from 15 February until 30 September. Salmon fishing from 1 February until 30 September. There are boats and gillies for hire. Tuck's fishing tackle shop in the heart of the village is a good source of information. Lal Faherty has an angling centre, The Lakeland Angling Centre, well signposted off the N59 just outside Oughterard, telephone 091–82121.

## COARSE FISHING

Moycullen and Ross Lake are the best locations for coarse fishing in Connemara. Free fishing stands are provided. Access through the forestry on the Callownamuck road, 1 mile/1.6 km from Moycullen towards Oughterard. Car park on left. Track leads to lake. Stand available for wheelchair users. Live bait from the Cloonabinna House Hotel nearby.

## SEA ANGLING

### Spiddle.

The *M.V. Killaree*, a modern 34' cabin cruiser, can cater for parties of up to 12 anglers and is available for weekly or daily charter. Telephone Joe O'Toole at 091–83412. A 33' catamaran purpose-built for deep-sea angling is available for intensive week-long trips or more easygoing excursions. Telephone Tom Curran, 091–83535 or call at the sea angling office at the boat pier in Spiddle.

### Letterfrack.

The *Lorraine-Marie* is available for fishing trips and is berthed at Derryinver Quay. Contact John or Phil Mongan at telephone 095–43473. Three–hour morning, midday or evening trips can be arranged. Sightseeing as well as angling. Full safety equipment carried on board. Trips at 10 a.m., 2 p.m. and 5 p.m.

The *Fiona-Jane* is available for trips to Inishbofin or for angling trips. Telephone 095–41041/41003. Full safety equipment carried.

### Roundstone.

Ask at the pier for Martin O'Malley (his boat is moored there), or telephone him at 095–35854 to book fishing trips or excursions to see sharks swimming.

## AQUA SPORTS

*Aquasport An Spidéal*, canoeing and kayakking courses daily in July and August opposite the strand in Spiddle. Beginners of all ages welcome; telephone 091–83307.
*Little Killary Adventure Centre*, Salrock, telephone 091–43411 for sailing, wind-surfing, canoeing courses and instruction.
*Renvyle House Hotel*, Renvyle, telephone 095–43511, open to non-residents for surfing (surfboards for hire) and row-boat hire. Reduced rates for family membership on a daily, weekly or monthly basis.
*Delphi Adventure Centre*, Delphi, telephone 095–42208, for wind-surfing, canoeing, sailing and water-skiing courses and instruction.

*Diving facilities* on board Tom Curran's catamaran, telephone 091–83535.
*Clifden Boat Club* for local information, telephone 095–21711.

## GOLF

*The Connemara Golf Club* is at Aillebrack near Ballyconneely. This is an impressive 18-hole links course which is edged by the Atlantic. The Connemara Mountains form a spectacular backdrop. Difficult course when windy. Modern clubhouse with bar and restaurant. Restricted access to children. No professional. Club and caddie car hire. Visitors welcome at all times but best accommodated Mondays to Saturdays. Sandy beach nearby for members of family who do not wish to play. Access to beach across stile near club car park. (Fencing is in place to help prevent erosion of foreshore.) Telephone 095–32502.

*Oughterard Golf Club* is an 18-hole wooded course in the grass-rich area near Lough Corrib. Visitors welcome at all times but best accommodated Mondays to Fridays. Modern clubhouse with bar and restaurant. Professional. Club and caddie car hire. Telephone 091–82131.

*Renvyle House Hotel* has a 9-hole course open to non-residents. Telephone 095–43511.

*Lettermore*, known as Gailf Chursa Gaeltachta Chonamara, 9-hole course. Clubhouse. Visitors are welcome any day. Telephone 091–72498.

## HORSE RIDING

*Cashel Equestrian Centre*, Cashel, telephone 095–31082. Open all year. Specialised day activities for children. Treks to beaches and mountains. Lessons with qualified instructors. Signposted off the N59 near Maam Cross.

*Cleggan Equestrian Centre*, telephone 095–63355. Beach treks.

*Errislannan Manor*, Clifden, telephone 095–21134. Open April until mid-October. Closed Sundays.

*Cluain Árd*, Lettergesh East, Rinvyle. Pony riding on quiet Connemara ponies. Telephone 095–43521.

*Oughterard Trekking Centre*, Telephone 091–82120. Guided treks. Telephone booking is essential.

Connemara coast trail and Connemara mountain/bog trail is organised on six day/six night basis with accommodation, picnic stops and luggage transportation, by Mr William Leahy, Aille Cross, Loughrea, telephone 091–41216.

## PITCH AND PUTT

*Spiddle.* 18-hole course located off coast road out of village towards Galway. Open morning until dusk during June/July/August/September.
*Recess.* On opposite side of lake from Joyce's. Open summer season only.
*Moycullen.* Beyond Celtic Crystal on Church Road. Open all year.

## SWIMMING

Outdoor heated pool available at *Renvyle House Hotel*, Renvyle, telephone 095–43511.
Small indoor heated pool available at *Connemara Gateway Hotel*, Oughterard, telephone 091–82328. Not open December and January.
Sea-bathing excellent throughout region. See beach guide, page 14.

## TENNIS

*Courts at Renvyle House Hotel*, Renvyle, telephone 095–43511. Open to non-residents.
*Connemara Gateway Hotel*, Oughterard, telephone 091–82328. Open to non-residents.
*Roundstone* public courts, opposite the Roundstone House Hotel.
*Clifden* public court on Quay Road.

## OTHER SPORTS

*Renvyle House Hotel* offers croquet, grass bowling and putting to non-residents.
*Pool tables* in a number of bars in Clifden and throughout Connemara.
Rock climbing and hill walking from Renvyle House Hotel, telephone 095– 43511, and Little Killary Adventure Centre, telephone 095–43411.

## ART COURSES

*The Irish School of Landscape Painting*, Clifden. Contact Miss C. Cryan, 095–21891.
Landscape painting courses at *Ballinakill Studios*, Letterfrack. Contact Ballinakill Studios, c/o Connemara West, Letterfrack, County Galway, or telephone 095–41044/41047. Fax 095–41112.

## LAKE CRUISE

Cruises twice daily, 10 a.m. and 2.45 p.m., from Oughterard pier. Telephone 092–46029. Visit Corrib Islands and Cong.

## SEA SIGHTSEEING TRIPS

Trips on the *Lorraine-Marie* from Derryinver near Letterfrack. Half-, full-day or evening excursions. Telephone 095–43473.
Scenic bus tours, booking and information at tourist offices. See page 8.

## WALKS AND TOURS

*Heritage Tours*, Market Street, Clifden. Tours of local archaeological sites (including Inishbofin) and natural history phenomena with Michael Gibbons and Dave Hogan.
*Corrib Conservation Centre*, Ardnasillagh, Oughterard, telephone 091-82519.
Residential wildlife and environmental education courses throughout spring, summer and autumn.
Western Way hill walking route maps are available at tourist information offices.
Connemara Coast and Connemara Gateway hotels have maps of local walking routes.
Cósta Conamara tourist office in Spiddle has maps and multi–lingual information brochures of walks in the Spiddle/Inverin area.

# EVENING ACTIVITIES

## INTRODUCTION

In Connemara, people start their evening out quite late. A pub will often not start to become lively until 10 p.m. Many pubs throughout Connemara have live music, especially at the weekend. You may see a sign outside the pub saying 'music tonight'. This music is likely to be Irish country music, and not Irish traditional music. If traditional music is offered the poster will say so. However, the musicians who play country music in the pubs will be familiar with traditional music and will often oblige visitors, if not with a reel, then with a traditional ballad. When entertainment is held in a pub there is usually no entrance charge. However, it is customary to buy something to drink. This may be non-alcoholic if you prefer. Impromptu traditional music sessions can often start in a quiet pub if one or two musicians happen to be there and feel like playing. Sometimes a lively session will occur during the day.

Entertainment in Connemara is advertised on Radio na Gaeltachta or in English in the *Connacht Tribune* newspaper, county edition, published weekly, every Thursday. 'Craic' is a word you may see on a poster advertising a function. Roughly translated it means 'fun'. 'Ceol agus craic' usually indicates a lively night of music and fun.

### Tully, near Letterfrack.

*Seisiún*, a show of traditional dance and music, in Teach Ceoil, every Tuesday mid-July to late August. Set dancing for beginners in Teach Ceoil every Wednesday at 9 p.m., July and August.

### Clifden.

Music nightly in *Barry's Hotel* during June, July and August. Weekends rest of the year.

Live music or disco in *Clifden House Hotel* during June, July and August. Weekends rest of the year.

Music and entertainment during festivals. (See festival guide, page 8.)

### An Spidéal (Spiddle).

*Cruiscín Lán*. Traditional music every night. Sound system used.

*Tigh Hughes* has set dancing every Tuesday night except during June, July and August. Hosts regular unscheduled sessions.

*The Connemara Coast Hotel* in Furbo organises live music, usually ballad singing, for visitors.

### Oughterard.

*The Connemara Gateway Hotel* arranges live musical entertainment (usually ballad singing) throughout the summer season.

*Faherty's Bar* and *The Boat Inn* have music on Saturdays and Sundays and every evening during the Queen of Connemara Festival.

## SEAN NÓS

Connemara is particularly noted for sean nós singing — the old style of unaccompanied singing. Sean nós singing is non-European in style and is closer to Eastern Mediterranean or Indian-style music. The singer learns three disciplines: ornamentation, melody and rhythm. These are developed as the song proceeds so that each verse has its own variation. These songs will be sung in Irish. If you are interested in listening to sean nós you will hear good singers during the Joe Heanue weekend in Carna (see festivals, page 8), or you may hear someone in Tigh Pheadar

Dick's pub near Ros a Bhíl (Rossaveel). If there is a celebration in a south Connemara village you are likely to hear sean nós singing in the village pub.

# What to see in Connemara

## OUGHTERARD (Úachtar Árd: The Upper Height) AND THE HILL OF DOON.

17 miles/27 km north-west of Galway City on the N59.

Often described as 'the Gateway to Connemara', Oughterard is a large, busy village with shops, bank, post office, bureau de change, pharmacy, hotels and pubs by the shores of Lough Corrib.

You can have a drink in a thatched pub or sit at a table outside another and watch the world go by. You're likely to see bullocks being herded down the wide street, or groups of anglers making their way to the lake for a day's trout and salmon fishing.

Access to Lough Corrib for fishing or a cruise is at the end of the lane beside the Health Centre on the Galway side of the village. Over the bridge on the other side of the village is a small riverside park with seats and grassy play area. For a pleasant stroll, continue up the hill from the park. A signpost on the left indicates a path to the waterfall. Go through the small iron gate. The path winds up between trees and fencing for a short distance before it slopes down to a narrow iron bridge across the falls.

The path continues on the other side of the bridge. Turn left when you reach the road and continue down this country lane, past mature trees and pleasant detached houses, for approximately just over a mile (2 km) to a T-junction. Turn left and you arrive back at the main road above the bridge near the church. Cross the bridge and return to the park and your starting point.

For a drive or cycle of almost 9 miles/14 km to a noted beauty spot, take the road signposted to Glann and the Hill of Doon.

The road swings along by Corrib's shore, moves inland through woodland and fields before returning to the shore a few miles further on. Here there are picnic tables under trees. The road then narrows as it climbs for about 2 miles/3 km to the car park overlooking Lough Corrib and the view of the Hill of Doon. For an even more spectacular view climb the hills behind you on foot. This road ends a little further on so you have to return the way you came.

It is possible, however, to vary your return journey by taking the scenic road route signposted to the right a few miles (approximately 2.5 km) before Oughterard. The road takes you up and over heather and forest-covered hills high above Lough Corrib (more superb views) before returning to the village below the bridge.

If you take the cruise of Lough Corrib from Oughterard you may visit Inchagoill Island, or you may be able to hire a boatman to take you out to the island although most boats will be engaged in fishing. The name roughly translated means 'island of the foreigners' or possibly 'island of the stone'.

There are indications of an early monastic settlement of which little is now known. Only two churches remain. St Patrick's was originally an early simple rectangular church with the tiny flat-headed doorway which is typical of the early Christian churches. Later on in its history a chancel was added.

A pillar found on the island has the inscription 'Lie Lugucredon Macci Menueh' which roughly translated means 'the stone of Luguaedon son of Menueh'. The inscription is thought to be a transliteration of an older Ogham inscription. The pillar is standing near a beautiful little 12th century church known as the 'saints' church'. This was extensively restored in the 19th century by Sir Benjamin Guinness. Notice the heads carved around the curve of the Romanesque arch. Look out for the Byzantine cross in the right-hand corner. Sir Benjamin Guinness had paths and walks made through the woods all over the island. (The Guinness family owned Ashford Castle further around the lake, and Inchagoill was once part of the Ashford estate.) The island's trees were extensively damaged in 1964 when hurricane 'Debbie' hit the west of Ireland. A caretaker, Thomas Nevin, lived in a small cottage on the island for many years. He looked after the paths and the graveyard on behalf of the Guinness family. At one time there were four or five inhabited cottages on the island.

Martin Kinneavy was the last boat builder to live on the island. A snapshot of him with his family in 1906, published in Maurice Semple's *Reflections on Lough Corrib*, shows him to be a young man with a pretty wife and four young children. The baby in the snap grew up to become the Reverend Father Kinneavy and another snap taken in the mid-1960s shows Father Kinneavy standing under the Romanesque arch of the saints' church. He is also shown with his brothers and their families when they were all back on the island in 1968 for the annual anglers' mass.

Aughnanure Castle (see page 28) is close to Oughterard, as is Ross Castle. (See page 32.)

It is possible to hire bicycles on the corner of the road leading to the pier and from Tommy Tuck in the main street. See cycle tours section for suggested routes from Oughterard, page 11. For information on shops, hotels and restaurants see appropriate sections, pages 57, 50, 60.

## How to get there.

Oughterard lies on the N59 Clifden/Galway road approximately 18 miles/29 km north of Galway City. It is often difficult to find a parking place in the centre of the village so it is advisable to park in the large car- park at the Galway entrance to the village. (The hotels have their own car parks.)

## AUGHNANURE CASTLE.

(From Achadh na n-Iubhar, 'field of the yews'.) Approximately 14 miles/22 km north-west of Galway City, 2 miles/3 km south of Oughterard off the N59.

Surrounded by shrubby woodland near Lough Corrib, Aughnanure is a superb example of a 16th century Irish Tower House. The original castle was probably built by Walter de Burgo, First Earl of Ulster, who took possession of Lough Corrib, its lands and castles, from the O'Flaherty clan in 1256. Before the close of the century the O'Flahertys had won back their lands and for the next three centuries were masters of Iar-Connacht (West Connaught). So powerful was the O'Flaherty clan during this period that the words 'From the ferocious O'Flaherties, Good Lord deliver us' were inscribed above the west gate of Galway City.

It was probably to Aughnanure that Donal Crone O'Flaherty invited Owen 'Black oak' O'Malley, chief of the powerful Mayo seaboard-based O'Malley clan, to discuss a marriage between their children, Dónal an Chogaidh and Gráinne. In 1545 Dónal an Chogaidh married Gráinne; she was later to become notorious as Granuaile. (See Inishbofin, page 39.)

In 1569, Edward Fitton, the Lord President of Connaught, declared on behalf of the English Crown that Murrough na Doe O'Flaherty was now Chief of the O'Flaherty clan and lands. Murrough had demonstrated his allegiance to the Crown by informing on his kinsmen and the sons of the Earl of Clanrickarde. They were plotting against the Crown and this was his reward. Murrough was to hold these possessions on behalf of the Crown.

Naturally this decree by Edward Fitton enraged many of the O'Flaherty clan, particularly Dónal an Chogaidh who was the rightful chief. He led a raid on Galway City in 1570 and was killed. His wife Gráinne and his son Owen refused to accept allegiance to the Crown. The O'Flaherty clan was now divided into the west branch based in Connemara, and the east branch under Murrough na Doe O'Flaherty. His lands stretched from Aughnanure to Galway (you can see ruined O'Flaherty castles near Moycullen), across to the sea at Spiddle and along the coast. Aughnanure was refitted and refurbished as Murrough's principal residence. During the Cromwellian period the castle was used as a stronghold by Cromwellians to defend the approach to Galway from the west and by Lough Corrib.

Roderick O'Flaherty, the scholar and writer, who was born in Aughnanure in 1630, petitioned the Crown after the Restoration for the return of the castle. It was returned to him, but the family was Catholic and the family fortunes suffered considerably during the penal times and Roderick died in poverty. The castle was allowed to fall into disrepair. It was still in private hands when it was bought a few years ago by the Office of Public Works who have done considerable reconstruction work.

The castle stands on a rocky promontory beside a narrow river, the Drimneen. The short path from the car park winds along by the river (notice the interesting caverns the river has cut into the rock beneath the castle), and up and over the natural stone bridge into the courtyard. The perimeter walls and towers are in ruins (reconstruction work is in progress), but the main tower house has been well restored by the Office of Public Works.

A plan and an artist's reconstruction is on a wall in each room. Above the front entrance is a hole, known as the Murder Hole, from which missiles could be dropped on intruders. A cubicle to the right probably housed a guard. The ground floor was for storage only. The other floors are divided into two: the larger room for living, the small narrow room for sleeping. There is a lavatory garderobe on the first floor. The fourth- floor room with its large fireplace and mullioned windows was obviously the main living-room. An opening off the garderobe on this floor is the only entrance to a secret room. Continue up the stairs to the walkway along the top of the castle for magnificent views of Lough Corrib and surrounding countryside.

Outside the main house there are two wards or courtyards. The smaller inner one which surrounds the main house, and the larger outer one which dates from a later period. A circular tower in the corner of the inner ward was obviously a watch-tower. Along the western face of the outer ward stood the banqueting hall. Only one wall with decorated stone window frames remains. The style of the windows suggests that this was quite a sumptuous building and was probably built once Murrough na Doe felt secure enough as clan chief to entertain on a lavish scale. A subterranean river ran under the hall. Local legend says that a trap door in the floor of the hall dispatched unwelcome guests into the river below. The castle is open from June until September. Small admission charge.

**How to get there.**

From Galway City take the N59 signposted to Moycullen, Oughterard and Clifden and watch out for the sign for the castle near the golf club before you reach Oughterard.

From Spiddle or Carraroe, take the coast road to Costelloe (Casla) and take the road inland to Oughterard. At Oughterard turn right and continue on the road out of the village towards Galway and watch out for the sign to the castle near the golf club. The road passes the golf course entrance before swinging right towards the castle. Wheelchair access to grounds is difficult.

Ecotour, Galway Corrib circuit, page 154, may be followed to the Stop at Ross Lake (M180362), page 156, and following link.

Bus Éireann operates a bus from Galway to Clifden which passes the turn-off every morning from June until September. Return buses in the afternoon and evening. Check times at CIE enquiry office at the railway station.

After visiting Aughnanure you may wish to continue into Oughterard for a stroll to the pier, the park, or a drive or cycle to the Hill of Doon (see page 26), or you may like to take a coastal drive to Galway via the Costelloe road, signposted to the left near the church.

Close to Aughnanure is Ross Castle, a 'modern' family-owned castle open to the public. (See Ross House section, page 32.)

If you are interested in looking for another O'Flaherty castle, you need to return to Moycullen. On the left, as you enter the village is a stone wall with arched doorway which marked O'Flaherty land. At the crossroads turn left to the church. Below the church a road on the right will bring you to a very ruined O'Flaherty tower and graveyard with O'Flaherty grave slabs. (Keep to the left fork when following the road.)

## PRE 1840 FARM AND HERITAGE CENTRE.

Located alongside the N59, a few miles from Clifden, is the Dan O'Hara pre–1840 Farm Visitor Centre.

When the present owners of this roadside farm discovered that Dan O'Hara had been a previous owner, a man whose life and times were celebrated in a popular ballad, they decided to rebuild the O'Hara ruins (house and cow barn) as they would have been before Dan and his family emigrated to the United States shortly before the Famine in 1845. The 8 acres of hillside surrounding the farmhouse are worked as they would have been by Dan in those pre–Famine times. You will see how a self–sufficient farm worked then: how potatoes, cabbages and oats were grown, how a bank of turf was cut and dried for the fire, and how the cow was milked. And inside the stone–built, thatched cottage you will see simple furnishings, typical holy pictures on the walls, and an open turf–burning fire. Potatoes may be boiling in the old black pot hung over the fire, or a cake of soda bread may be baking in an iron pot oven, heated solely by burning turf. You will be told of the life of a peasant farmer over a hundred years ago and a little of the life of Dan O'Hara, who went from this spot in Connemara to sell matches on the streets of New York.

Other attractions are a re–constructed *crannóg* (an artificial island created and lived on by people in pre–Christian times, for protection from marauding animals and neighbours) and a dolmen (a type of tomb from around 2000 B.C., see page 169). And as the old Galway to Clifden road used to run through this land, the bridge which Daniel O'Connell crossed on his way into Clifden in 1820 may be seen and celebrated as the 'Smallest O'Connell Bridge in Ireland'. Children will enjoy feeding the ducks swimming around the crannóg, or riding in the horse–drawn trap to the farmhouse on the hillside. Those who wish to avoid the horse–drawn vehicle may walk or drive the short distance up the hill to the farm.

Close to the car park is the craft shop, for tickets and information as well as souvenir gifts, tea, coffee and home–baked snacks.

The track to the crannóg and dolmen may be muddy after heavy rain, so wear stout footwear.

Even if you are not interested in early 19th–century farms, a visit to the old O'Hara farmstead on the hillside is worth it for the air and views alone.

31

## How to get there.

From Clifden take the N59 Galway road for 3.75 miles/6 km. Farm is well signposted on the left–hand side of the road. From Galway and Oughterard, take the N59 towards Clifden. The farm is located on the right–hand side, approximately 4.75 miles/7 km beyond the turn off for Loch Inagh. Open from 1 April until 30 September, 10 a.m.–6 p.m., seven days. School tours catered for. Telephone 095–21808. Fax 095–21246.

## ROSS CASTLE.

Located on the shore of Ross Lake off the N59, 5 miles/8 km from Oughterard.

This restored and modernised family home was originally an O'Flaherty castle. The remains of the castle in the basement of the present house indicate a building of the 15th century. In the 17th century the castle was sold to the Martin family of Galway who bought an extensive estate in Connemara. (See Ballynahinch Castle Hotel and Literary Galway for information on 'Humanity Dick' Martin, pages 51 and 131.) The Martins built a 17th century fortified mansion on the site of the castle.

Major Poppleton, who was dismissed from his post as one of Napoleon's guardians on St Helena for being too kind to the fallen Emperor, married one of the Martin girls and came to Ross House to live, and eventually die.

Violet Florence Martin was born here in 1862. She was injured in a fall from a horse in 1898 and began writing. She collaborated with her cousin Edith Somerville and took the pen name of Martin Ross. The two women wrote *Stories of an Irish R.M.* and *The Real Charlotte* which were immensely popular. In the 1980s a television adaptation of some of their work introduced Somerville and Ross to a new audience. Violet died in 1915 and she is buried with her cousin in Castletownsend in County Cork.

In the early 1980s the house had become dilapidated and an Irish-American family, the McLoughlins, bought it and had it renovated to a very high standard. A swimming pool, modern plumbing and a fully equipped kitchen were installed. Every restoration and alteration was done using the best possible material available. Outside in the grounds, one of the old stone outhouses was converted to a chapel. Stained glass from an Irish-American church in New Jersey was brought over and installed.

In their search for replacement stone which would be in keeping with the period of the house, the McLoughlins located stone window sills which had formerly been part of Coole Park, the house owned by Lady Gregory who was one of the founders of the Irish National Theatre. Unfortunately Coole Park was demolished in the 1950s. (See Tour to Thoor Ballylee and Coole Park in the Galway section, pages 140–44.) Work on

*Derryclare Lake*

the old castle foundation is still being done by staff from University College, Galway. When the base of the O'Flaherty Castle was revealed it was felt that the house could once again be called a castle.

Ross Castle is a family home. A member of the family will show you around during May, June and September between 10 a.m. and 4 p.m. This is not a visit for those who want gift shops or tea shops. It is a visit for those who are interested in how an old house can be modernised without obliterating its past. The setting by the shores of Ross Lake is superb and well worth seeing. The grounds, lakeshore and woodlands are also open to visitors. As the family do not keep a large staff, the castle will be closed when it is inconvenient to admit visitors. Telephone 091–80183 to check.

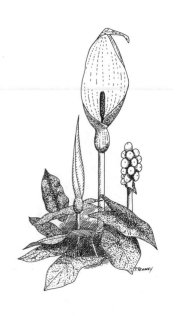

**How to get there.**

From Galway take the N59 through Moycullen for approximately 3.5 miles/6 km. As the road descends through woodland, watch out for a wall and stone pillars on your right. If you reach Kinneavy's pub you have gone a short distance past the castle entrance. Return to the stone gateway which leads to a lane past modern houses to the entrance gates to the castle.

From Oughterard take the N59 to Kinneavy's pub and follow directions as above.

**KYLEMORE ABBEY.**

10 miles/16 km from Clifden, 45 miles/72 km from Oughterard, 62 miles/ 99 km from Galway. The grounds of the Abbey, tea rooms, pottery and craft shop are open to visitors.

The story of Kylemore started in 1852 when Mitchell Henry, a surgeon and financier with addresses in Manchester and London, married Margaret Vaughan from County Down. They honeymooned in Connemara. It is said that when the couple entered the lovely valley of Kylemore they stopped the carriage to picnic. Margaret looked up and noticed a tiny dwelling on the side of the hill overlooking the lake (it may have been a shooting box). She is said to have exclaimed: 'How I would love to live there!'

Back home in England, Mitchell Henry found out who owned the tiny dwelling and learnt that 9,000 acres of moorland, bog, water and woods went with the property. This was the period when wealthy Englishmen aspired to be landowners and built themselves castles and created estates. Mitchell Henry decided that Kylemore would be his estate.

The architects were instructed to incorporate the following rooms in the plans: drawing-room, dining-room, morning-room, breakfast-room, library, study, billiard-room, ballroom with sprung floor, 33 bedrooms, a few bathrooms and apartments for the staff. There was also to be a model farm with up-to-date farm buildings, a saw mill, a turkish bath, a laundry and a chapel. There were to be walled gardens, and glasshouses for rare flowers and fruits. The boggy hillside was to be drained and planted with shrubs and specimen trees. As an interesting feature to walk to, perhaps alone or with guests, a small church was to be built a short distance from the house. The church was to be a replica of Norwich Cathedral.

The building of Kylemore took seven years. No doubt it provided welcome work in an area so recently devastated by the Famine. The style of the building was 'Gothic Revival', a style popular in the 19th century. At that time the novels of Walter Scott, which evoked a nostalgia for the supposed romantic times of earlier centuries, were very much in vogue.

If you consider how far away the valley is from any major centre of industry and supply, building the castle must have been a monumental task of organisation. The stonework is magnificent. The stone carving on the capitals at the entrance were obviously done by a master craftsman. Nearly all the labour was local. A few specialists came from Dublin, and Italian craftsmen were brought in for the ceiling details. Finally, fresh water was piped from a spring on the Mweelin mountain and the castle was ready. It cost about £1.25 million.

The Mitchell Henrys settled happily into their dream home which was finally completed in 1868. Mitchell Henry took an interest in his estate and from 1864 to 1868 he represented Galway in Parliament. But the couple's years of happiness together were short-lived. They had only been living in their Kylemore castle for seven years when Margaret, by now the mother of nine children, decided to join a woman friend on a visit to see the wonders of Egypt. Tragically she fell ill with Nile fever while there and died in Cairo after a few days. Mitchell had her body brought back and placed in the mausoleum which had been part of the original plan. Mitchell Henry seems to have spent most of his remaining time in London attending to his business. Later, another tragedy struck the family. Mitchell and Margaret's daughter Geraldine was killed when the pony pulling her trap shied and hurled her on to the rocks at Derryinver. Shortly afterwards Mitchell Henry's business interests began to fail and he was forced to find a buyer for Kylemore. Mr Zimmerman, a Chicago businessman, bought it for his daughter when she married the Duke of Manchester. However, the new owners do not seem to have been very interested in the estate.

In 1903 there was a rumour that King Edward VII was looking for an estate in Ireland and Kylemore was a possible choice. The beautiful ballroom with its sprung floor was converted into a kitchen. No doubt the Duke hoped to entertain the King with such magnificence that Edward would be sure to buy Kylemore, but when the King and Queen Alexandra toured the area they preferred to stay on the royal yacht and merely took a cup of tea at Kylemore. In 1913, the Duke mortgaged the estate to a moneylender in Liverpool.

The following year at Ypres in Belgium, the nuns of St Benedict felt threatened by the events of the First World War. A short time before shells and explosives wrecked their abbey, they set out to walk to safety with as many of their precious treasures as they could carry. One sister died of exhaustion *en route*. Eventually they reached the coast and got a boat to Dover. From there they went first to Benedictines in Staffordshire, then to Macmine Castle in Wexford.

The Archbishop of Tuam gave the nuns his support. Eventually the money to buy Kylemore Castle for the gallant nuns from Belgium was raised through public subscription. In 1920 Benedictine nuns from Ypres settled into Mitchell and Margaret Henry's beloved Kylemore. The Pope transferred the rights and privileges of the abbey in Ypres to Kylemore and it ceased being a castle and became an abbey. It is an interesting coincidence that Norwich Cathedral, which was the model for Mitchell Henry's Gothic church, was originally built by English Benedictines.

The kitchen, which was converted from the ballroom, has now become a chapel which contains some of the magnificent treasures the nuns carried with them from Ypres. Downstairs in the hall are more treasures: vestments embroidered with gold and silver thread on velvet, a chasuble dating from the time of James II, and a damaged silver figure of Our Lord torn from a cross (it was found in the rubble of the abbey after the war and returned to the nuns). Also hanging in the hall is a flag captured from Marlborough's army at Ramillies by the Irish Brigade fighting for the French in 1706. (Lord Clare, the Commander of the Irish Brigade was a kinsman of a nun at Ypres.)

Following a fire in 1956 a new wing was added which was built in the Gothic style. The Abbey is now an exclusive girls' school, but the nuns will permit visitors to see the hall. The grounds with the statute of the Sacred Heart standing above the Abbey, and the replica of Norwich Cathedral along by the lake, are open to visitors. Ecotour stop L753583, page 76, refers.

In the craft shop a window allows you to watch the pottery being made. The nuns decided to start making pottery in the mid-1970s and sent one of their sisters to learn the craft at Youghal Pottery, and so the pottery, craft shop and tea rooms were built in the grounds.

Kylemore pottery is not available anywhere else as the small pottery can only supply their own craft shop's needs. The shop stocks a good range of Irish gift items like tweeds, knitwear, Connemara marble, crystal, and other china and pottery.

The grounds are open all year. The craft shop and tea rooms are open from Easter until November.

### How to get there.
From Clifden take the N59 Westport road through Letterfrack to Kylemore. For a scenic return route, continue on the N59 and turn right along the R344 through the Inagh Valley. Turn right on to the N59 and back into Clifden.

For a longer scenic drive, continue on the N59 to Killary harbour and the village of Leenaun. See Ecotour stop L833620, page 77, and subsequent link, page 79. Leenaun was the setting for the film 'The Field'.

Follow the R336 along the Maum Valley to Maum. Keane's pub was the house Alexander Nimmo lived in while he was surveying the bogs, roads and harbours of the West. (See 'Roundstone', below.) Turn right (still the R336) to Maam Cross. A right turn brings you back into Clifden on the N59. This circular route is approximately 40 miles/64 km long.

From Galway or Oughterard, follow the N59 to Maam Cross. (See Ecotour stop L978461, page 69). Continue along N59 and turn right along the R344 along the Inagh Valley. A left turn at the T-junction brings you back on to the N59 to Kylemore. Return through Clifden on the N59 or take the route on the N59 to Leenaun through the Maum Valley on the R336 (as above). Turn left at Maam Cross on the N59.

From the coast at Spiddle or Carraroe, take the road from Costelloe to Oughterard (R336) and turn left on the N59 and follow as from Galway.

### ROUNDSTONE
### (Cloch na Rón, 'The Stone of the Seals').
14 miles/22 km from Clifden. 30 miles/48 km from Oughterard.

Located on the coast, this village was established as a fishing village by the Scottish engineer Alexander Nimmo in the 1820s. He was born in Perthshire in 1783. He came to Ireland in 1822 as Surveyor to the Commissioners for the reclaiming of Irish bogs and as engineer of the Western Districts. Nimmo was responsible for 30 stone piers around the Irish coast and the construction of Connemara's roads. He designed a harbour at a place known as the 'The Quay' close to Roundstone. (Tim Robinson says that some people had thought Roundstone an erroneous translation of the name, but as he points out in his *Connemara Gazeteer*, the rock which gave its name to the bay is round.)

There was no village prior to Nimmo's harbour, only a small quay beside a store. The Fisheries Board had the harbour built to Nimmo's design between 1822 and 1825. Nimmo bought land around the harbour and let it out in plots, offering inducements to those who would build two-storey houses, and fisherfolk from Scotland came to settle in the new village.

The Catholic church was built in 1832, and Franciscans established a monastery there in 1835. The friars had a farm and ran the national school. The last friar retired to Clifden in 1974. The IDA park was built on the site of this monastery, and the church tower and gateway have been preserved. The Protestant church was consecrated in 1843. A Presbyterian chapel was built in 1840, but it fell into disuse earlier this century and was demolished. A Protestant school was built in 1891 opposite the harbour.

William McCalla, the discoverer of the rare Mackay's heath (*Erica Mackaiana*) is buried near the site of the old Presbyterian chapel. Born in 1814 the son of the local innkeeper, he acted as a guide for some visiting botanists and was inspired to study botany himself. He made several important discoveries and was financed by the Royal Dublin Society to undertake a botanical expedition to New Zealand. He never carried this out and died of cholera in Roundstone during the aftermath of the Famine.

The novelist Kate O'Brien lived for a few summers during the 1960s in the Old Fort. The building once served as an auxiliary workhouse. The name 'The Fort' was bestowed on it by her. The building housing the Folding Landscape Studio was once a lace school set up by the Congested Districts Board in 1900 to give work and training to local girls. The IDA park was named after Michael Killeen who was chairman of the IDA at the time the park was built in 1983. He was a frequent visitor to Roundstone and the park was renamed in memory of him in 1988.

**How to get there.**
From Oughterard, take the N59 west towards Clifden. Take the R341 signposted to the left past Ballynahinch Castle to Roundstone village. (The road may be indicated as the coast road to Clifden.)

From Clifden, follow the R341 south through Ballyconneely and continue on this road as it heads eastwards to Roundstone.

## INISHBOFIN
### (Inis Bó Finne).

This inhabited island lies close to the fishing village of Cleggan and may be reached very easily from there. The Irish name comes from a legend which told of two fishermen who decided to light a fire on the island which was always shrouded in mist. Once the fire was lit, the mist began to disappear. An old woman driving a white cow approached, passed, and drove the cow towards the lake. There the old woman struck the cow and it turned into stone. No doubt incensed at what they saw as waste, the two men rushed at the woman, wrenched the stick from her hand and struck her. She too turn-

ed to stone. Until 1893 it was still possible to see the two white stones beside the lake. Since then, the rocks may have been chipped away by people needing pretty white stone to decorate a grave or a house wall.

In A.D. 664, the Synod of Whitby in England decided to adopt the Roman instead of the Celtic Church's date for Easter. St Colman, the Irish bishop of Northum-
bria, left England in disgust and came to Inishbofin with some of his followers. They built a church and small monastic settlement, traces of which can still be seen.

During Elizabethan times the island was fortified by a pirate called Bosco and his ally, Grace O'Malley (Gráinne Ní Mháille), who is popularly known as 'Granuaile'. Gráinne was the daughter of the O'Malley chief and she was first married to Donal An Chogaidh O'Flaherty. He was killed in 1570 while on a raid to Galway City. (For background information, see page 29.) Gráinne then married Richard Bourke on condition that she could divorce him after a year if the marriage wasn't satisfactory (under Brehon law divorce was legal). By this time Grace was a competent and fearless sea captain, known and respected up and down the west coast. The merchants of Galway had to make deals with her so that their ships would have safe passage in and out of Galway Bay. It is said that Gráinne gave birth to her and Richard's son while her ship was engaged in battle with a Turkish trader. Her crew were losing the battle so she got up from the bed where she had just given birth, pulled on her britches and marched on deck to direct and win the battle. Later, Richard

Bourke capitulated to the English forces and accepted a knighthood. Granuaile was disgusted with him and threw him out.

Granuaile was a thorn in the side of the English forces for the rest of her life. She easily defeated any ships sent against her. Her castle strongholds were all around the coast. Bosco had chains stretched across the harbour mouth on Inishbofin to protect his and Granuaile's fleet — a fleet she was constantly adding to by capturing the ships she defeated. On one occasion, Gráinne was captured and brought to Galway to be hanged, but her son Owen O'Flaherty rescued her. Finally, members of her family were taken hostage. At the age of 63, Granuaile sailed across the Irish sea, around the coast and up the Thames to London to plead successfully with Queen Elizabeth for the release of her family.

The castle Granuaile and Bosco built on Inishbofin was later taken over by Cromwell's soldiers when they captured the island in 1653. The island was a centre of O'Flaherty and Catholic resistance to English rule in Connemara. Once Cromwell's men were established on Inishbofin, all of Connemara succumbed. Catholic priests and scholars were imprisoned on the island before they were transported into slavery. They were kept in what were nothing more than blow-holes on the north-east side of the island. At low tide the poor wretches could climb down into the caves for shelter, but at high tide they would have been exposed to the rain and cold. Many died. The fortress Cromwell's engineers built had 24 gun placements, a walkway around the top and a well in the central courtyard. There were small rooms around the walls.

During this period Catholic families forced out of other areas were sent into Connacht. In 1900 there were still people who had Ulster and Meath surnames living on Inishbofin. Some of Cromwell's soldiers settled in the district.

When King Charles II came to the throne, the Earl of Clanrickarde was created Baron Bophin and given Inishbofin and neighbouring Inishshark. Later on in the century, the island was held by Jacobite supporters of Catholic James, but they surrendered to King William's troops in 1691.

For a while Inishbofin was owned by a succession of absentee land-lords. The last landowner was Cyril Allies who built a hotel in Victorian times. (Day's Hotel is built around the original house.) The Allies family stayed on Inishbofin until 1908 when the Congested Districts Board bought most of the island to distribute to the tenants. The Allies emigrated to South Africa and started a farm there which they called 'Inishbofin'. The island has beautiful beaches and a small population. In the summer it becomes a popular holiday island for those who want sea, sand, caves to explore, easy walks and night-time music sessions. At low tide you can walk out to the remains of the Cromwellian fort. East of the fort is the roofless 13th century chapel associated with St Colman's monastery. Nearby is a holy well dedicated to St Flannan.

**How to get there.**
Cleggan lies 10 miles/16 km from Clifden. There are regular boats out to Inishbofin from Cleggan in the morning, afternoon and evening. Go down to the pier and you will be advised by the signs which boats are going out. As all the boats are independent of each other, be careful you don't buy a ticket for one boat, then get on another by mistake, as tickets are not transferable! For information on cost and times, telephone 095–44649/44690/44761.

**PATRICK PEARSE'S COTTAGE.**
37 miles/59 km from Galway City, 31 miles/50 km from Clifden, 9 miles/14.5 km from Maam Cross.
On the far side of the lake at Turlough, a townland of Rosmuck in the heart of the Connemara Gaeltacht, is the small whitewashed cottage used by Patrick Pearse as a summer home. (Patrick Pearse, writer and poet, was one of the leaders of the 1916 Rising and was executed for his part in it.) It is in a superbly isolated setting surrounded by granite and heather high above the lake. The interior was burned out in 1921 during the War of Independence in a reprisal action by the soldiers known as the 'Black and Tans' (because of their uniform which was a mixture of army khaki and police black). The cottage has since been restored and furnished as it was in Patrick Pearse's time.
Many of Pearse's stories contain references to places and events in this district. In addition to writing, Pearse improved his Irish and knowledge of the people of Connemara while staying here. In his small cottage he discussed with other leaders of the 1916 uprising the possible future of an independent Ireland. The cottage contains many mementoes of Patrick Pearse and is open to the public from April until September from 10.30 a.m.–6 p.m. A guide is present at the cottage during these hours to give a short talk on Pearse. A small charge is made for admission. If you wish to visit the cottage out of season, the key is available at the bungalow opposite the access road.

While in the area, you may be interested to know that nearby in Camas Uachtair (Camus Oughter), is the national school which the Irish language writer, Máirtín Ó Cadhain (1907–70), taught in when he was a young man; Cill Bhriocáin (Kilbracken) was the home of the Irish language poet, singer and activist, Caitlín Maude (1941–82), and Pádraig Ó Conaire (1883–1928), one of the most important figures in modern Irish-language literature, was brought up by his uncle in Garafin House which is in Gairfean (Garrivinnagh).

**How to get there.**
From Galway, Oughterard or Clifden take the N59 to Maam Cross. At Maam Cross turn left if approaching from Galway, right if approaching from Clifden. At Screeb the road forks. Take the right fork for 5 km. The cottage is visible from the road and is well signposted. Park on the road or drive to the small car park half-way along the access road. Beyond the cottage gate the path is steep and uneven and probably difficult for wheelchairs.

For Cill Bhriocáin and Garafin House, return towards Screeb and take the first right for 2.5 miles/4 km for Caitlín Maude's home and 3.75 miles/ 6 km for Pádraic Ó Conaire's childhood home. For Camus Oughter, return to Screeb junction and take the R336 to the right for 1 mile/1.6 km. The school Máirtín Ó Cadhain taught in is now the headquarters of An Comhlachas Náisiúnta Drámaíochta.

To vary your return journey to Galway, stay on the R336 for a route which takes you back to Galway along the shores of Galway Bay through Inveran and Spiddle. If returning to Oughterard, turn left at Costelloe.

If returning to Clifden, turn left on the R340 from Pearse's cottage and take a tour through Carna, Cashel and Glinsk before rejoining the N59 for Clifden.

## CLIFDEN ('An Clochan': the stepping stones, crossing place across the river).

Approximately 50 miles/80 km north-west of Galway City. This is a 19th-century market town tucked picturesquely into a valley between the mountains and the sea.

In 1812 a local landowner, John D'Arcy, who was High Sheriff of Galway, dreamed of a centre of law and order on his lands in what he regarded as the wild and lawless countryside of Connemara. He used government grants and generous lease agreements to help to establish the town, which was completed by the mid-19th century. The castle, which was John D'Arcy's residence, was the first construction. Fifteen acres of sloping land overlooking Clifden Bay were drained and planted with shrubs and trees. The house is a ruin now as the D'Arcy family became bankrupt during the famine years and sold the castle and estate to Thomas Eyre of Bath who was an absentee landlord.

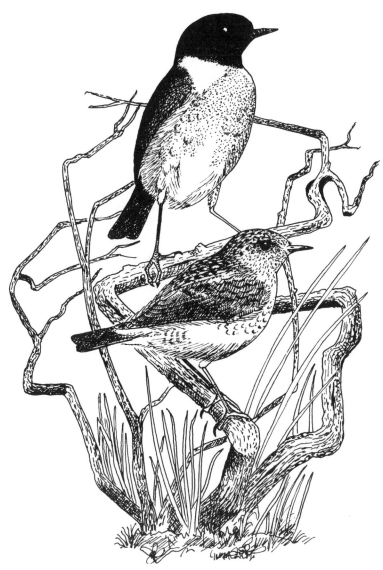

The castle is reached off the Sky Road which is signposted in front of the Alcock and Brown Hotel. Cars must be parked at the entrance gate. The cart track to the castle is very muddy in winter and after heavy rain. Four standing stones at the side of the track may have been removed from an ancient site nearby and placed there during the castle's construction. The building is unsafe to enter, but its dimensions and scope can be adequately seen from outside. It was obviously a typical gentleman's residence of the time with castellations and heraldic decorations on the exterior. Opposite the rear entrance, on the other side of the wall, is a 19th century stone drainage channel. Nearby are ruins of extensive stables, barns and walled gardens. On the shore are the remains of a beach, or marine, house which was decorated with shells.

Two church spires dominate the skyline of the town. The Protestant Church, on the hill behind the Alcock and Brown Hotel, is a simple undecorated mid-19th century church. A replica of the silver Cross of Cong stands on the altar and the decorated organ pipes are well worth seeing.

The first rector of the church was Hyacinth D'Arcy, eldest son of John D'Arcy. The D'Arcy family became Protestant in name in 1800 in order to keep their lands in accordance with the penal laws. Hyacinth, who contracted a painful disease of the knee joints while a teenager, and who later lost a leg, was a fairly idle youth who spent a lot of time on his yacht on Clifden Bay. When his father died prematurely in 1832, Hyacinth became landlord, magistrate and leading citizen overnight. During the famine years he took his role very seriously and bankrupted the family estate trying to alleviate the distress of the starving peasants. Distressed at his inability to help, Hyacinth was influenced by Robert Dallas, the founder of the Irish Church Missionary Society, when he visited Clifden. Hyacinth became a committed convert of Protestantism and subsequently a clergyman.

The Catholic Church on the other side of the town has beautiful stained glass and an interesting modern icon of Our Lady of Knock. The Stations of the Cross are traditional framed oil paintings.

The Sky Road is worth driving, cycling or walking on for spectacular views. Keep to the right fork and stop at the car park and viewing point on the left. Return the way you came or continue for a few metres and turn left for the low road which hugs the cliff face back into Clifden. The circular route is approximately 7 miles/11 km long. The roads are narrow, so drivers are advised to go slowly.

The Alcock and Brown Memorial is 3 miles/5 km south-west of the town on the road to Ballyconneely. John Alcock and Arthur Whittier-Brown were the first people to fly non-stop across the Atlantic: on 15 June 1919 they landed near the Marconi wireless station in the middle of the bog. They were able to travel on the small train the wireless station staff used to get on to firmer land. When they got into Clifden they sent a telegram from the post office to announce their feat to the world. A concrete memorial which evokes an aeroplane has been erected on the roadside overlooking the bog where they landed. The large car park is an ideal site to look back at Clifden nestling between the hills and the surrounding coast and countryside.

The Marconi Wireless Station was built on Derrygimlagh bog (near the Alcock and Brown memorial) in 1906. It was the first transatlantic wireless station. There were no obstructions between it and the receiving station on Cape Breton Island, Nova Scotia. The bog supplied the fuel to power the steam-driven power plant. A set of rails and a small narrow-gauge train enabled the staff to reach the turf banks for the fuel and the road. The station was burned down in 1922 during the Civil War.

Omey Island and Inishbofin lie close to Clifden and are worth a visit. Letterfrack and the Connemara National Park Centre are a short distance from Clifden. *En route* to Letterfrack you will pass Kylemore Abbey. (See page 34.) For information on hotels, where to eat and shop, see pages 50, 60 and 57.

### How to get there.

Clifden lies on the N59 from Galway. In the late 19th century a railway line ran from Galway to Clifden, but unfortunately the line was closed in 1935. Steam railway buffs may like to spot the remains of the old track on the road out from Galway.

Bus Éireann operates a daily service to Clifden which takes just over 2½ hours. Times of departure are available from the enquiry office at the railway station.

### CONNEMARA NATIONAL PARK AND LETTERFRACK.

The Connemara National Park covers over 2,000 hectares of mountain, heath and bog, which are publicly owned, near Letterfrack village in west Connemara. Some of the mountains in the park area are part of the Twelve Bens or Beanna Beola range. Glanmore, the large glen, forms the centre of the park and from it the Polladirk River flows through a scenic gorge just south of Kylemore Farm.

The Visitor Centre is located on the side of a hill behind the old Industrial School in Letterfrack. The entrance is on the left-hand side of the Clifden road. A good tarred road leads to an excellent car park. The

*Aughnanure Castle*

Visitor Centre, which is comprised of low, white-washed buildings, is in a landscaped setting with furnished picnic area. There is an audio-visual theatre, informative displays, leaflets and an indoor picnic area. Leaflet guides for two well laid out nature trails are available for those who prefer to follow a set route into the park. During July and August there are special evening films, and talks and guided walks during the day. Special children's events and walks are arranged. The summer guided walks take two to three hours and usually start at 10.30 a.m. on Mondays, Wednesdays and Fridays during July and August. You need to wear boots or stout shoes and you are always advised to bring rainwear. Wheelchair access to the Visitor Centre may be difficult as the approach path from the car park is quite steep.

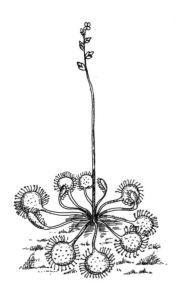

Letterfrack was developed by two Quakers, John and Mary Ellis, who settled in the district in 1849. They drained land, planted trees, built cottages, a temperance hotel and a shop to sell local produce. Because of ill health, John and Mary returned to England and their estate was bought by the Diocese of Tuam in 1882.

The Church established an orphanage first, which later became an industrial school, then a reform school which became notorious for the harsh way the boys were treated. (The writer Mannix Flynn has recorded his time here.) In the graveyard behind the church is a headstone with the name of 60 boys who died while at the school. Eventually the school was closed in 1973.

An enterprising local development company bought the old school and transformed it. It now houses a health centre, sports and leisure centre, offices and a school of woodworking design — the only one of its kind in Ireland. The students' work is displayed during the summer months. On the grass outside the centre is an exhibition of wood sculptures. If you walk around the village you will notice the substantial 19th century buildings.

While in Letterfrack you may wish to visit the Church of Christ the King at Tully Cross to see the Harry Clarke stained-glass windows in the east gable.

Marconi erected a receiving station in 1913 on the hilltops between Letterfrack and Tully Cross. (The Clifden station could not transmit and receive simultaneously.) Eventually the high winds proved too much and the Clifden station was adapted and the Letterfrack station abandoned.

The foundations of the boiler can still be seen near the road and the base of the masts on Shanaveg and Currywongan.

The beaches at Lettergesh, Glassilaun and Renvyle are worth visiting (see beach guide, page 14).

For those interested in traditional music and dance, the Teach Ceoil at Tully (a very short distance out of Letterfrack) is a regular venue for music and dancing. Visitors are encouraged to learn to dance an Irish set in special beginners' and advanced dancing sessions.

**How to get there.**

If approaching from Galway, stay on the N59 through Recess. Then turn right on the R334 through the Inagh Valley, and left on the N59 past Kyle-more Abbey, to Letterfrack and through the village for the Park entrance.

From Clifden, come through Moyard into Letterfrack. An interesting return route would be to continue on to Kylemore, then a right turn through the Inagh Valley and back on to the N59 for a return to Clifden.

Letterfrack can be reached by Bus Éireann from Galway and Clifden, but the timetable allows only restricted access in winter, and is impossible for day trippers in winter or summer.

**CONG.**

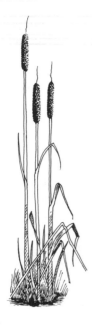

28 miles/45 km from Oughterard, 50 miles/80 km from Clifden, 28 miles/ 45 km from Galway (via Headford).

Cong is a small village just inside the Mayo border on the shores of Lough Corrib. It is famous for its Abbey, and for being the location of Ashford Castle. Interesting sights like 'the rising of the waters' and 'Kelly's Cave' are also in the village vicinity. Walking tours of the location of the classic 1950s John Ford film, 'The Quiet Man' are held daily during high season.

The Abbey was founded by St Feichin in the 6th century. King Turloch Mór Ó Conor had it rebuilt and dedicated to the Augustinian Canons Regular in the early 12th century. Turloch's son Rory, the last High King of Ireland, retired to the monastery in 1183 and lived there for 15 years until he died. He is buried at Clonmacnoise, County Offaly.

Access to the Abbey is off the main street. The locked gate has a sign indicating where the key may be obtained. However, access through the cemetery near the modern church appears to be possible all the time. Access to the cloisters and grounds is through the Ashford Castle gateway (but no entry to Ashford Castle is allowed) immediately to the right. The most substantial remains are the cloister, chapter house, monks' fishing house and the bridges. An outline plan of the Abbey is sited by the approach path to the cloister garth.

The beautiful Romanesque doorway in the north wall dates from A.D. 1200. Stairs lead from the sacristy to the upper levels. Part of two vaulted rooms and part of the walls of the chapter rooms remain. The sculptures on the west wall of the chapter room date from the 13th century.

The decoration on the cloister arches is quite lovely and thought to be the finest example of this type of work in the west of Ireland. The work largely dates from the 15th century, but during the late 19th century, a local family, the Foys, were hired by Sir Benjamin Guinness to do some restoration work. The cloister garth, with the sound of the river filtering through the trees, has a wonderfully peaceful atmosphere.

Well-kept paths lead through the grounds past ancient yew trees to a stone bridge over the river. The arches at either end of the bridge have carved heads on them; one is of the last abbot and the other is of Rory O'Connor.

The monks' house sits over the river. You can see the hole where a fishing line was dropped into the river. It was so rigged that a bell rang in the kitchen when a fish was on the line. Beyond the river, paths wind through the woods. The abbey is open all year and admission is free.

Ashford Castle started out as a De Burgo Norman tower castle in the 13th century. It was rebuilt during the 15th and 16th centuries, then rebuilt in the style of a French château during the 18th century. In the 19th century it was in a dilapidated state and was bought by Sir Benjamin Guinness. It was subsequently extensively rebuilt in the Gothic style which was popular with landowners during the 19th century. The interior of the castle has been modernised and is a luxury hotel. President and Mrs Reagan stayed here duing their visit to Ireland. The castle is in a superb spot by the shores of Lough Corrib. Cruises go from the pier beside the castle down the lake to Oughterard.

Many of the scenes for the film 'The Quiet Man' were shot near the castle and a local man takes parties on walking tours of the location sites. He has a fund of interesting anecdotes about the 'stars' of the film, John Wayne and Maureen O'Hara, and of events which occurred while the film was being made. Tours leave every 90 minutes, starting at 8.45 a.m., from the ticket office which is further down the street from the Abbey. 'Quiet Man' devotees may like to know that some scenes were shot near Maam Cross, the racing scenes were shot on the beach at Lettergesh and the station used was Ballygluin, now featured in West Rail steam train tours (see Galway section, page 121).

The base of the stone cross in the centre of the village dates from the 12th century.

There is an outlet of Lough Mask near the village. When the waters in the lake rise, the underground river flowing through the limestone gurgles and rushes to the surface. This is known as 'the rising of the waters'. The Pigeon Hole is a natural rocky cavern descended by a flight of rough-cut steps to where a branch of the Cong River flows underground.

A huge cairn of loose stones, approximately 150 ft/50 m in diameter and 70 ft/23 m high, is said to contain the body of the last Firbolg King of Ireland who was killed in the 3rd century B.C. during a battle with the De Dannan army. Experts agree that the cairn probably covers a passage grave from this period. Called the 'Giant's Grave' locally, it is signposted through woods off the road approaching the village. Kelly's Cave, a natural cave, is also signposted off the approach road to the village.

The village caters for visitors with the Quiet Man coffee shop and Danagher's pub which serves meals all day.

**How to get there.**

From Galway and Oughterard, take the N59 to Maam Cross and a right turn on the R336 to Maum. Another right turn at Keane's pub on the R345 takes you along the shores of Lough Corrib into Cong. Ecotour Galway Corrib circuit, page 154, follows this route. If not following the Ecotour return route through Headford to Galway, return the way you came.

# WHERE TO STAY IN CONNEMARA

'**Gaeltacht**' has been indicated after placenames for those who would like the opportunity to speak Irish.

## HOTELS

This is a comprehensive list of hotels in Connemara. The Irish Tourist Board and the Irish Hotels Federation use a star rating for hotels ranging from 5 stars to indicate international standard luxury to 1 star for simple, often family run, hotels. All will have a high standard of cleanliness and hygiene.

As inflation may alter the accommodation rates, a rough indication of the single overnight accommodation is given as follows:

| | |
|---|---|
| Economy: | £15 to £25 |
| Budget: | £25 to £35 |
| Moderate: | £35 to £45 |
| High: | £45 plus |

Hotels offer a cheaper rate during their low season. High season is June, July and August unless otherwise indicated. If the hotel closes for part of the year, this also is indicated. Hotels may add a 10% or 12% service charge. You should check when booking.

## Ballyconneely.

*Erriseask Hotel.* Telephone 095–23553. **. 10 rooms, 8 en suite. Overlooks Mannin Bay. Peaceful and quiet. Bicycles available to guests. Open turf fires. Open end of March to end of September. Rating: budget.

## Ballynahinch.

*Ballynahinch Castle Hotel.* Telephone 095–23553. ****. 28 rooms en suite. Located in extensive wooded grounds overlooking famous salmon river. Hosts autumn and winter woodcock shooting. Gothic style 19th century castle. (The original castle is now a ruin in the lake.)

In the 17th century a large castle or manor house was built on the present site. This burnt down in the 19th century. 'Humanity' Dick Martin lived there. He was the MP who introduced legislation in the British Parliament which led to the setting up of the RSPCA – hence the nickname. The Martin estate stretched from Oughterard almost to Clifden, and the avenue to Ballynahinch Castle was said to be the longest in Ireland. But 'Humanity'Dick was a lavish spender. By the time his son Richard inherited in 1883, the estate was largely in debt. Earlier this century the Castle was owned by the Maharajah Ranjitsinhji, the famous cricketer.

Ballynahinch has been thoroughly modernised, but it still retains the air and style of a grand country house. It is a member of the Manor House hotels group. Rating: high. Open all year.

## Carna (Gaeltacht).

*Sceirde House Hotel.* Telephone 095–32255. Fax 095–32342. **. 12 rooms en suite. Modern building. Rating: budget.

## Casla (Gaeltacht).

*Cashel House Hotel.* Telephone 095–31001. Fax 095–31077. ****. 32 rooms en suite. Once a family home at the head of Cashel Bay, now an elegant hotel. Landscaped gardens, tennis, horse riding, private beach, rowing boats and bicycles for guests only. General and Madame de Gaulle spent two weeks here in 1969. Open mid–February to mid–November and Christmas. Irish, French and German spoken. Cesar award for highest standard of Irish hotelmanship, 1987. Winners of National Garden Award, 1983. Rating: high.

## An Ceathrú Rua (Gaeltacht).

*Hotel Carraroe.* Telephone 091–95116. Fax 091–95187. **. Modern hotel. All rooms en suite. Parents with children catered for (special children's tea and entertainment which is videoed. While parents have dinner the children watch themselves on the video.) Outdoor heated swimming pool, tennis court, games room, sauna, solarium. About ten minutes' walk from the village, 15 minutes' walk from the beach. Open spring to late summer. Rating: budget.

*Óstán an Dóilín.* Telephone 091–95169/95177. *. Open all year. Modern building. 10 rooms en suite. 1 mile/1.5 km from the 'coral strand'. Rating: economy.

## Clifden

*Abbeyglen Castle Hotel.* Telephone 095–21201. Fax 095–21797. ***. Located on Sky Road overlooking the Bay. 42 rooms en suite. Tennis courts, outdoor heated swimming pool, pitch and putt, table tennis, sauna. Closed January. About ten minutes' walk from the town centre. Rating: high.

*Alcock and Brown Hotel*, The Square. Telephone 095–21086. Fax 095–21842. **. 20 rooms en suite. Central position. Open all year (not Christmas Eve or Christmas Day). Rating: budget.

*Barry's Hotel*. Telephone 095–21287. Fax 095–21499. **. Family owned and managed. Centrally located. All rooms en suite. Music in bar most nights, every night during high season. Rating: budget July/August, economy rest of year.

*Clifden House Hotel*. Telephone 095–21187. Fax 095–21479. *. In the centre of town with own grounds. Open April to end of September. 20 rooms en suite. Family run. Disco or live music nightly. No single rooms. Rating: economy.

*Foyle's Hotel*. Telephone 095–21801. Fax 095–21458. ***. Centre of town. 28 rooms en suite. Family owned and run. Open May to October. Rating: economy to budget.

*Ardagh Hotel*. Telephone 095–21384. Fax 095–21314. ***. 2 miles/3 km from Clifden. Facing west overlooking bay. Log and turf burning open fires. Restaurant regularly mentioned in Egon Ronay guide. Family run (member of Coast and Country Hotels of Ireland). French, German and Dutch spoken. Rating: moderate.

*Rock Glen Manor House Hotel*. Telephone 095–21035. Fax 095–21737. ***. 1.5 miles /2 km from Clifden. 29 bedrooms en suite. Modernised 18th century shooting lodge. Open from mid–March to end of October. Tennis court. Snooker. Overlooking inlet of sea. Family run (member of Manor House hotels group). Rating: high.

## Na Forbacha.
*Connemara Coast Hotel*. Telephone 091–92108. Fax 091–21737. ****. Overlooking Galway Bay. Recently refurbished to luxurious standard. Sauna/gymnasium. Video link to rooms. Booklet of walks available to guests. 83 rooms en suite. Open all year. Rating: moderate.

## Glinsk (Gaeltacht).
*Glinsk House Hotel*. Telephone 095–32279. Fax 095–32342. **. Modern hotel on the side of the road in splendidly isolated position on the Glinsk peninsula. 12 rooms en suite. Open all year. Rating: budget.

## Inishbofin.
*Day's Hotel*. Telephone 095–45827/45829. **. Near sandy beach. Cycle hire. Rating: economy.

*Doonmore Hotel*. Telephone 095–45804. **. Near sandy beach. Facilities for children. Pets welcome. Cycle hire. Rating: economy.

## Letterfrack.
*Kylemore Pass Hotel*. Telephone 095–41141. **. Located 1.5 miles/2 km from Kylemore Abbey. Has own fishing. Pool table. Rating: budget.

*Renvyle House Hotel*. Telephone 095–43511. ***. About 3 miles/5 km from Letterfrack right beside the sea. Own beach, boating, swimming pool, croquet. Once the home of Oliver St John Gogarty who entertained, among other celebrities, W. B. Yeats and Augustus John. The principal actors from the film 'The Field' stayed here while on location in Leenaun. Rating: high July and August, moderate low season.

## Moycullen.
*Cloonabinna House Hotel*. Telephone 091–85555. **. Modern hotel on shore of Ross Lake. 15 rooms en suite. Family owned and run. Rowing boats. Angling centre, particularly coarse fishing. 9 miles from Spiddle beaches and Galway City. Open all year. Rating: economy.

## Clifden.
*Clifden Glenn Holiday Village*. Telephone 095–21491. Fax 095–21818. 83 luxuriously appointed houses and some single apartments located in a wooded valley alongside the N59, a short drive from Clifden. Pitch and putt, tennis courts, restaurant and bar on site. Tours and excursions arranged. Open all year.

## Oughterard.

*Corrib Hotel.* Telephone 091–82329/82204. Fax 091–82522. **. Comfortable, modernised country hotel on the main street in Oughterard. Gardens at rear. Family run (member of MinOtels Ireland). Babysitting service. Wheelchair facilities. 26 bedrooms en suite. Closed January/February. Rating: budget.

*Egan's Lake Hotel.* Telephone 091–82275. **. 20 bedrooms. Has been popular with fishermen for years. Wash–hand basins with hot and cold in bedrooms. Open all year. Rating: economy.

*Connemara Gateway Hotel.* Telephone 091–82328. ***. Luxurious modern hotel on outskirts of Oughterard. Heated indoor swimming pool, sauna, tennis courts, booklet of walks (at all levels) from the hotel provided for guests. Video facilities to each room. Children catered for with special meal times and entertainment. Closed January. Live music – ballads and sing–along most evenings during summer season. Rating: high.

*Sweeney's Oughterard House Hotel.* Telephone 091–82207. ***. 29 rooms en suite. A few have four–poster beds and five have king–size beds. Comfortable country house at the side of the road surrounded by pretty, mature gardens. River and riverside park opposite. Quiet. Only well–behaved children encouraged in bar. Specialises in fresh shellfish (sea water tank in dining–room) and gourmet food. Rating: high July/August, moderate rest of the year.

## Recess.

*Lough Inagh Lodge.* Telephone 095–34706. Fax 095–34708. ***. Located in a stunning valley. 56 en suite rooms. Open April to October. Rating: moderate to high.

## Rosscahill.

*Ross Lake House Hotel.* Telephone 091–80109. Fax 091–80184. ***.  Located approximately midway between Moycullen and Oughterard 1 mile/2 km off N59 in woodland setting. Georgian House. 13 rooms en suite. Tennis courts. Ideally located for gentle hill walking. Fishing within short driving distance. Rating: budget in high season, economy low season.

## Roundstone.

*Roundstone House Hotel.* Telephone 095–35864. **. Family run, member of Village Inns Group. Centrally situated in village with views over harbour to bay. Open late March to end of September. Rating: economy.

*Eldons Hotel.* Telephone 095–35933. Fax 095–35921. **. 13 rooms en suite. Open March to December. Rating economy.

*Seals Rock Hotel.* Telephone 095–35860. *. Open April to September.

## An Spidéal (Gaeltacht).

*Park Lodge Hotel.* Telephone 091–83159. Fax 091–83494. **. 23 rooms en suite. Family run. Open June to September. 10 minutes' walk along coast road to village and beaches. Uninterrupted views of Galway Bay. Open June to September only. (Other months, minimum number 20 groups or conferences only.) Rating: budget.

*Bridge House Hotel.* Telephone 091–83118. **. 16 rooms en suite. Centre of village. Gardens to rear. Comfortable, established, family hotel. Closed for a month at Christmas. Rating: budget low season, moderate July and August.

## BED AND BREAKFAST

Offered throughout Connemara, but cluster in and near to Oughterard, Spiddle, Moycullen, Clifden, Roundstone, Letterfrack/Rinvyle, Leenaun, Cleggan.

## SELF-CATERING

### Carraroe (Gaeltacht).
*Carraroe Holiday Village.* Telephone 091–95116. Fax 091–95187, or write to Carraroe Holiday Village, Carraroe, County Galway. Ten two-storey slate roofed cottages in the grounds of Hotel Carraroe on the outskirts of Carraroe. Gallery bedrooms. Open all year. (Hotel open from May to October only.) Use of hotel bar, restaurant and video screening facilities. Use of tennis court and outdoor swimming pool. Direct dial telephone. Babysitting service. Pets welcome. Centrally heated. About 10 minutes' walk from grocery shop, butchers, pharmacy and post office. About 15 minutes' walk from beaches.

### Cleggan.
*Cleggan Farm Cottages.* Telephone 095-44648. Five slate-roofed, stone built, converted farm buildings located on working sheep farm by the sea. Two-person and eight-person cottages available. Open fireplaces plus central heating in smaller cottages. Beach, Martello tower, and megalithic tomb nearby. Open all year. Pubs and shops in the village.

### Clifden.
*Clifden Glenn Holiday Village.* Telephone 095–21491. Fax 095–21818. 83 luxuriously appointed houses and some single apartments located in a wooded valley alongside the N59, a short drive from Clifden. Pitch and putt, tennis courts, restaurant and bar on site. Tours and excursions arranged. Open all year.

### Indreabhán (Cnoc) (Gaeltacht).
Telephone 01–571437/571439/593138. Fax 01–592068, or write to Spiddle Holiday Homes, An Grianán, Ballymount Road, Clondalkin, Dublin 22. A group of single-storey, slate roofed, semi-detached, modern traditional looking cottages on the side of the R336 at Inveran. Beach on opposite side of road about 15 minutes' walk away. Tennis court and amenity building with washeteria, games room.

### Lettermore (Gaeltacht).
Telephone 091–72120, or write to The Hooker Bar, Bealadangan, Lettermore, County Galway. A small group of traditional thatched modernised cottages tucked into trees right on the edge of the sea. Entrance opposite The Hooker Bar. Stone flagged floors, open fireplace and old-fashioned dresser in the sitting-room. Carpeted bedrooms. Hooker Bar serves seafood snacks. Nearest small shop is a good 15 minutes' walk away.
Telephone 091–81163/72348. Fax 091–81146, or write to Island Holiday Cottages, Annaghvaan, Lettermore, County Galway. A larger group of modern old-style slate-roofed cottages in more open setting. Portacabin has a pool table and football game tables, and automatic washing machine and dryer. Grass area between houses for children's play and some rudimentary swings. A ten-minute walk from post office/local shop with newsagents. Babysitting service. Television and open hearth fireplace. Close to sea but not to strand. Ideal for anyone interested in sea angling. game fishing, exploring Connemara or improving their Irish. English is the second language of the local people. Nine–hole golf course.

### Furbo.
Telephone 091–92335, or write to Marino Holiday Cottages, Furbo, Spiddle, County Galway. Marino cottages are a small complex of traditional style cottages on the Galway to Spiddle road, behind the Furbo petrol station. Approximately ten minutes' walk from the beach. Small shop for groceries, or use Galway supermarkets at

*Lough Ahalia*

*The Twelve Bens*

Westside, Terryland or Headford Road, avoiding the city centre.
Galway Bay Cottages. Telephone 091–92491 or write to Galway Bay Cottages,
Barna, Galway. Small estate of slate-roofed traditional style houses on slightly
elevated site off main road. Landscaped, each cottage has own small front garden. 10
minute walk into Barna village for shops and restaurants.

### Inishbofin.
Telephone 095–43473 or write to West Coast Cottages, Derryinver, Letterfrack,
County Galway. Traditional style cottages available. Eight minutes' walk from pubs,
shops and beaches.

### Letterfrack.
Renvyle Thatched Cottages. Contact Connemara West plc, Letterfrack, County
Galway. Telephone 095–43464/41044/41047. Fax 095–41112. Nine traditional style,
modern thatched cottages built and run by the local community organisation. Located
about ten minutes' walk from Letterfrack, at Tully Cross. Close to bars, shops and
church. Ten minutes' drive from beach.

### An Spidéal (Gaeltacht).
Park Lodge. Telephone 091–83159/83207 or write to Rent-a-cottage, Park Lodge
Hotel, Spiddle, County Galway. 11 traditional slate-roofed-style cottages tucked in
behind the Park Lodge Hotel on the outskirts of Spiddle. (See hotel section, page 50.)
Cottages close together. No sea view. Use of hotel facilities. Open all year. T.V. hire
available. A few minutes' walk along the main road to the beach. Spiddle has two
supermarkets and a pharmacy.
Spiddle Holiday Homes. Telephone 01–571437/571439/593138. Fax 01–592068, or
write to Spiddle Holiday Homes, An Grianán, Ballymount Road, Clondalkin, Dublin 22.
A group of traditional style slate-roofed cottages spaciously laid out on site
overlooking Galway Bay. Located up a side road on the outskirts of Spiddle towards
Galway. Site has tennis courts, swings and slide. Pets not welcome. Open all year.
Babysitting service available. A few minutes' walk down to the main road and along it
to the beach. Narrow road to rear of cottages leads across bog to Spiddle/Moycullen
road.

# HOSTELS

A hostel will provide basic accommodation (usually dormitory or shared) and a kitchen
for self–catering. It is advisable to have your own sleeping bag or sheet. Some
hostels will rent you a duvet or sleeping sheet. As they offer cheap accommodation,
hostels are popular with young visitors, but there is no age limit in any hostel. Some
will offer family rooms.

### Carna (Gaeltacht).
Mac's Bar in the village has a hostel at the rear of the bar (it used to be a hotel).
Telephone 095–32240. Open from May until end of September. 4 beds to a room.
Free showers.

### Cleggan.
The Master's House, Knockbrack, Cleggan. Telephone 095–44746. Open all year.
Free hot showers, a private room and a family room available.

### Clifden.
Leo's Hostel, Sea View, Clifden. Telephone 095–21429. Open all year. Free hot
showers. A few private rooms and one family room available.
An Óige Hostel at Ben Lettery outside Clifden on the N59. Telephone 095–34636.

### Inishbofin.
Inishbofin Island Hostel. Telephone 095–37164. Open from St Patrick's weekend in
March until the end of September. Free hot showers. One family room available.

**Indreabhán (Gaeltacht).**
*The Connemara Tourist Hostel* at Aille, Inveran. Telephone 091–93104. Open all year. Free hot showers. Two family rooms available.
*An Óige hostel* off R336 Spiddle to Costelloe road. Telephone 091–93154.

**Oughterard.**
*Lough Corrib Hostel,* Camp Street, Oughterard. Telephone 091–82634. Open from 1 March until end of the year. Free hot showers. Three family rooms. Good library of books, tapes and videos.

**An Spidéal (Gaeltacht).**
*Village hostel.* Telephone 091–83555. In heart of village. Short walk to strand.

## CAMP SITES AND CARAVAN PARKS

**Carna (Gaeltacht).**
*Mac's Bar and Hostel.* Telephone 095–32240. Camp site available. Use of hostel kitchen and showers.

**An Ceathrú Rua (Gaeltacht).**
*Coillean Caravan and Camping Park.* Telephone 091–95266/95189. Open 1 April to end of September. Food shop. Ten minutes' walk into village. 15 minutes' walk to beach.

**Cleggan.**
*The Masters' House Hostel* has camping facilities. Telephone 095–44076. Use of kitchen and showers.

**Letterfrack.**
*Rinvyle Beach Caravan and Camping Park.* Telephone 095–43462. Open Easter to end of September. Food shop. No dogs allowed.
*Connemara Caravan and Camping Park.* Telephone 095–43406. Near Lettergesh beach. Open 1 May to end of September. No dogs allowed.

**Roundstone.**
*Gorteen Beach Caravan Park.* Telephone 095–35882. Located on beach, 2 miles/3 km from Roundstone village. Food shop. Children's play room. Open 1 March to 30 September.

**An Spidéal (Gaeltacht).**
*Pairc Saoire an Spidéal.* Telephone 091–83372. Open 1 May to end of September. 1 mile/1.6 km from village/beach. Children's play area.

# SHOPPING FOR GIFTS AND SOUVENIRS

**Cashel.**
*Connemara Marble Studio* for original items in Connemara marble. Turn off the Cara/Cashel road by Glinsk House Hotel. Proceed for a short distance, turn towards the sea and take second left.

**Clifden.**
*The Weaver's Workshop* sells original design, locally made, handwoven rugs, wallhangings and tweeds. Open from Easter to October, Mondays to Saturdays. If visiting out of season telephone 095–21074.
*Millar's shop* is a long-established supplier of quality, traditional tweed, knitwear, crystal and original depictions of landscapes. Millar's of Clifden started making tweeds for the Victorian tourists and have been in the business ever since. Open all year, Mondays to Saturdays.

*Clifden Pottery.* Open 11 a.m.–12 noon, 2 p.m.–5 p.m., or telephone 095– 21259 if you see anything you like through the window.

*Gerard Stanley and Sons* are suppliers of Barbour jackets, Aran knits, tweeds and sportswear. This is a typical market town countryman's shop.

*Heritage Crystal Shop*, Main Street. Crystal made by local ex–Waterford craftsmen sold at half the Waterford price. Closed November to March. Will open on request, telephone 095–21827.

*Connemara Woollen Mills Handcraft Shop.* Thatched cottage shop selling knitwear and a wide variety of gifts. Located on the road to Westport. German and French spoken. Large car park.

*Smoked Salmon at Salt Lake Manor.* Wild Irish salmon smoked on the premises. Visitors may sample and buy a small quantity for picnic or heat-sealed pack to take home. Located about 1.6 miles/1 km from Clifden on the Roundstone road.

## Furbo/Barna.

*Kilraine of Connemara.* Large souvenir house on the sea side of the coast road to Spiddle. Tweeds, knitwear, wide range of gifts. Specialises in miniature traditional cottages, old road signs. Coffee shop overlooking bay. Good parking. Summer only.

*Timber Leaves* in Barna village. Wood craft workshop. Lamps, clocks, toys, ear-rings, brooches. All Irish wood. Open all year.

## Cornamona.

*Galway Woollen Market* stocks wide range of knitwear, tweeds and a smaller range of other gifts. On the side of the road approaching from Maum. Open seven days a week during the summer.

*Joe Hogan*, telephone 092–48241, is a traditional basket-maker who makes a wide range of baskets from 'sally' rods he grows on his land. Baskets from large creels to smaller fruit or vegetable baskets. Although his address is Finny, Cornamona, he is located on the road beside Lough Nafooey. If coming from Clifden via Leenaun, or from Maam, turn up by the Maam Country Knitwear shop (see below) and follow the road down to the lake. Joe's house is the first stone cottage on the left-hand side of the road. Open Mondays to Saturdays all year.

## Letterfrack.

*Connemara Handcrafts* is an Avoca handweavers' shop. Located just outside village on quay side on road to Moyard.

*Stoneworks Connemara Ltd* for Connemara marble gifts. Located just outside Letterfrack at Derryinver on the shores of Ballynakill Harbour.

## Maum and Maam Cross.

*Peacock's* for an extensive range of quality gifts: tweeds, knitwear, crystal, books, sheepskins and some pocket-money souvenirs.

*Maam Country Knitwear and Gallery.* Paintings, photographs, knits. Coffee shop. Open all year.

## Moyard.

*Cottage Handcrafts* for a large selection of sweaters and other gifts. Coffee shop. Open all year.

*Roger Walker Pottery.* Stoneware pottery. One mile off Clifden to Letterfrack road beside Ballynakill church. Open six days, closed Mondays all year.

## Moycullen.

*Celtic Crystal* make distinctive crystal glasses, vases, clock casings, even napkin rings using unique cutting method and traditional Celtic designs, including the Claddagh ring design. Some coloured crystal. Factory showroom. Parties will be allowed to watch cutter at work. Popular with bus tours, so there is a coffee shop and outlet for other Irish gifts next door to showroom. Located down the road past the church. Continue down the road to where road bends through trees, over a small stone bridge and watch out for sign indicating a right turn. Open all year.

*The Luck Penny.* Thatched craft shop next door to the marble factory on the N59. Sweaters and a wide range of goods. Specialists in mail order. Open March until October.

*Connemara Marble Factory and Shop.* Popular with bus tours whose passengers are given a talk on the origin, colour and forms of Connemara marble. Most gifts in the shop use this green marble. Coffee shop for visitors to the shop and factory. Located on side of the N59 on the Oughterard side of Moycullen village. Parking available.

*This 'n' That.* Antiques, gifts and curios. Open all year. Located on the N59 near centre of the village.

## Recess.

*Joyce's.* Wide range of quality Irish goods: clothes, paintings, unique locally–crafted Connemara marble carved pieces, antiques and a wide range of Irish interest books. Next door to Joyce's bar/lounge on the N59. Car park overlooks lake. Open 17 March until October, to 6 p.m., seven days.

## Oughterard.

*Monahan's crafts and coffee shop.* Also a tourist information centre. Has sheepskins, goatskins, Aran knits and tweed. Look out for terra cotta figures from Tipperary and miniatures of Irish cottages made by a thatcher from the south-west. (As he travels around to ply his trade he photographs the cottages he thatches and makes colourful ceramic models of them during the winter.) The location of each cottage is indicated on the base.

*J.P. Keogh's* for an excellent range of tweed capes, scarves, sweaters, Aran knits. Look out for the knitted 'tams' (caps) and the pampooties (slippers) for small children. Also stocks Irish interest videos, spoken word as well as singing.

*Fuchsia Craft Shop* for wide range of goods, Royal Tara china, Galway crystal, jewellery, decorated bodhrans (Irish hand-held drums). Look out for small watercolours of local scenes at reasonable prices. Also Diarmuid Boyd framed prints.

*Candle Maker*, about 1 mile/1.5 km outside village. Take Galway road out and turn right about 0.5 miles/800 m along narrow winding road. Showroom behind cottage on your left. Well signposted. Pretty handpainted, scented, and special occasion candles.

*West Shore Gallery* in Camp Street for quality art work by local artists.

## Roundstone.

*Malachy Kearns* in the IDA park for musical instruments: decorated goatskin bodhrans (Irish hand-held drums), flutes, harps and tin whistles. Miniature bodhrans personalised with name, or design of choice ready within one hour. Open seven days a week, 8 a.m.–7 p.m. May to October. Five-day week out of season. Coffee shop.

*Seamus Laffan and Rosemary O'Toole* in the IDA park for porcelain jewellery, decorated domestic and garden stoneware and pottery. Open all year.

*Folding Landscapes* for Tim Robinson's quality maps. His map of Connemara with gazetteer surpasses all others. Studio in Nimmo House on the quay. Open May until September, 11 a.m.–6 p.m.

**Rosmuck.**
*Rosmuck Knitwear* for original design knitwear. The modern showroom in front of the factory is open all year, Mondays to Saturdays, 9 a.m.–7 p.m. Located on R340 near Pearse's Cottage.

**Spiddle.**
*Standún's (Staunton's) Shop* is probably the largest souvenir shop in the west. Located on the side of the road outside Spiddle towards Galway. Staunton's have been selling quality Irish gifts to passing tourists for a lot of years. If it is Waterford crystal, Belleek, Aran knitwear, or Irish tweeds you want, this shop holds a large stock. Open all year.
*Ceardlann (Craft Village)* opposite blue flag beach for a variety of gifts made in the village. All the 'cottages' have workshops and showrooms with goods for sale. In some it is possible to watch the craft being made. The Ceardlann is open all year, seven days a week. The landscaped area around the cottages has seats and a coffee shop. Visitors are encouraged to wander through the village and in and out of the showrooms. The following crafts are available:
*An Spailpín Fánach* for original design screen-printed quality T-shirts, sweat shirts and track suits. The Irish language is featured on the shirts. Also screen-printed tiles, linen stationery sets.
*Sliding Rock Pottery* for hand-thrown pottery at reasonable prices.
*Proinsias* for practical and attractive machine-knit woollen sweaters and jackets.
*Galway Gold.* Jewellers and goldsmiths. Original jewellery designs.
*Róisín Conamara* for pretty paperweights, penholders and other gifts using dried wild flowers.
*One of Susan's* for designer handknits.
*Máire Ní Thaidhg.* Hand weaver who makes spectacular wallhangings and smaller items like tweed scarves.
*An Damhlánn* has regular exhibitions of work by local artists, sculpture, paintings, drawings, wallhangings. A lot of the work has a Connemara theme or depicts Connemara scenery. Reasonable prices.
*Mike Wilkins*, stone worker.

# WHERE TO EAT IN CONNEMARA

This is a guide to places to eat while you are touring Connemara. It is not a good food guide. A brief indication of location, style and price range of the restaurant/café is given so that you may check before setting out on a visit or tour whether you need to take a picnic. The price rating is only a rough guide as some people eat very little and consider themselves well fed.

| | | |
|---|---|---|
| Economy: | under | £5.00 |
| Budget: | under | £10.00 |
| Moderate: | under | £15.00 |
| High: | over | £15.00 |

All restaurants are required by law to display their menu and prices outside the premises. Pubs along the route may offer sandwiches or soup and home-made brown bread. If they do they will indicate 'snacks, teas, coffee' on a displayed sign. 'Children's menu' indicates that chips are served.

**Ballynahinch.**
*Ballynahinch Castle Hotel* is open to non-residents. See hotels section, page 50. Bar snacks and full dinner menu. Dining-room overlooks river. Rating: economy to high.

## Ballyconneely.
*Erriseask Hotel.* Open to non-residents. See hotels section, page 50. Rating: budget to moderate.

## Carna.
*Sceirde House Hotel* is open to non-residents. See hotels section, page 50. Has children's menu. Rating: budget.

## Carraroe.
*Hotel Carraroe restaurant* is open to non-residents. See hotels section, page 50. Rating: moderate to high.

*Óstán an Dóilín* is open to non-residents. See hotels section, page 50. Located *en route* to the 'coral' strand. Substantial meals (meat and two vegetables). Rating: economy to budget.

*An Ciseóg.* Restaurant open from the end of May to the end of August. 10 a.m.–11 p.m. Takeaway side open until 3 a.m. Small café with polished wood tables, place mats. Steaks, seafood, salads, children's menu. Rating: economy and budget.

*An Cistín.* Bar lounge. Snacks, salads, and outside seating. Open pub hours. Rating: economy to budget.

*An Realt* coffee shop is on the road to the 'coral' strand. Modern décor. Rating: economy.

## Cashel.
*Cashel House Hotel.* See hotels section, page 50. Lunch, snacks and dinners. Cuisine. Rating: high.

## Cleggan.
*Oliver's Seafood Restaurant and Bar* overlooking the harbour.

## Clifden.
*Mitchell's Restaurant*, Market Street. Stone walls, polished wood floor, open fireplace. Children's menu, locally caught seafood dishes, home–baked snacks. Open seven days all year. 11.30 a.m.–10.30 p.m. (6 pm. for snack menu). Rating: budget to moderate.

*Derryclare Restaurant*, Market Street. Wood panelled, tiled floor, modern PVC table covers. International cuisine. Open all year for lunches and dinners. Wine. Rating: economy/budget.

*Cullen's Coffee Shop*, Market Street. Stews, salads, home–baked snacks. Open Easter to October, 10 a.m.–10 p.m. Rating: economy.

*Doris's Restaurant*, Market Street. Telephone 095–21427. Polished wood tables. Intimate rustic simplicity. Broad menu including Asian and vegetarian. Will cater for special needs menus if contacted in advance. Open all year. 12 noon–10 p.m. Wine. Booking advisable during summer months.

*The Olde Skillet*, Market Street. Stews, seafood, special tourist menu. White–washed walls. Carpeted. April to October. 6 p.m. until late. Open for lunch June/July/August. Wine. Rating: budget to moderate.

*Destry's*, Market Square. Fun decor. 'Boys from the Backroom' memorabilia. Casual but stylish. Inventive menu. Open Easter to October. Wine.

*E. J. King's*, Market Square. Two–storey bar restaurant. Salads, seafoods, steaks and bar menu. Stone walls, open fires. Full licence. Open all year. Rating: economy to budget.

*Quay House.* Telephone 095–21722. Located along the quayside. View across the bay from the window seat. White–washed walls, carpets, candles, original paintings, inventive menu. Booking advisable.

*Atlantic Fisherie*, Main Street. Seafood specialists. Pine tables. Carpeted. Open April to October, 12 noon–3 p.m., 6 p.m.–10 p.m.

*D'Arcy Inn*, Main Street. Upstairs restaurant has view of a terraced garden. Table linen co–ordinated with docor. Tiled floor. Downstairs bar has booth seating and open fireplace. Irish/international cuisine. Open all year. 12 noon–3 p.m., 6 p.m.–10 p.m. Full licence.

*O'Grady's Seafood Bar.* Family run. Award-winning restaurant. Table linen. Lunch 12.30–3 p.m. Dinner 6.30–10 p.m. Wine bar. Lunch rating: budget. Dinner rating: budget to moderate

*High Moors restaurant.* Telephone 095–21342. 2 miles/3 km outside town, overlooking moorland and lakes. Dinner only, Wednesdays to Sundays, 7 p.m.–9 p.m. Wine. Rating: budget to moderate.
*Connemara Woollen Mills Craft Shop* on Westport road outside the town. Seafood restaurant open 10 a.m.–8 p.m., seven days a week. Wine. Home baking. Rating: economy to budget.
*Ardagh Hotel.* Telephone 095–21384. 2 miles/3 km towards Ballyconneely, overlooking bay. Gourmet food in spectacular location. Open to non-residents. Rating: high.

### Furbo.
*Connemara Coast Hotel.* Open to non-residents. Provides snacks and full dinner. Rating: budget to moderate.

### Glinsk.
*Glinsk House Hotel* is open to non–residents. See hotels section, page 50. Rating: moderate to high.

### Inagh Valley.
*Inagh Valley Inn.* Telephone 095–34608. Oldest coaching inn in Connemara. Modern dining–room overlooks the lake. À la carte from 10.30 a.m.–9 p.m. Locally–caught salmon and fresh seafood. Rating: budget to moderate.

### Inishbofin.
*Day's Hotel* restaurant. Open 10 a.m.–10 p.m., snacks and meals. April to September. Rating: economy to budget.
*The Lobster Pot* for locally caught seafood. April to September. Rating: economy to budget.
*Doonmore Hotel* restaurant. Open to non–residents. April to September.

### Leenaun.
*Portfinn Lodge.* Telephone 095–42265. Seafood restaurant. German spoken. Rating: budget to moderate.
*The Field Restaurant* and coffee shop. Steaks, salads, seafood, home–baked snacks. Open April to September.
*Interpretative Centre* restaurant. Open April to September.

### Letterfrack area.
*Bard's Den* lounge bar in the centre of Letterfrack serves full means and snacks. Open all year. Rating: economy to budget.
*Veldon's Lounge Bar* in village serves substantial meals and snacks. Open all year. Rating: economy to budget.
*Kylemore Abbey* coffee shop and tea rooms for snacks and meals. Rating: economy to budget.
*Kylemore Pass Hotel*, a short distance from the Abbey has tourist menu in restaurant, bar and snacks. Rating: budget to moderate.
*Cottage Handcrafts*, Moyard, tea rooms for home baking and lunches. Open seven days a week. Rating: economy.
*Derryglen restaurant* in Tully Cross. Open 9 a.m.–9 p.m. Children's menu. Rating: economy to budget.

### Maam Cross.
*Peacock's.* Full meals and snacks all day and evening in the lounge bar or restaurant. Full à la carte, seafood, salmon, steaks, salads. Rating: economy to budget.

### Moycullen.
*Drimcong House.* Telephone 091–85115/85585. Georgian country house in beautiful grounds located 1 mile/1.5 km out of Moycullen towards Oughterard. Gourmet food at reasonable prices. Chef uses freshly picked herbs and salads from own gardens. Also uses wild hedgerow ingredients when available and pike fresh from the lake near the house. Awarded a star by the Egon Ronay good food guide (and regular winner of Ballygowan/Bord Fáilte awards for excellence). Chef named 'Egon Ronay Chef of the Year' 1994. Excellent wine cellar. Simple but elegant dining–room can seat 50. Full à

la carte and also vegetarian. Popular, so advisable to book in advance. Closed
January/February. Rating: moderate children's dinner, budget vegetarian, high rest of
menu.
*White Gables.* Charmingly renovated old two–storey cottage at the side of N59 in
village. Dining–room ground floor only. Small but good selection of gourmet food –
particularly fish dishes. Rating: moderate to high.
*Ferryman Inn lounge bar.* Recently refurbished, offers snacks and salads, coffee and
tea.
*Country Chip Café.* Takeaway and café. Salads and snacks as well as fast food.
Open from 1 p.m. until after midnight throughout the year. Closed Sundays, but open
Sunday nights. Extremely clean and cheerful. Order food at counter. Rating:
economy.

## Oughterard.
*Corrib Hotel Restaurant* is open to non–residents. 7 p.m.–8.30 p.m. Hot and cold
snacks all day until 11 p.m. in bar. Good plain food. See hotels section, page 50.
Rating economy to moderate.
*The Boat Inn.* Bar food at lunchtime. Restaurant open 6 p.m.–10 p.m. Salmon, steaks,
salads. Prettily decorated dining–room with lots of natural light. Rating: budget.
*Keogh's Restaurant and Bar.* Restaurant at rear of bar. Gleaming wood tables.
Subdued lighting. Children's menu. Rating: budget to moderate.
*Waterlily Restaurant.* Telephone 091–82737. Overlooking river near bridge at side of
N59. Table linen, wine. Open evenings. Rating: moderate to high.
*Sweeney's Oughterard House Hotel Restaurant.* Telephone 091–82207. Picturesque
old house opposite river park on N59. Gourmet food, specialises in seafood. Wine.
Rating: moderate to high.
*Corrib Country* restaurant, Main Street. Snacks, lunches, dinners. Children catered
for. Open Easter to October. Rating: economy to budget.
*Ó Fatharta Coffee Shop and Restaurant.* Home–baking, seafood, children's menu.
Wine. Open Easter to October, seven days a week. Rating: economy to budget.

## Ros a' Mhil (Rossaveal).
*Le Morganou.* Breton chef. Owned and run by family who operate fish factory and
export business next door. Seafood, fresh from the bay, is cooked French style at
moderate prices. Informal French country–style décor. Rating: budget to moderate.
*An Ghleoiteóg restaurant.* Open seven days a week, breakfast to dinner. Wine.
Home–baking. Tourist menu and à la carte. Rating: economy to budget.

## Roundstone.
*Beola Restaurant.* Telephone 095–35871. Centre of village. Steaks, salads, seafood.
Locally caught lobster a speciality (20 lobsters a day consumed during height of
season). Table d'hôte and à la carte. Wine licence. Open April to 30 October. Lunch
12.30 p.m.–2.30 p.m. Dinner 6.30 p.m.–9.30 p.m. Full table linen. Rating: moderate.
*Malachy Kearn's* craft shop coffee shop in IDA park. See shopping guide, page 59.
Rating: economy.
*O'Dowd's Bar and Restaurant.* Telephone 095–35809.

## Spiddle.
*'Boluisce'* steak and seafood bar and restaurant. Winner of the 1990 'Best Seafood
Bar' award. Family run. Children's and vegetarian menu. Full bar licence. Open
midday until late. Particularly noted for shellfish dishes and home–made brown bread.
Open all year. Charming country cottage décor. Closed Sundays and Mondays out of
season. Bar downstairs, restaurant upstairs. Rating: budget to moderate.
*An Droighnean Donn.* Restaurant at rear of the bar. Lunch menu from 12.30
p.m.–2.30 p.m. Hot meals, salads and children's menu. Soup and sandwiches all day
in the bar. Pretty dining–room arranged in booth style. Restaurant closed in winter.
Rating: economy to budget.
*An Cruiscín Lán.* Hot meals, salads, soups, sandwiches and children's menu in the
bar. Good views of the bay. Rating: economy.
*Craft Centre Café.* In Ceardlann opposite the beach. Cheerful décor. Seating
available outside. Home–baking and international–style lunch dishes including
vegetarian. Order food at counter. Open from 10 a.m.–6 p.m. all year. Open until 7
p.m. during the summer. Rating: economy.

# CHILDREN'S ACTIVITIES

See the aqua sport section (page 22) for canoeing, sailing, boating and windsurfing. *Cashel Equestrian Centre* specialises in children's activities. See horse riding (page 23). Older children may like to learn to fish. The Spiddle Angling School will hire out tackle and give lessons. Telephone 091–83510.

Visit *Spiddle Animal Farm* 1 mile/1.5 km from village on Moycullen road. Open seven days, June to September. Open 11 a.m.–8 p.m.

There are free fishing stands on Ross Lake, near the Cloonabinnia Hotel, Moycullen. A cheap rod may well be as good as an expensive one for catching coarse fish. Live bait from the hotel.

*Cruises on Lough Corrib* are always popular with children. See Oughterard section, page 24.

*Aughnanure Castle* near Oughterard. The 'Murder Hole', the secret room and the climb to the battlements always seem to interest younger people. See page 28.

*The Connemara National Park Centre* organises special children's mornings on Tuesdays and Thursdays during July and August, 10.30 a.m.–1.30 p.m. Boots and rainwear advisable. Telephone 095–41054 to check details.

*Teach Ceoil* in Tully, near Letterfrack, arranges Irish dancing lessons for visitors, 11 a.m.–1.30 p.m. during July and August. The set-dancing sessions during the evening may interest older children. (See evening activities, page 25.)

Boat trips will often entertain children. Telephone John or Phil Mongan at 095–43473 for information about trips on the *Lorraine-Marie*, and 095–41041 for information about trips on the *Fiona-Jane* in the Letterfrack/Clifden area.

On a fine day nowhere is nicer for children than a beach. See beach guide for information on amenities and location, page 14.

Indoor swimming pools at *The Connemara Gateway Hotel*, Oughterard and the *Connemara Coast Hotel* in Furbo are open to non-residents.

*Leisureland amusement park* and swimming pool in Salthill is a perennial favourite with children of all ages.

A day in Galway City may be a popular activity, especially if a tour of toy shops is included. See page 104. See also children's activities Galway City, page 150.

*Westport House and Zoo.* Open May to September, Rowing boats on lake. Miniature railway. Slides. See rainy day activities.

Boat trip to Heather Island near Letterfrack. June to September 2 p.m.–6 p.m. Closed Sunday/Monday. Telephone/fax 095–41028.

# RAINY DAY ACTIVITIES

*Visit Westport House in Mayo.* 36 miles/57 km from Clifden. Home of Lord Altamont. Open from May to September to visitors. Telephone 098–25711 (Westport Tourist Office.) Ceilings by Cassells, who designed Powerscourt and Leinster House, and a superb James Wyatt dining-room. Early 19th century Waterford glass chandeliers, 18th century handpainted Chinese wallpaper and rooms of classical furnishings.

In the grounds there are children's activities, a miniature railway, slides, and a zoo with llamas, ostriches, camels and monkeys. Inside the house in the basement is a ball pond for active toddlers and young children.

*Go into Galway City.* See 'rainy day activities', page 150.

Visit Aughnanure Castle (see page 28); Ross Castle (see page 32); Pearse's cottage (see page 41).

Go swimming (see pages 14, 24)

Visit the Connemara National Park centre (see page 45)

Visit *Cultural Centre* in Leenaun. Audio visual displays connected with local sheep and wool industry. Demonstration, crafts for sale, restaurant and coffee shop. April to September daily.

Visit V'Soske-Joyce carpet/rug factory in Oughterard. Open all year.

Visit the *Clifden Heritage Centre for Alcock and Brown*, and Marconi exhibitions.

# ECOTOUR

## GALWAY — SCREEB VIA ROSSAVEEL/COSTELLOE/LETTERMULLAN.

**Link** 7 miles/11 km from Silver Strand/Loc Ruisin.

Travelling westwards along the coast road we have a continuous view of Galway Bay against a backdrop of bare, limestone terraces of the Burren. In clear, calm conditions the Aran Islands gradually rise above the horizon as we approach Spiddle. The landward side of the road is now a ribbon of modern bungalows, carelessly scattered along what was once a most scenic and agreeable route. Beyond the houses, though, there is still an extensive area of open countryside — blanket bog, rock and lakes interspersed with forestry plantation. The road northwards from Spiddle to Moycullen captures the essence of these low, rolling granite hills and is an ideal cycling route for a tour from Galway City. (The increasing use of this road by large coaches is to be deplored.)

**Stop** Spiddle (M126227), on the bridge at the western end of the village.

Beneath the bridge the Owenboliska River tumbles over granite boulders at the end of its short but turbulent journey to the sea. From its source in the peat-covered hills to the north it crosses open bogland, skirts conifer plantations, expands into lakes and finally, just above the village, passes through Shannawoneen Wood — probably the only surviving native woodland in the coastal area of southern Connemara. The wood is dominated by sessile oak, but birch, rowan and beech are also present. Of particular interest, however, are the mosses and lichens which live on the surface of the rocks and on the trees. Many species are typical of western woodland, but have a restricted distribution elsewhere in Ireland.

Oak woodland was at its most extensive in Ireland about 6,000 years ago after the expansion and decline of post-glacial birch, hazel and pinewoods. This is evident from the pollen preserved in the peat in many parts of the country. The analysis of pollen in the sediments of a small lake near Spiddle has confirmed this sequence of events in south Connemara and shown that the blanket bog started to form about 4,000 years ago. The appearance of cereal pollen and then charcoal in the bog over 3,000 years ago indicates substantial human impact on that ancient landscape. Changes continue as the bog is cut for turf or planted with trees. Drainage alters the course and flow of the river and a dam has turned Boliska Lough into a reservoir to serve the growing human population in the area. Salmon, which run up the river to spawn in its headwaters, are becoming scarce as drift-nets catch them at sea before they have a chance to enter the river. Grouse, too, which were once common on the surrounding hills, have become scarce and are not often seen these days.

**Walk.**

A short walk westwards leads to a left turn which takes us down to Spiddle beach and pier and an interesting rocky shore beyond.

**Link** 18 miles/29 km.

Beyond Spiddle the density of housing diminishes a little, but many of the new homes, with their 'suburban' gardens look incongruous in such a naturally harsh landscape. For the walker or cyclist a detour to the north along any of the small by-roads will lead into the heart of one of the most extensive areas of, until recently, untouched blanket bog in Connemara.

After Inveran the road swings northwards towards Costelloe. The coast road takes us via Rossaveel — primarily a fishing harbour, but used increasingly by ferries serving the Aran Islands (see Link Rossaveel (L962252) to Kilronan (L882087), page 69). Like all fishing harbours it is an important haunt for gulls and enthusiastic gull watchers. Returning to the main road we turn left towards Costelloe. However, the cyclist or motorist who wishes to cut short the journey to Galway can take the road signposted to Oughterard which offers a picturesque, though somewhat bumpy, route across country towards Lough Corrib. At Costelloe we can make a choice to venture first on to the causeway-linked islands of Lettermore, Gorumna and Lettermullan or to continue northwards towards Screeb.

Heading to the islands we turn right at the Radio na Gaeltachta station (which serves the Irish-speaking community) a short distance to the west of Costelloe and follow the road through a landscape of bare rock and small fields which merge into seaweed-rimmed inlets, creeks and bays. Exploration of Gorumna is best carried out by bicycle or on foot. The narrow roads, high stone walls and humps and hollows in the landscape bring endless visual surprises which require time to savour — time that travel by motorised vehicle does not permit.

**Stop** near causeway between Lettermore Island and Gorumna Island (L896274).

The causeway was built in 1897 and replaced a swing bridge. This permanent link between the islands, which has prevented sailing boats passing between them, marked the end of an era of regular coastal commerce. Today, only the tide races between the pillars of the causeway from Greatman's Bay in the east to the island-studded inlet of Kilkieran Bay to the west.

The tiny island just to the east of the causeway is Geabhróg, Tern Island, and, true to its name, Arctic and common terns nest on the island, just a few centimetres above the high tide level.

**Link** 4 miles/6.4 km.

On Gorumna Island we pass some of the island's few mature trees on the hill to our right. The island's industrial complex (still under the sign of Comharchumann na nOileáin) is on the left with the island Heritage Centre beside the road. Here we can learn about the history of the island and some of the crafts which were practised by the resilient people who worked so hard to survive in this difficult environment. A little further on at the crossroads we see, to the right, the last remaining bog on the island with its ancient pine stumps. Lough Illauntrasna is now the island reservoir and much lower than it used to be before its waters were tapped for domestic and industrial use, as is evident from the wetlands which remain around it.

**Stop** opposite the church (L882238).

It is hard to believe that much of the ice-smoothed granite landscape which stretches before us was once covered with peat. Generations of turf cutting, coupled with extensive grazing and burning have, through sheer necessity, stripped the landscape to its rock skeleton. Only in the damp hollows and on the few remaining dry peaty knolls can life maintain a presence. Bog asphodel, bog cotton, bog bean and sundew grace the wet peat and pools, while western gorse and heather cling, prostrate, to the exposed summits.

A diversion along the second road to the left will bring the energetic walker or cyclist to a summit which commands fine all-round views of the Connemara mountains, the Aran Islands, the Burren and the Cliffs of Moher.

**Link** 0.5 miles/0.8 km.

We keep going southwards past small walled fields and gardens to the parking area beside Lough Hibbert.

**Stop** at the parking area beside Lough Hibbert (L882234).

The highlights of this shallow, rocky lake are the scrubby islands, wildlife havens in the midst of a rocky desert. Herons nest on the islands, though they are hard to see as they crouch low on their nests which are firmly incorporated into the foliage of the bushes. Woodpigeons and mallard nest on the islands, too, and gulls come inland to roost on the lake. In the shallows at the lake edge the delicate heads of water lobelia sway in the almost ceaseless summer breeze.

**Link** 1 mile/1.6 km.

Continuing south-westwards we pass Lough Awallia with its crannóg, not far offshore from the car park. This ancient artificial island, on which there would once have been a dwelling, was a safe haven from marauding neighbours. Nearby, but far removed in time, thatched cottages and new slated houses signal further changes in human habitations, but turf is still neatly stacked against protective stone walls in a comforting traditional manner.

**Stop** Ballynakill Lough (L863223), at the parking area beside the lough.

Looking southwards across the lough we see a change in the landscape from the bare rolling granite which occupies the northern part of the island to a line of low, sometimes cliff-girt hills, clad with bracken on their lower slopes and generally better vegetated than the land to the north. The low hills are the 'country rocks' thought to be Ordovician in age (about 500 million years old) into which the younger granite intruded some 400 million years ago. Still and silent now, this boundary zone would have been the scene of immense geological upheaval all those millions of years ago. To the right of the hills we can glimpse the sea and, in the background, Inishmore, a relative newcomer in geological terms, being only about 300 million years old.

**Link** to Screeb 18 miles/28.8 km.

We continue westwards and then take the switch-back road to the north along the coast of Coonawilleen Bay with its 'coral' strands and salmon-rearing cages or return towards Lough Hibbert and take the road along its southern shore towards the coast of Greatman's Bay. Both routes lead back to the crossroads at Lough Illauntrasna and the main road back to Costelloe.

From here we take the road to Screeb and then a left turn takes us along the northern shore of Camus Bay. (Alternatively, we could return to Galway by turning right and taking the road northwards to Maam Cross.)

From Costelloe, we can take the road back to Rossaveel to catch the ferry to Kilronan.

**Link** Rossaveel (L962252) to Kilronan (L882087) 12 miles/19 km.

The ferry journey between Rossaveel (Ros an Mhíl) and Kilronan can be a treat for the naturalist. The fish docks at Rossaveel attract many gulls, amongst them glaucous and Iceland gulls and, on occasions, even rarer species. Seals often venture into the harbour and appear and disappear tantalisingly into the murky water. However, it is once we are outside the bay and into the North Sound that we start to see birds that are rarely seen from the mainland shore. Manx shearwaters, gliding effortlessly over the waves, first showing their dark upper parts and then the white below. During the summer months it is possible to see many thousands on this short journey. In August, as the migration season gets under way, the discerning birdwatcher will see, amongst the Manx shearwaters, small parties of sooty shearwaters, easily distinguished by their sooty underparts. Many of the Manx shearwaters breed on Irish offshore islands, but the sooty shearwaters breed in the southern hemisphere and visit our waters only in summer and autumn.

The diminutive storm petrel, with its distinctive white rump, is another summer visitor to our coastal islands. It also flies close to the sea surface and appears to be in perpetual danger of being engulfed by breaking waves. A close, but larger relative is the fulmar, which also inhabits the Cliffs of Moher in large numbers. It is common around Inishmore where it breeds on the cliffs on the south-west side of the island.

Terns often fly close to the boat, demonstrating their superb aerial skills, plunge-diving to catch small fish in the surface waters. The occasional gannet, too, may display its fishing prowess, diving with partly closed wings in pursuit of herring or mackerel. Many of the gannets seen here at the outer limits of Galway Bay are immature birds with grey, mottled plumage, rather than the sparkling white of adults. Guillemots and razor-bills are a common sight, often sitting on the water, generally unconcerned by the passage of the ferry.

Less common, but well worth keeping an eye out for, are the dolphins and harbour porpoises which visit the area during the summer. A school of dolphins leaping clear of the water beside the boat is a breathtaking spectacle.

## CONNEMARA CIRCUIT — MAAM CROSS — VIA SCREEB/CASHEL/ BALLYCONNEELY/KYLEMORE/ LEENAUN/MAUM.

**Stop** Maam Cross (L978461), near crossroads or at Peacock's.

Maam Cross is the gateway to Connemara and in a glance you can sense the essence of the region — craggy mountains, sparkling loughs and pools, turbulent streams, hummocky blanket bogs.

The road to the north takes us past Loughanillaun and Maumwee Loughs, set in a granite basin, over a windy coll into the Maum Valley and the village of Maum nestling beneath the hills of Joyce's Country. To

*Gorteen Bay*

*Fishing on Lough Corrib*

the east of this road there is a fairly easy walk from the coll to the summit and the reward of panoramic views of upper Lough Corrib, Joyce's Country, the Maumturk Mountains and south Connemara — a preview of the tour to come.

To the west of the Maam Cross–Maum road, where the quartzite crags steepen on the slopes of Corcogemore, it is possible to find St Patrick's cabbage blooming in late spring in damp, shady crevices. Ravens nest on the crags in early spring and hooded crows and kestrels are regularly

in evidence. In winter, before the weather gets too cold, woodcock roost on the hillsides. Lower down, on the blanket bog, Greenland white-fronted geese feed on the nutrient-rich bulbils of sedges which they uproot from soft, wet peat. The bog at the foot of Corcogemore also supports several uncommon grasses and sedges and is considered to be of national conservation importance.

The main road to the west (N59) follows the ice-sculptured corridor of softer schists and gneisses through bogland, lake and mountain to Clifden. Lough Shindilla, to the north of the road, contains charr — small, trout-like relics of colder times. These fish were once more widespread in the west of Ireland, but pollution and eutrophication have now restricted their distribution to the cold, deep and nutrient-poor loughs of the far west. Little grebes appear regularly on the roadside loughs and in winter whooper swans and pochard visit these cold, dark loughs to feed and roost.

**Link** 13 miles/21 km.

The road to the south takes us towards An Ceathrú Rua (Carraroe) and Ros Muc (Rosmuck). A quarry on the left provides an opportunity to study the local metamorphic rocks with prominent whitish, quartz-rich granite intrusions. Across the road there is an incongruous limestone wall built with stone brought into the area from a distant quarry. At the top of the north end of the quarry ancient Scots pine roots project from the peat — reminders of the landscape 4,000 years ago. Blanket bog with pools and rocky knolls dominate the scene, though new coniferous plantations are beginning to change the colour and texture of the landscape, just as intensive fish production cages are affecting the waterscape of Connemara. Upper Camus Bay is the regular haunt of up to 100 mute swans, and small islands in the vicinity of the former power station host breeding common terns and black-headed gulls. Industrial activity is not new to the area: Lough Nafurnace testifies to an 18th century iron smelting industry which has long since disappeared. At the head of Kilkieran Bay continue westwards towards Cashel along the small road which takes us into the heart of the Connemara blanket bog.

**Stop** Gowlan East (L867400), at the head of a sandy bog road.

Here, the northern prospect, seen through ubiquitous electricity wires, is a basin of blanket bog and loughs set against the stark quartzite cones of the Twelve Bens and Maumturks. The rolling, stream-incised bog extends up to 4.5 miles/7 km to the low, fringing hills of ancient, basic, intrusive rocks. Brown is the dominant colour of the landscape. Only on the lake islands, where livestock are absent, have trees and shrubs managed to survive. Until recently it was thought that the vegetation on Connemara lake islands was a snapshot of the natural communities which had survived undisturbed since the distant past, but now it seems that this is not the case and the analysis of pollen grains in soil cores and the discovery of charcoal layers in the earth indicate grazing by livestock and burning of the vegetation by our recent ancestors.

The bog vegetation is composed of plants which can thrive in (or at least tolerate) the wet, acid peat. Purple moor-grass dominates the moorland landscape these days with its tall, green tussocks which turn golden brown as summer slips into autumn. Sedges are also important components of the vegetation, and bog cotton is easily recognised in summer by its white, cottony tufts. Though less conspicuous, the white-beaked sedge, with its small, narrow leaves and numerous spikelets of white flowers, is an important member of the flora because its nutritious underground bulbils are a preferred food of the white-fronted geese which spend the winter in the area.

Heather and cross-leaved heath find refuge on the drier knolls and, in turn, provide food and cover for the few remaining grouse and Irish hares. On the drier margins of the bog, golden plover, spectacular in their breeding plumage, nest in small but probably declining numbers. Meadow pipits are the commonest birds and they provide a steady food supply for merlins which nest on some of the wooded lake islands. Small numbers of teal nest at the lake edges and cormorants also visit these to feed on small brown trout, fish which, no doubt, the common but secretive otters also prey on from time to time.

But the bog is changing. Turf cutting and afforestation are making huge inroads into what was once one of the largest areas of natural blanket bog in Connemara. The ecological changes wrought by these developments are likely to drive away the white-fronted geese and the few remaining breeding golden plover and probably the merlins for which Connemara is a nationally important haunt. Continuing drainage, fertilisation, road building and unremitting disturbance will have destroyed the nature and essence of this wild area by the end of the century — the product of 5,000 years of evolution obliterated in just 25 years.

**Link** 8.5 miles/13.5 km.

Continue westwards through the stony bogland — a landscape first scoured by ice, then clothed with trees and later turned to bog by wet weather and, probably, the hand of man. Fishing stands along the Owengowla River testify to the importance of Connemara rivers for sea trout and salmon. Turn right and then take the first turning left to Cashel and Roundstone, past the wooded grounds of two well-known hotels, the Zetland and Cashel House, and on to the calm, open waters of Cashel Bay, studded with seaweed-draped granite boulders.

**Stop** west of Cloonisle (L767442), on grassy pier by roadside.

This quiet, enclosed bay is typical of the south Connemara coast. Gentle tides and currents encourage the rich growth of seaweeds along

the shore. Bladder wrack and egg or knotted wrack lie thick upon the boulders of the upper shore, giving way to green alga where freshwater collects in hollows or seeps on to the shore from springs. The incoming tide brings life to the shore. The seaweeds float erect to form a marine forest through which shore crabs and periwinkles can be seen going about their business from the top of the pier.

Grey herons stalk their prey in the shallows. They are common birds in south Connemara where the sinuous shoreline provides numerous feeding stands. Red-breasted mergansers breed in the vicinity and family parties can often be seen diving for fish offshore in late summer.

At this time, too, the hillside on the other side of the road is at its most colourful. The Connemara speciality, St Dabeoc's heath, with its large, reddish-purple flowers and thick, glossy leaves, mingles with the smaller flowered bell heather and the distinctive western gorse with its bright yellow flowers.

**Link** 7.5 miles/12 km.

Travelling north-westwards along the shore the road leads to a junction at Toombeola where a left turn takes us across the Ballynahinch River, famous for its sea trout and salmon, and on towards Roundstone. Near Roundstone we pass through the wooded grounds of Letterdife (Letterdyfe) House. Beyond Roundstone village the road turns westwards again beneath the rocky slopes of Errisbeg which sweep down to the edge of Gorteen Bay and Dog's Bay.

**Stop** Dog's Bay (L691386) at car park beside bay.

Port na Fadóige, as indicated on the road sign, means 'plover's shore' and is certainly apt because ringed plovers nest on the beaches, laying their four cryptically coloured eggs in shallow scrapes in the sand. Little terns also nest on the beaches and care should be taken to avoid stepping on the eggs of both species. Sandwich terns fish offshore regularly through the summer. Many common gulls feed on the island, particularly when June chafers are flying and lesser black-backed gulls sometimes roost here in large numbers, too. During the summer the short island sward comes alive with colourful flowers like the delicate bog pimpernel and knotted pearlwort.

The sandy spit linking the mainland to the granite island was built up by local currents and is called a tombolo. The 'sand' is not composed of the usual quartz grains, but of countless tiny, snail-like shells and shell fragments of single-celled, planktonic animals called Foraminifera — seen easily with x10 hand lens. Over 120 species of various shapes and sculpture have been recorded from these beaches.

Overgrazing by livestock and rabbits, excessive recreational pressure and storms have taken their toll of the machair (coastal sandy grassland

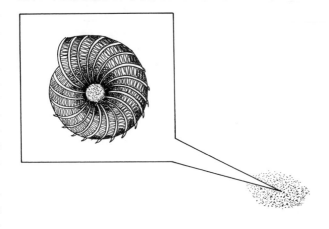

maintained by heavy grazing) and the dunes. Bare sand on the machair and blow-outs in the sand dunes testify to a deterioration in this uncommon and fragile habitat. However, remedial action is now being taken. The worst affected areas of the dunes have been fenced off and are being planted with sand-stabilising marram grass.

Nevertheless, 'it's an ill wind which blows nobody any good'. In January 1991 a violent storm exposed an important archaeological site in the south-east corner of Dog's Bay. Although the existence of pre-historic settlements at this site had been known since the last century, this storm has given archaeologists the opportunity to study the four horizons of settlement, probably dating back to the Bronze Age.

**Link** 7.75 miles/12.3 km.

Continuing westwards, we skirt Errisbeg, with its dark, upper gabbroid rocks atop the lighter granite and pass lough-studded bogland where pipewort grows beside water lobelia in the shallow waters of the loughs. (Unfortunately, agricultural intensification appears to be damaging some of these lakes which are said to be losing plant species, including rare and protected species.)

Then on to more open coast where breakers smash almost constantly against the rocky islands and the shore. Ahead are Bunowen Castle, a sometime home of Grace O'Malley, and Doon Hill, a conspicuous dolerite volcanic plug which dominates the lowlands of Slyne Head. Heading northwards through Ballyconneely we come to the green waters of Mannin Bay.

**Stop** Mannin Bay (L628455), at lay-by overlooking the bay.

Mannin Bay is a broad, shallow bay, punctuated here and there by drumlins — grassy topped, boulder clay hills with their steepest slopes facing the open Atlantic. The white fringing beaches here are also unusual and known locally as 'coral strands'. They are not composed of true coral fragments, which would be of animal origin, but of smooth, rounded fragments of the remains of calcareous red algae — *Lithothamnion* and *Phymatolithon* — which once grew on the seabed offshore. Common and sandwich terns nest on some of the small islets in the bay and common seals breed and haul there, too.

Along the south shore of the bay is an unusual type of habitat called machair, a short grassy sward developed on lime-rich sand and maintained by relatively heavy grazing. This is a very fragile habitat which is, as will be obvious on closer inspection, liable to overgrazing by livestock and rabbits and by excessive recreational use. It is an important breeding habitat for ringed plover, lapwing and redshank and is, of course, ideal for rabbits. Where the machair grassland has not been subjected to over-use it is carpeted through the spring and summer with a rich and colourful array of flowers. Early purple orchid, fragrant orchid, sea holly, storksbill and harebell to name but a few of the 50 or so species recorded in a recent brief survey.

In this area there is also one of the largest archaeological sites in the region, with remains dating back nearly 3,000 years. These include huge middens which contain vast numbers of shells of periwinkles and other shellfish.

Inland from the machair there are small, damp fields enclosed by dry stone walls and it is here that we may be lucky enough to hear some of the few remaining corncrakes in the west of Ireland during May and June. Part of this area has recently been designated as an Environmentally Sensitive Area so it is to be hoped that, with the low intensity agricultural management which this designation demands, the natural habitat and the rich archaeological heritage will be conserved.

**Link** 15.5 miles/25 km.

The narrow, bumpy road leads northwards towards The Twelve Bens and Clifden. New buildings punctuate this landscape, often in defiance of environmental considerations such as prevailing weather, aesthetics and road safety. Turbulent rapids issue from Salt Lake, now adorned with the varied structures of an industrial fish production unit. In Clifden we take the N59 northwards to Letterfrack through rolling moorland. 2 miles/3 km beyond Clifden a left turn will take us towards Cleggan and the ferry to Inishbofin (see page 39).

Here, too, the landscape is undergoing rapid change as the controversial 'sausage machine' mines turf from under the bog surface leaving tell-tale striations and a ruined flora on the surface. Fencing and afforestation are evident, too, in this once wild part of Connemara. The headquarters of the Connemara National Park are at Letterfrack where there is an exhibition centre, nature trails and Connemara pony and red deer enclosures. There are also basic laboratory and domestic facilities for serious naturalists and visiting school and university groups.

Continuing northwards, we pass an extensive quarry to the right and reach Kylemore Lough and an unexpected sight in the Connemara landscape.

**Stop** Kylemore Abbey (L753583), near the bridge overlooking Kylemore Abbey and Lough.

Kylemore Abbey was built by Mitchell Henry in the 19th century. Today it is a girls' school and craft centre. It is set against a backdrop of oakwoods growing on the steep slopes of Doughruagh. The extensive canopy of oak belies the health of the wood which is being 'strangled' by rhododendron as we will see if we climb the track to the statue high above the abbey. Although beautiful in the hedgerows when in flower in spring, this aggressive introduction has become established through-out the oakwood, cutting off light from the woodland floor and preventing the establishment of oak seedlings.

On the other hand, fuchsia, another introduction, rarely reproduces naturally in Ireland and has remained in the hedgerows where it was originally planted. The delicate, drooping, crimson and purple flowers bring welcome colour to Connemara roadsides in late summer and autumn.

In contrast to the well-stocked slopes of Doughruagh, the slopes of Benbaun and Knockbrack to the south, are short cropped and largely devoid of even shrubby vegetation as a result of prolonged over-grazing by sheep — a problem common to most of the upland areas in the west. When grazing is withdrawn a surprisingly rich flora returns in quite a short time.

**Walk.**

An energetic climb up the track through the oakwoods leads to the prominent white statue above the abbey and rewarding 'bird's-eye' views of the Kylemore Valley.

**Link** 5.5 miles/9 km.

The Kylemore Valley opens out eastwards to reveal the broad, afforest-ed Inagh Valley which runs north–south between The Twelve Bens and the Maumturks. Passing Lough Fee, to the north of the road, Mweelrea comes into view as the road sweeps down to Killary Harbour.

**Stop** Killary Harbour (L833620), at parking space overlooking the elbow of Killary Harbour.

Killary Harbour, said to be a fjord though thought otherwise by some geologists, is over 9 miles/14.5 km long and 100 ft/30 m deep near the

mouth where Mweelrea rises directly from its shores to a height of 2,688 ft/800 m. This Ordovician grit and sandstone massif is the highest mountain in the west of Ireland and offers unparalleled recreation for the properly equipped hill walker and naturalist. Lazy beds (ancient cultivation ridges) on the lower slopes remind us of hard times when attempts were made to wrest potato crops from the few patches of good soil available.

Mussels grow in profusion on the rocky shore, but in the past many of the countless young mussels produced each year perished because there was no space left for them to settle on. Now, enterprising local groups are tapping that lost surplus by suspending ropes from the rafts and buoys anchored out in the harbour. The tiny mussels, after several weeks floating in the sea, attach themselves to the ropes by means of a

special thread called a byssus. Relatively safe from predators, and with a plentiful supply of food carried to them by the currents, they grow rapidly and can be harvested in less than two years.

In contrast to this type of fish-farming, which works with nature and has only a limited environmental impact, industrial salmon production, as practised in many Connemara bays, involves the importation into the area of expensive, high protein foods, the unnatural incarceration of high densities of non-shoaling fish and the use of pesticides to control parasites and fouling organisms which inevitably afflict such enterprises. Clearly, careful consideration will need to be given to the long-term environmental and social impacts of salmon production if this industry is to fit harmoniously into such a sensitive environment.

**Link** 8.75 miles/14 km.
The coast road winds down to Leenaun, overshadowed by hills at the head of Killary Harbour and then rises on its southward journey to Maum village. Terraced, sandy hills border the road leading out of the village. These are the remnants of a delta formed by Ice Age lakes which were possibly held back by ice dams in the vicinity of Leenaun.
The Maum Valley opens out with the smooth, green hills of Joyce's Country to the north and the bare, quartzite hills of the Maumturks to the south. To the south of the road, just before the turning to Lough Nafooey at Kendrick's craft shop, there is a cashel-like mound in the field, set against a backdrop of coniferous forest. Such monuments, which may be of prehistoric age, are rare in Connemara. Below, in the valley, Joyce's River meanders its sluggish course through the bog towards Lough Corrib.

**INISHBOFIN.**
Inishbofin, the Island of the White Cow, is, apart from Dursey Island off Cork, the most westerly of Ireland's permanently inhabited islands. It is an island of low relief with no point reaching 300 ft/90 m in altitude and in this respect and many others contrasts with Inishmore and the other Aran Islands.
The rocks of Inishbofin are some of the oldest in the region dating back over 600 million years to the Pre-Cambrian Period. Most are quartzites and schists belonging to the Dalradian Group, those at the north of the island being younger than the rocks which form the bulk of Inishbofin. Just to the west of the harbour the schists contain serpentine and talc (soapstone) — the latter being of some attraction to the mining industry.
The central part of the island is covered with a deep deposit of glacial gravels which have produced fertile soils and good farmland. Upland heath with exposed rock and occasional bogs make up the rest of the island which is given mainly to sheep grazing.
The north and west shores are very rocky, being fully exposed to the open Atlantic. Occasional stretches of cliff which are 50–100 ft/15–30 m high support small numbers of breeding fulmars, guillemots, shags, choughs and ravens. Several species of gulls and terns nest on the offshore rocks and Manx shearwaters and occasional kittiwakes and gannets can be seen offshore.
On the land the corncrake is the main celebrity, but sadly, as elsewhere in Ireland, its numbers are declining rapidly and in 1990 only four birds were heard calling. Another Irish rarity which still, hopefully, breeds on Inishbofin is the corn bunting. This small, rather nondescript bird was fairly common and widespread in Ireland at the beginning of the century, but is now confined to isolated pockets of open farmland and scrub, mainly on remote headlands and islands. More common, though, is the colourful stonechat, which can often be seen perching on the walls.

The underlying rocks and glacial deposits of Inishbofin provide conditions for plants which contrast markedly with those which can be seen on the limestone Aran Islands. Up to 370 species of flowering plants have been recorded in the past, but more recent surveys suggest that the intensification of farming, the removal of peat and the depredation of rabbits have led to the disappearance of up to 20 per cent of the flora. Overall, the vegetation is similar to that of the mainland and for further details of this and other aspects of the natural history and archaeology of the island *Inis Bó Finne*, written by David Hogan and Michael Gibbons, is indispensable.

Less obvious to the casual eye, but of considerable ecological importance, are the lichens which cover the rocks, grow on the peat, wooden fence posts, the stems of bushes and shrubs and inhabit mortar and cement. These fascinating plants, which are an association between a fungus and an alga, are ubiquitous. On Inishbofin alone almost 200 species have been recorded.

Mammals are few on Inishbofin and only the rabbit, field mouse and house mouse have been recorded. Butterflies such as the small heath and peacock are amongst the seven species so far reported. The snail enthusiast will be kept busy locating the island's 48 terrestrial and freshwater species — representing a remarkable one-third of the Irish total.

**Walk.**

Inishbofin, being only 3.5 miles/5.5km long and 2 miles/3km wide and of low elevation, is ideal for walking.

Starting from the pier, there is the option of taking an eastward or a westward circuit. Travelling eastwards we pass Knock Hill to the right, then Church Lough with its lush vegetation and nesting waterbirds, and the modern graveyard which marks the site of St Colman's 7th century ecclesiastical community. A turn to the right takes us to the dunes. Beyond East Village an inconspicuous track leads to the cliffs. We can return to the pier by the 'high road'.

Walking westwards from the pier we can follow the edge of the harbour to a right turn which leads to Lough Bofin and the North Beach Bay. A track to the west takes us across cut-away peat towards a spectacular double sea cave and a well-earned view of the Stags of Bofin. Turning south we pass Royal Oak cave and then Dún Mór, an Iron Age promontory fort. Returning to the east, an ascent of Cnoc Mór provides some of the best views on the island, before we join the 'green road' running along the shore on our way back to the pier.

# THE ARAN ISLANDS (OILEÁIN ÁRANN)

These three small islands — Inis Mór (Inishmore), Inis Meáin (Inishmaan) and Inis Oírr (Inisheer) lie at the mouth of Galway Bay. Morning and evening ferries to Inis Mór go from Rossaveel (Ros an Mhíl) (bus connection from Galway) and Galway City docks. Ferry offices are in the tourist office at the bottom of Eyre Square in Galway City and opposite the tourist office below the Allied Irish Bank in Eyre Square. Ask about times when buying your ticket: extra boats may be put on in the summer, but if the weather is bad the boats may not sail at all. Expect to be on board for at least 40 minutes from Ros an Mhíl (the Aran Flyer, a new, fast boat, can do it within half an hour) and sometimes a little longer. The ferries have comfortable seating and can carry bicycles. It is possible to go out to Inis Mór on the morning ferry and return that evening.

Many people prefer to fly by Aer Arann. Stormy seas do not affect flight schedules, and the trip takes only six minutes from the new airstrip at Inveran. (There are road connections from Galway and Galway Airport). The airstrip was only opened in late 1991, but Aer Arann has been flying out of Galway airport to Aran for many years.

The landing strip is near the sand dunes at Killeany, where there is a small terminal building. A minibus will transport you either to your accommodation or into Kilronan. It is advisable to book in advance, particularly in winter when the plane is often the only way the islanders can travel to and fro. Aer Arann also operates an inter-island shuttle service. For enquiries and booking, telephone 091–93034/93054 or 099–61109.

You don't need a car on the islands although on Inis Mór there are minibuses to transport you around; if you prefer a slower, more traditional method of transport, you can hire a pony and trap at Inishmore pier.

A list of accommodation with telephone numbers is given for those who wish to stay overnight and book in advance.

The Aran Islands were immortalised by the playwright Synge, but there has also been a vigorous tradition of indigenous twentieth-century writing. To date, 63 islanders have had their books published! The best known are Liam O'Flaherty, Brendan O'hEithir and Mairtín Ó Direáin.

The hard work of the islanders is evident in the stony, almost bare rock fields. Next to a stony field there is often a stone wall enclosing a patch of rich green grass. The earth to grow the grass was created from sand and seaweed dragged up from the beaches. Those green fields bear witness to the indomitable spirit of the islanders.

# INIS MÓR (INISHMORE)

This island is roughly 8 miles/12.8 km long and 2 miles/3.2 km at its widest part. Irish is the first language of the islanders, but they understand and can speak English. The ferries land at Kilronan and the plane lands at the nearby airstrip. Minibuses and ponies and traps meet the ferries. Bicycles may be hired at the pier or it is possible to walk comfortably around the island.

There is no pharmacy, although there is a doctor. The supermarket sells simple painkillers, antiseptics and indigestion remedies. It also stocks a wide range of groceries, a good selection of paperback books, the daily newspapers and wine.

### A BRIEF HISTORY.

The first settlers on Aran may have been the people known as the Fir Bolg. It is said that after their defeat by the Celts at the Battle of Moytura the Fir Bolg first went to Meath, then retreated to Aran when they would not pay the rents imposed by the King of Tara. The huge fortresses of stone were possibly built by these people around 500 B.C.

In the 5th century Christians made what must have been a difficult, and at times perilous, journey across land and sea to join St Enda in his monastery on Inis Mór. Here the founders of the other great Irish monasteries (St Ciaran of Clonmacnoise, St Finnian of Moville and St Jarlath of Tuam) studied and meditated with Enda before they left to found their own establishments.

When the Normans reached the west coast of Ireland in the 14th century, Inis Mór was first plundered by the Lord Justice and then the Lordship of the islands was granted to the O'Briens, principal landowners of Clare, in return for their co-operation and goodwill.

In the 16th century there was an internal feud among the O'Flaherty clan and one branch fled to Aran to find refuge with the O'Briens. The rest of the O'Flahertys assisted by the English, pursued them and both the O'Briens and the O'Flahertys of Aran were defeated. The islands were then handed over to the O'Flahertys who had sided with the English. The O'Briens appealed to the Crown and a Commission met in Galway in 1587 to decide the ownership of the islands. Since the English feared attack by the French and Spanish the position of the islands at the mouth of Galway Bay was strategically important. The English authorities held that as the Aran Islands were monastic lands (and under the Act of Reformation all church lands became Crown property) they were legitimately owned by the Crown, but someone had to be found who would run them with the Crown's interests at heart. The man chosen was John Rawson of Athenry, who was given Aran on the condition that he would maintain a garrison of soldiers on Inis Mór.

After Rawson, the islands passed through the hands of many landlords. Eventually, the Lynchs, one of Galway's leading families, gained possession. However, Robert Lynch supported the Royalist side in the English Civil War, and was declared a traitor in 1652 by the victorious Parliamentary forces. His possessions were confiscated, and his Aran Island lands were given to Erasmus Smith, a loyal Parliamentarian. Parliamentary forces were dispatched to Inishmore to build and garrison a fort. Erasmus Smith then sold Aran to Richard Butler who received the title Earl of Aran. (This Butler line died out, and later holders of that title had no connection with Aran.)

During the 18th and 19th centuries the islands were owned by a succession of absentee landlords too numerous to detail in this brief history. Their land agents extorted heavy rents from a people who were struggling on poor land. In 1825 an annual rent of £2,000 was raised from the islands, an extraordinarily high sum.

In 1800 Irish was the language of the people, but successive potato crop failure led to mass emigration from the islands, and the people began to learn English in order to prepare themselves for work in England and America. All official business was transacted in English. When the national school system started in 1831, English was the language of instruction. However, despite these historical pressures, the first language of the people of Inis Mór is still Irish. Father O'Donoghue, whose memorial cross is near the harbour, wrote to the authorities in Dublin Castle in 1886 saying, 'Send us boats or send us coffins.' In 1891 the Congested Districts Board began helping the islanders to buy their own land, but it was not until the foundation of the State in 1922 that the road to economic independence began.

**What to see on Inis Mór.**
The tour buses usually take visitors to the 'seven churches', to the other side of the island where there is an old-style village with thatched roof cottages, then to Dún Aenghus, one of the great Iron Age cliff forts. As the bus drivers are all island men they are the perfect tour guides, and will probably be willing to change their route if asked.

As you drive, cycle or walk around the island, notice the stone cattle troughs which are an Aran 'invention'. Rainwater slides down the rock or cement slope and is collected and held for cattle in the trough. Notice, too, the square roadside monuments topped with crosses. They commemorate people who have died. Although they appear to date from the last century, it is said that they were built on sites dating from a much earlier period. Any antiquities which are national monuments are signposted.

**NA SEACHT DTEAMPAILL — 'THE SEVEN CHURCHES'.**
There are really only two actual churches, the rest of the ruins were domestic buildings. The oldest church dates from the 8th century and is dedicated to St Brecan. It was enlarged over the centuries, but the west gable shows the original dimensions. In the graveyard is a stone erected to seven Roman saints. To the west is St Brecan's grave and in the rocks above it are the remains of an ornate cross. Teampall a Phoill, 'the church of the hollows', was a 15th century church and is situated a little further up the valley from St Brecan's church. Nearby are the remains of domestic buildings, some built as late as the 16th century. There is a good supply of spring water on the site. Access from the road is a short walk down a gravelled track.

**DÚN AENGHUS.**
This massive stone fort dates from the Iron Age, around 500 B.C. In other regions earth forts were used to surround the dwelling places and keep livestock in, predators out, and could also be used for defence if necessary. As stone was so plentiful and earth so precious on Aran, the forts were built of stone, and the cliff edge was obviously used as a natural defence. It is claimed that the Fir Bolg chiefs built the Aran stone forts, but this one could not have been intended for a lengthy occupation as there is no source of fresh water within the walls.

The fort has three rows of defences in roughly concentric circles around a cliff edge which has a sheer drop of 200 feet to the sea. The inner wall has walks and wall chambers and a massive entrance passage. Beyond the third wall are a number of sharp stones standing close together. Enemies approaching from the landward side would be so concerned about their footing that the defenders would be able to attack them quite easily. This type of sharp stone defence is known as a chevaux-de-frise. Beyond these stones is another wall. A path leads through the stones into the fort. If it was dark a stranger would not know where the path was. The buttresses outside the wall are modern as the fort was renovated and tidied up in the 19th century.

Over the years the many visitors to the fort have worn a track over stones and grass up to the top. At the foot of the track there is a small café with seats outside and inside. There are plans to build a more substantial refreshment area, probably with a gift shop, in old stables near the foot of the climb.

## THE BLACK FORT, DÚN DÚCHATHAIR.

This is a similarly impressive stone fort of the same period. Although now smaller than Dún Aenghus it is thought to have been much larger before sea erosion caused a collapse of the walls. It is located on the cliffs south of Dún Aenghus, in a direction almost due west from Kilronan.

## TEAMPALL CHIARÁIN (ST CIARAN'S CHURCH).

This is an early church within easy walking distance from Kilronan, roughly north of the village. (Take the road past the post office.) It dates from the 8th or possibly 9th century with modifications in the 12th century. It was St Ciaran who established Clonmacnoise in County Offaly, shortly before his death.

## TEAMPALL ASSURNUIDHE (ST SOORNEY'S CHURCH).

This is another small church signposted from the road (further on from St Ciaran's church). The track to it crosses a number of tiny fields to where the church stands on a sheltered ledge affording wonderful views. Very little is known of this female saint although there are wells on the mainland in County Clare, and in County Galway near Kilcolgan, dedicated to her.

## CILL ÉINNE (KILLEANY).

A short walk from Kilronan around the bay is the site and remains of the monastery founded by Saint Enda in A.D. 490.

Cill Éinne appears to have been a typical monastic settlement: the monks would have lived in beehive cells; there would have been workshops for blacksmiths and scribes and perhaps a building to house strangers and travellers. A stone wall would have surrounded the settlement as in the farming homesteads. A round tower would have been erected in the 12th or 13th century to function as belfry, lookout tower and place of refuge when attacked. The monks lived a disciplined life of fasting and prayer. St Enda was born in Leinster and was converted to Christianity by his sister, Faenche, who was a nun. He founded a monastery in the Boyne Valley, went to Scotland and finally returned to Ireland to establish his monastery on Inis Mór.

The settlement stands close to a wide strand. All that remains today are the stump of the round tower, the fragments of an inscribed cross, and two small churches. Cromwell's soldiers apparently plundered the buildings for stone to build Arkin's Castle here.

**Teaghlach Éinne** is a small church standing in the middle of a small graveyard among the sandhills. Saint Enda is said to be buried here.

**Teampall Bheanáin (Temple Benan)** is a well-preserved little church thought to be the smallest church in Europe. It is aligned north to south in contrast to all other Aran churches which are aligned east to west. Near the ruins are a number of clocháin (beehive cells) and the remains of a wall which may have enclosed the settlement. The round tower, of which only the stump remains, blew down in the 17th century.

Five hundred years after Enda's death the monastery was still flourishing, but in A.D. 1017 it was raided by Norsemen, set on fire in 1020, and again raided by Norsemen in 1081. The last recorded abbot died in 1400, but apparently the morale of the monks was low. The Franciscans came in the 15th century and established a friary, but they were suppressed after the Reformation.

### TEAMPUL AN CHEATHRAIR ALUINN — 'THE CHURCH OF THE FOUR BEAUTIFUL SAINTS'.

They were St Fursey, St Brendan of Birr, St Conal and St Berchan. This is a medieval church with a trefoil-headed east window and a pointed north door. It stands in a field just beyond the small village of Chorruch. The legend of the holy wells of these four saints is said to have inspired the plot of Synge's play, *The Well of the Saints.*

A climb to the top of the hill will bring you to a restored clochán (beehive cell). Beyond it are the scattered remains of buildings and a shell midden, indicating the site of an early village, possibly medieval or even earlier. It is known as Baile na mBocht ('the village of the poor'). If you continue walking on, you will join a road which will bring you back into Kilronan.

# DAYTIME AND EVENING ACTIVITIES

There are two superb strands on Inis Mór; one is on the south side of the island, beside Cill Éinne. The sand dunes have almost enclosed the bay to form a lagoon. No amenities. The other beach is towards the north side, at Cill Mhuirbhigh. This is another fine stretch of sand (although not quite as large as Cill Éinne). Safe bathing and toilet facilities.

Near the beach are thatched cottages which Robert Flaherty built in 1932 for the making of his classic film 'Man of Aran'. The film is regularly shown in the village hall in Kilronan during the tourist season. The hall is used for dances as well as films and shows.

The pubs often have live music. Traditional music sessions often start when a group of musicians get together and feel like playing.

Sea angling can be arranged. Ask in the tourist office in Kilronan.

The Heritage Centre in Kilronan shows history, geology, wildlife and examples of traditional crafts like currach making.

The Inis Mór walking route is clearly way marked around the island or take a guided mini–bus or pony and trap tour.

Scrigeen Art Gallery has work by local and national artists.

## SHOPPING AND WHERE TO STAY

*The Carraig Donn craft shop* is near the pier. It stocks Irish knitwear, tweeds and linen. It also stocks waterproof jackets and has a changing room.

*Aran Islands hand crafts* is housed in the wooden hut near the pier. It stocks screen–printed T–shirts, and a good range of local crafts including small baskets made in the traditional style.

*Snamara*. Small, well–stocked shop selling the traditional woven belt (called a crios, pronounced 'kris') which used to be worn by the islanders. It has beautiful pressed seaweed cards and book marks, door mats recycled from old sea ropes, wooden rosary beads made on the island and a selection of knitted hats, caps and Aran–pattern knitwear.

*Siopa Uí Mhaoláin*. Small, well–stocked shop selling T–shirts, locally made jewellery, locally made Aran knitwear and other design knitwear, and pocket–money novelties.

*An Pucán*. This cottage with open hearth has local knitwear and a good selection of books and other gift items. Sells a T–shirt which is exclusive to the shop with a charming drawing of the shop's exterior.

### BED AND BREAKFAST

The following places offer bed and breakfast accommodation. Some provide dinners. Those not near the pier will arrange for transport to meet your boat or plane if you ask. The telephone code for calls from the mainland to the Aran Islands is 099.

Ard Einne, Kilronan. 61126. Fax 73052.
Johnston Hernons, Kilmurvey House, Kilmurvey. 61218.
Tigh Fitz, Killeaney. 61213.
Bay View, Kilronan. 61260. Fax 61260.
Mrs Beatty, Kilronan. 61115.
Mrs B. Conneely, Oatquarter. 61141
Mrs M. Conneely, Kilronan. 61139.
Mrs C. Flaherty. 61208.
Marion and Bartley Hernon, Kilronan. 61111.
Mrs Bridie McDonagh, Kilronan. 61150.
Mrs Pauline McDonagh, Upper Kilronan. 61167.
Mrs M. O'Flaherty, Oatquarter. 61226.
Mrs B. Connolly, Manister. 61185.
Cliff House. 61286.

## HOSTEL ACCOMMODATION

*Mainister House.* Telephone/fax 099–61169. Purpose–built hostel. Breakfast included in price. Has family rooms. Member of Independent Hostel Owners' Association.
*Aran Islands Hostel,* Kilronan. Telephone 61255. Fax 68538.

## CAMPING

There is a *camp site* — a field with basic washing/toilet facilities, within walking distance of Kilronan.

# WHERE TO EAT ON INIS MHÓR

Food available from prices under £5 to over £15. Choice ranges from takeaway chips at An Sean Céibh, to excellent home-baking and good coffee at Peig's, to quality food with wine at Dun Aonghasa, an excellent restaurant which is open seven days a week all year round for lunch and evening meals.

# INIS MEÁIN (INISHMAAN)

This is the middle island, and for a long time it was the most difficult to get to, because it was more remote than the other islands. Possibly because of this, Inishmaan was regarded as a stronghold of the Irish language. It was to this island that J.M. Synge and Patrick Pearse came to improve their command of Irish.

The boat docks at the pier at An Cora. The small slipway at the side of the pier is used to launch currachs, the tarred canvas boats which have been used for fishing by the islanders for centuries.

**What to see on Inishmaan.**

Turn left when you leave the pier, cross some rough ground and you will come to **Cill Cheannannach**, 'the church of St Gregory' (the name could be a reference to Gregory's fair hair). The church is a small typical 8th/9th century church.

A short distance north-west up a cobbled track brings you to a square stone fort dating from the 1st to the 7th century.

If you return down to the main road and walk through the village, you will come to a fairly modern church. The altar was designed and made by James Pearse, father of Patrick Pearse, and the windows are from the Harry Clarke studio.

On the other side of the road, a little further on, is the traditional cottage which was used by J.M. Synge every summer from 1898 to 1902. It is said that while on the island Synge heard the story of the man called O'Malley from the mainland who had accidentally killed his father. The islanders hid him until he could get a boat to America. It is supposed that Synge used this story as the seed of the plot of his most celebrated play, *The Playboy of the Western World.*

Just beyond Synge's cottage, is a stile leading to the path to the impos-
ing structure known as **Dún Chonchuir**. This stone fort dates from the
1st or 2nd century A.D.

Return to the main road and continue along. On your left watch out
for a clochán, a small stone beehive hut. It is possible to climb above the
clochán and look through a hole in the roof to see the construction of
this early stone building.

As you continue walking, the road becomes a grassy track until you
reach bare rock; the enclosure of stones with the magnificent view out
to sea was J.M. Synge's favourite seat.

**Leaba Dhiarmada (Dermot and Gráinne's bed)**. This is a dolmen
with two standing stones and a capstone. Dolmens are Bronze Age
single-chamber tombs. The word comes from the Breton for stone table.
The dolmen is situated off the road which runs parallel to the main road
back to An Cora. The freshwater tanks, the knitwear factory (a major
employer on this island of 250 people) and the generating station are on
this road.

# OTHER ACTIVITIES

The safest bathing beach and strand is Trá Leitreach, located close to the pier.
There are shops on the island and a folk museum.
The island Co-operative runs a successful knitwear factory which exports fashion
garments to Tokyo, Milan, Rome, Frankfurt, Paris and New York.
The Inis Meain walking route is clearly way marked around the island.

# WHERE TO STAY ON INIS MEÁIN

## BED AND BREAKFAST

The telephone code for calls from the mainland to the Aran Islands is 099. Bean
(pronounced 'ban') is the Irish language version of 'Mrs' in English.
*Angela Bean Uí Fhátharta* 73012
*Máire Bean Uí Mhaolchiaráin* 73016
*Máire Bean Uí Fhátharta* 73027
Most of the Bed and Breakfast houses will provide evening meals.

## SELF-CATERING ACCOMMODATION

*Nóra Bean Uí Chonceanainn* 55893
*Pádraig Ó Fátharta* 62402
*Máirín Bean Uí Fhátharta* 73001
*Pádraig Ó Fátharta* 73047
*Paul Williams* 73029
*Margaret Millane* 68796.

## HOW TO GET THERE

*Inishmaan* can be reached by boat from the pier at An Spidéal (Spiddle), from Inishmore or Inisheer and Rossaveel (Ros an Mhíl).
*Island Ferries* opposite the tourist office at the bottom of Eyre Square, Galway, telephone 091–61767.
*Inter-Aran Boat Service Ltd*, Spiddle, telephone 091–83322, or Eircell 088–551663.
Aer Arann fly regular flights. (See Inis Mór section, page 82).

# INIS OÍRR (INISHEER)

This is the smallest island and it lies only 5 miles/8 km from the coast of County Clare. The island is approximately 2.5 miles/4 km long and 1.5 miles/2.5 km wide.

**What to see on Inis Oírr.**

The Inis Oírr Way is signposted around the island and is approximately 6.5 miles/10.5 km long. Watch out for the distinctive arrows on rocks along the way.

Walk past the strand (which is safe for swimming). Cattle are herded out through the water from this beach to the supply ship which is too big to dock at the pier.

Continue along the road until you see the gravestones around **Teampall Chaomhain**. The church dates from the 10th century and has a nave and chancel. The chancel arch and south door are later insertions, possibly dating from the 14th century. The church has to be dug out of the sand regularly! At the entrance to the graveyard the mass of shells indicates a kitchen midden of the early Christian or Medieval period.

Continue around the east side of the island on a grassy track. The wrecked ship is *The Plassy*, which was wrecked during an Atlantic storm in 1960. Later, high winds tossed it above the high-tide mark. The stone pedestals you see are used to dry seaweed.

The trail turns north above the lake, An Loch Mór, and then south again along a walled track to the high point at the middle of the island. You will reach **Cill na Seacht n-Iníon** ('the church of the seven daughters'). This is a ruined monastic settlement which was built within an ancient stone fort. There is an altar and a stone inscribed with a cross.

Walk back to the generating station and cross a valley to reach **Caisleán Uí Bhríain and Dún Fhormna**. This is an O'Brien castle dating from the 16th century, built within a cashel dating from the 1st or 2nd century. From the hillside you can see the floating salmon farm anchored off the north coast.

The trail continues past the water tanks and the signal tower built in 1804–5. The trail zigzags down and past the church. In the spring there are fields of daffodils as the island co-op is now organising daffodil growing as an industry.

A short distance beyond the church, the trail swings left to **Tobar Éinne**. This is the holy well of St Enda who is said to have lived in a clochán nearby. The trail turns back north and follows the coast to Cill Ghobnait (St Gobnait's church) which dates from the 8th or 9th century. It was said that St Gobnait of Ballyvourney in Cork fled here when she was threatened by enemies.

A short walk brings you back to the pier.

# WHERE TO EAT ON INIS OÍRR

A caravan near the pier sells take–away food and snacks, and the *Óstán Inis Oírr restaurant* is open to non-residents. Many of the bed-and-breakfast houses provide evening meals for their guests and will also cater for non-residents.

# OTHER ACTIVITIES

The island co-op stocks locally produced crafts of the highest quality: knitted socks, island shawls, fishermen's shirts and waistcoats, and miniature model currachs. It also houses a small folk museum with artefacts and old photographs.

# WHERE TO STAY ON INIS OÍRR

## BED AND BREAKFAST ACCOMMODATION

The code for telephone calls from the mainland to the islands is 099.

Bríd Póil 75019
Óstán Inis Oírr (Hotel) 75020
Sarah and Paddy Crowe 75033
Barbara Bean Uí Chonghaile 75025
Monica Bean Uí Chonghaile 75034
Delia Bean Uí Fhlatharta 75107
Tigh Ruairí (Pub) 75002

## CAMPING

There is a camp site with modern toilet and shower block close to the pier and beach. Telephone 75008.

## HOW TO GET TO THE ARAN ISLANDS

*Island Ferries* operates a service from Rossaveal (Ros an Mhíl) with bus connection from Galway, telephone 091–61767. *Doolin Ferries* operates two modern boats which sail daily from April to October from the small port at Doolin. Parking facilities at pier. *Aer Aran* operate daily flights from Inverin. Booking in advance essential. Telephone 091–93043. Fax 091–93238. *Aran Ferries* operate daily service from Rossaveal (coach connections from Tourist Office Galway) and from Galway Bay. Telephone 091–68903.

# RAINY DAY ACTIVITIES

The film 'Man of Aran' is shown in the hall in Kilronan (Inishmore) every afternoon during July, August and early September.

Visit the *Heritage Centre* on Inishmore and craft shops on all three islands.

Visit the *Scrigeen Art Gallery* on Inishmore. Work by local and national/international artists. Open all year. Located beside Cliff House guest-house. (With your back to the sea, turn left and follow the road around to your left for ten minutes to a small electricity pumping station and walk up the road towards the house overlooking the cliff.)

Stay indoors and read a good book.
Put on waterproof clothing and set out for a walk. If you have dry clothes to change into on your return, a walk in the rain, particularly if it is very blowy, can be a very exhilarating experience, and one you are unlikely to forget.

# CHILDREN'S ACTIVITIES

For children, the best entertainment is the beach for swimming, beach games or investigation of rock pools. On Inishmore during the summer, groups of ten or more children are taught Irish set dancing so they may take part in the evening ceilidhs. If you can organise a party of ten or more, contact Michael Gill at Kilronan 61286.
On Inishmore, children may enjoy a trip around the island in a pony and trap. Drivers assemble at the pier when a ferry is due.

# ECOTOUR

**INISHMORE.**
The first impression of Inishmore is of sand dunes and sandy beaches set against a background of grey, craggy limestone, reminiscent of the Burren. Then we notice the dry-stone walls enclosing small, flower-rich pastures which carpet the thin mantle of soil, so assiduously maintained by generations of islanders. Only in sheltered hollows can patches of stunted hazel and hawthorn scrub eke out a living, for over most of the island the salt-laden winds have laid low all but the hardiest of plants.

However, the harshness of the environment belies its interest for the naturalist. The geologist will find its simple, but clearly exposed, stratified and fossil-rich limestone well worthy of study and the botanist can take up the challenge of comparing the flora of Inishmore with that of the Burren, not too far away across the water to the east. Some Burren species are missing, but there are some arable weeds on Inishmore which are now rare or no longer found on the mainland. Well over 400 flowering plants have been recorded on the island.

With such a small range of habitats, it is not surprising that bird life is not as diverse as on the mainland, though about 60 species have been recorded breeding on the island. Choughs and peregrines can be seen on the cliffs, and herons breed in low trees on the side of the valley beside the track leading up to Dún Dúcathair. On the cliffs near the fort there are breeding kittiwakes, fulmars, guillemots, razorbills, black guillemots, shags, herring gulls and the occasional pair of great black-backed gulls (but large numbers of these nest on Brannock Island and Straw Island off the western tip of Inishmore). Kittiwake numbers have declined on Inishmore from 820 pairs in 1970 to 664 pairs in 1982 and further to a low point of 350 pairs in 1989. Numbers increased to 560 pairs in 1990 but dropped again by about 10 per cent in 1991. The reason for the population decline is not known, but may

be due to a shortage of suitable food during the breeding season — a factor which may be affecting other animals in the area, too.

The most prominent wild mammal on the island is the rabbit, especially along the cliff top where it burrows in the soil-filled hollows, often right to the edge of the precipice. However, its arch enemy, the stoat, also lives on the island along with the ubiquitous brown rat, the field mouse, and Ireland's smallest mammal, the pygmy shrew.

In calm moments butterflies appear in the sheltered pastures. Speckled wood, grayling, meadow brown, small heath, ringlet, peacock, small blue and orange tip are amongst the 15 species recorded on Inishmore, and in warm weather the viviparous lizard comes out on to the rocks to bask in the sun.

## INISHMAAN AND INISHEER.
Though similar in geology, the other Aran Islands, Inishmaan and Inisheer, are much smaller than Inishmore and are proportionally less varied in

their landscapes and wildlife. Inishmaan has about 352 species of flowering plants while only 289 have been recorded on Inisheer. Both islands lack substantial cliffs and, therefore, have no major seabird colonies. However, Inishmaan is noted for its small colony of little terns which nest on the machair (flat, sandy grassland) beside the airstrip, and ringed plovers breed on the beaches of both islands.

Inishmaan also possesses what is probably the largest storm beach in Ireland. Ferocious Atlantic storms have thrown large boulders up on to the western flank of the island to a height of over 170 ft/50 m.

**Walks.**

Colourfully illustrated walking guides have been produced for each island and can be obtained locally. When used in conjunction with Tim Robinson's map, *Oileáin Árann*, and his excellent book, *Stones of Aran*, the visitor cannot fail to gain insights into the history and life of the islands.

# GALWAY CITY

B efore the 11th and early 12th centuries, it is probable that the fishing village now called the Claddagh was already substantial. The other side of the river, where Galway City now stands, was merely pasture land. Then the O'Connors built a castle near the mouth of the River Corrib opposite the Claddagh.

Later, in the 13th century, Norman knights called De Burgo came west and captured the O'Connor castle. Subsequently the De Burgos built other castles (simple stone towers) in the fertile hinterland to the east and south of the river. This fertile land produced a surplus which could be traded, along with fish from the river and the sea.

Galway began to develop into a trading post with an export trade to Europe, particularly Spain. Wine and brandy were imported, whilst wool, meat, fish and kelp were exported.

Merchants of Norman descent, many from Wales, were attracted to the trading potential of Galway and came to settle here. Subsequently the city was walled and fortified. In 1396 Galway was given a Royal Charter. The De Burgos, who by now had 'gone native' and become the Burkes, were no longer 'Lords' of the city.

In 1484, King Richard II of England gave the Galway merchants a charter which gave them the sole right to run the town; it became an area of English influence, a city-state run by merchants surrounded by hostile Gaelic clans.

The O'Flahertys of west Connemara were the city's greatest foes. An inscription erected over the gate of the city in 1549 read: 'From the ferocious O'Flaherties, Good Lord deliver us.'

Galway City was devastated by a fire in 1473 and following this merchants built splendid mansions throughout the 16th and early 17th centuries. They were prosperous: the wine and brandy trade was brisk, the good agricultural land and the sea produced a surplus for trading, and the city merchants had control of the import and export trade. Although nominally owing allegiance to England, the merchant families ran the city for themselves. They traded with native Gaels although the relationship was kept firmly at an economic level. Anyone wearing Gaelic-style clothing was to be excluded from the city by nightfall. Anyone called Kelly or McWilliams or with an 'O' prefix to their surname was not to be entertained on feast days like Christmas or Easter without the city fathers' approval. The merchant families arranged marriages between their sons and daughters to ensure the continuation of these arrangements.

The best known of the families were the 14 who were nicknamed 'the tribes' by Cromwell's men in 1652. They were the families named Athy, Blake, Bodkin, Browne, D'Arcy, Deane, Font, French, Joyce, Kirwin, Lynch, Martin, Morris and Skerret. A free school was founded in the city in 1580 and had 1,200 students at one time. It became an important centre for Catholic culture nationally. A celebrated headmaster was John Lynch, who wrote *Cambrensis Eversus*. Ruairi O'Flaherty (1629–1718), the historian and author of *Iar-Connacht,* was a pupil.

The merchant families took the Royalist side in the wars of the 1640s. Parliamentary troops under Cromwell, flushed with their victories in England, came to Ireland and dispatched a force to Galway in 1652. The siege of Galway lasted nine months before the city fell, whereupon the Cromwellians ransacked it. Leading families like the Lynchs were accused of treason and dispossessed.

At the end of the century, the city fathers again supported the losing side when they championed the cause of King James rather than King William. Once again the city was besieged. Galway's importance as a trading port declined along with the influence of its leading families, most of whom lost possessions and land. However, some, like the Martins, bought cleverly when land became available with the final defeat of the O'Flahertys in Connemara.

During the 18th century Galway City was merely an administrative centre. But by the beginning of the 19th century, commerce was once again beginning to flourish. Mills and distilleries were established, and Alexander Nimmo, an engineer appointed by the British government to advise on the development of harbours and roads in the western region, proposed the development of the city harbour with land drainage and new piers.

Galway was all set to become a thriving city once again when the surrounding countryside was devastated by the potato blight, and the subsequent Famine, during the years 1845–48. The population of the city and county was drastically depleted by death and emigration.

Even in the midst of this tragedy however, there were positive developments. Queen's College, Galway (now University College, Galway), opened its doors to 68 students in October 1849. The railway line between Galway and Dublin was opened in 1854. A western extension of the line reached Oughterard in 1862 and eventually ran all the way to Clifden by 1893. A regular steamer service between the Aran Islands and Galway was established by the Congested Districts Board in 1896. Under the influence of the Gaelic Revival of the 1890s, cultural nationalists came west to experience at first hand the Irish language and a traditional way of life which had all but disappeared elsewhere.

The Irish Free State was established in 1922. Galway was no longer just a regional capital; it was developed as the centre of Gaelic culture. The university became a centre for bilingual studies. The Irish language theatre, *An Taibhdhearch na Gaillimhe*, was launched in 1928.

In 1967 the Industrial Development Authority established the first of Galway's industrial estates. Five years later, a Regional Technical College opened, offering, among many other courses, hotel and catering studies to degree level.

The 1970s were boom years. The university continued to develop and expand, and by the early 1980s the city's population had regained its pre-Famine level. Urban renewal followed. Because of the previous neglect of the inner city, Galway's planners and architects were able to avoid the mistakes made by other Irish cities. The inner city area was carefully rebuilt to accommodate the best of the old with the new. Emphasis was laid on maintaining it as a place where people live. The centre of Galway does not become empty when the shops and offices close. The suburbs, of course, continue to expand as the population reaches 50,000.

Because of UCG and the Regional Technical College, there is a predominance of young people on Galway's streets, in the restaurants, pubs and night-clubs. Young people from England, America and Europe, as well as other regions of Ireland, came to Galway in the 1980s, liked what they found and stayed. Many opened restaurants or craft workshops, started organic farms, made cheese, or joined the arts community. Consequently, mingled with local and regional Irish accents, you will hear English, European and American accents, and because the city is the regional capital for the Connemara Gaeltacht, you will also hear Irish spoken.

Galway is small enough to be enjoyed at a leisurely pace. The shops offer everything you can get in a much larger city and the quality and standard of the resident street musicians and performers is high. Plans exist to pedestrianise the narrow inner city streets. Every Saturday that almost happens anyway: from 9 a.m., when the market opens, the streets begin to fill with people shopping and meeting friends, until by mid-afternoon the throng almost blocks the streets to motor traffic.

Galway today is a thriving commercial and industrial centre. It is also a city which recognises the value of tourism to the region. The emphasis on catering and hotel skills at the Regional Technical College has resulted in high standards in the restaurants, pubs, hotels and guest-houses. Competition is lively and anyone who does not offer the visitor good value is soon out of business.

Salthill, with its promenade, amusements and night-time entertainment, has been a seaside resort for over 100 years. However, it has always adapted to changes in styles, and unlike many seaside resorts it does not close down entirely in the winter. Because it is so close to the city centre (1 mile/1.6 km), it remains an entertainment centre all year round. For many Galway people the promenade at Salthill must be walked at least once a week, whatever the weather. The visitor is encouraged and enabled to enjoy the city and Salthill, as much as the inhabitants do.

# USEFUL TELEPHONE NUMBERS AND INFORMATION

## BANKS

All banks close on Saturdays, Sundays and bank holidays.
Allied Irish Banks (A.I.B.), Bank of Ireland (B.o.I.) and Ulster Bank have branches in Eyre Square; A.I.B. are also in Shop Street, and B.o.I. in Mainguard Street.
They are open from 10 a.m.–12.30 p.m. and 1.30 p.m.–4 p.m. Mondays, Tuesdays, Wednesdays and Fridays; open until 5 p.m. on Thursdays. Eyre Square branches remain open lunchtime.
Cash points for after–hours banking are located at A.I.B. (Eyre Square and Lynch's Castle); B.o.I. (top of Eyre Square and Mainguard Street); Ulster Bank (Eyre Square).
The Cork and Limerick Savings Bank in Prospect House, Prospect Hill are open from 10 a.m. until 4 p.m. every day except Fridays, when they stay open until 6 p.m.

## BUREAUX DE CHANGE

Bureau de Change facilities are located at:
The Galway Tourist Office, Victoria Place
Post Office, Eglinton Street
Faller's Jewellers, Williamsgate Street
Great Southern Hotel, Eyre Square
Imperial Hotel, Eyre Square
Irish Permanent Building Society, Eyre Square
Lazlo's Jewellers, Shop Street
Western Union and information on all exchange facilities from Áras Fáilte, Eyre Square. Telephone 091–65202/63689.

## CAR EMERGENCIES

### Puncture and Breakdown repairs

*Free–Fit Exhaust Centre* does all car repairs and is open seven days a week. Breakdown recovery, telephone 091–57378 or 091–57734 after hours. Located 2 miles/6 km out on the Headford Road beside Ballindooley Castle.
*Patrick Francis*, B.P. filling station on Newcastle Road is open six days a week for puncture repairs, Mondays to Saturdays from 9 a.m.–6.30 p.m.
*Austin's Tyre Services*, located to the rear of the Tourist Office on Victoria Place, is open Mondays to Saturdays from 9 a.m.–6 p.m. for puncture repairs.
*AA breakdown service*, telephone 091–64438.

## 24–HOUR PETROL SUPPLIES

*Renmore Service Station*. Located on the Dublin road (soon to be the Old Dublin Road) before you reach the Corrib Great Southern Hotel.
*Arch Motors* at Westside on Séamus Quirke Road.

## CAR HIRE

*Avis* have a desk in the Tourist Office, telephone 091–68901.
*Budget*, telephone 091–66376.
*Capitol*, telephone 091–65296.
Johnson and Perot, telephone 091–68886
*Hertz*, telephone 091–61837.
*Murray's*, telephone 091–62222.
*Euro–dollar*, telephone 091–61427, Fax 091–64611.

## CONVENIENCE STORES (open until 11 p.m. at least)

*Patrick Francis*, Newcastle Road Service Station, shop open until 11.30 p.m. Sells groceries and fuel. Located near route R337 over New Bridge.
*Arch Motors* is open for groceries 24 hours.
*Esso Service Station shop*, opposite University College Hospital, stocks groceries. Open until 11 p.m.

## CRÈCHE AND BABYSITTING SERVICES

*The Eyre Square Centre Crèche* will look after small children (not babies) for up to two hours Mondays to Saturdays.
Galway Shopping Centre, Headford Road. Crèche open from 10.30 a.m. until 6 p.m. Mondays to Saturdays.

## CHURCHES

Mass times are usually posted outside churches.
Mass in the Cathedral is on Saturdays at 8 p.m., Sunday mass times begin at 8 a.m.
and continue on the hour until 12 noon, and 6 p.m.
Latest mass in the city is at St Patrick's Church, Forster Street, at 7.30 p.m.
*Church of Ireland service*, St Nicholas Collegiate Church, at 11.30 a.m.
*United Methodist Presbyterian Church* in Victoria Place (near the Tourist Office) at
11.30 a.m.

## CYCLE HIRE

*Europa Bicycles*, telephone/fax 091–63355. Located opposite the main entrance to
Galway Cathedral. Open all year. Guided tours arranged.
Cycle hire shops located next door and to rear of Áras Fáilte (Tourist Office), Eyre
Square. Open summer months only.

## CYCLE REPAIRS

*Hughes' Cycles* in the Headford Road Shopping Centre.
*Harry's Cycles*, Bohermore. (Take the road at the top of Eyre Square past the
American Hotel. Harry's is less than 1 mile/1.6 km away on the left–hand side of the
road.)
*Walsh's Cycles* on the Headford Road.

## EMBASSIES

These embassies are located in Dublin, and the telephone numbers are:
American 01–6688777
Australian 01–6761517
British 01–2695211
Canadian 01–4781988
French 2694777
German 01–2693011
Italian 01–6601744

## EMERGENCIES AND MEDICAL MATTERS

In case of emergency, dial 999 from any telephone, private or public; this will connect you with the emergency services. The call is free.

The hospital accident and casualty unit is located at University College Hospital near the Cathedral and the University.

If you need a General Practitioner, ask at your accommodation.

## GARDAÍ (POLICE)

The principal station is located on Mill Street, telephone 091–63161.

If you have lost your credit cards contact:

*American Express* c/o John Ryan Travel, William Street, Galway, telephone 091–67375

*Diner's Club International*, telephone 01–779444 (Dublin telephone number)

*Access*, telephone 01–719555 (Dublin telephone number)

*Visa*, Allied Irish Banks, Lynch's Castle, Galway, telephone 091–65794.

## LAUNDERETTES

*Prospect Hill*, opposite the County Buildings. Open six days a week, 8.30 a.m.–6 p.m., and 7.30 p.m. on Fridays.

*Galway Shopping Centre* on Headford Road. Open from 8.45 a.m.–6 p.m. and 7 p.m. on Fridays. Ironing service.

*West Side Shopping Centre.* Open from 9 a.m.–6 p.m.

*Olde Malte Arcade Launderette*, off High Street. Open from 9 a.m.–6 p.m. Mondays to Saturdays.

*Bubbles Launderette* in Mary Street. Open from 9 a.m.–6 p.m. six days a week.

## LIBRARY SERVICES

*The Galway City Library* is on St Augustine Street. A visitor's membership card is available for £1.00. Any current Irish library ticket may be used. Open from 11 a.m.–8 p.m. Tuesdays to Fridays; open on Mondays from 2 p.m.–5 p.m. Open on Saturdays from 10 a.m.–5 p.m. Open during lunch hour except Saturdays, when it closes from 1 p.m.–2 p.m. (Any change in these times will be posted on the front of the library.) Always closed on the Saturday preceding a bank holiday.

## PHARMACIES

These are located throughout the city and suburbs and are open during usual shop hours (9 a.m.–5.30 p.m.). Closed Sundays.

Those opening beyond these hours are:

*Matt O'Flaherty*, William Street (next to Moon's), open until 9 p.m. on Fridays.

*Matt O'Flaherty*, Shopping Centre, Headford Road, open until 9 p.m. on Thursdays and Fridays.

*McLoughlin's*, West Side Shopping Centre, open until 9 p.m. on Thursdays and Fridays.

*McLoughlin's*, Dunne's Stores, Terryland, open until 9 p.m. on Thursdays and Fridays.

*Paul Hennigan*, Cooke's Corner, open on Sundays from 11 a.m.–1 p.m.

*Salthill Pharmacy* is open on Sundays from 10.30 a.m.–1 p.m.

## POST OFFICE

The main post office is located on Eglinton Street (Moon's department store is on the corner). Open six days, Mondays to Saturdays 9 a.m.–5.30 p.m., except on Wednesdays when it opens at 9.30 a.m.
Suburban offices close on Saturdays at 1 p.m.

## TAXIS

Galway taxi firms run a late night/early morning service. Telephone or call at the office. Waiting room provided.
*Apollo Taxis*, Seaport House, near the Docks. Telephone 091–64444.
*Big-O Taxis*, near Monroe's Tavern, Upper Dominick Street. Telephone 091– 66166.
*Corrib Co-op Cabs*, Eyre Street (beyond Roches Stores entrance), telephone 091–67888.
*Galway Taxi Co-op* in Mainguard Street (opposite Murray's shop), telephone 091–61111.
There are taxi ranks at the top of Eyre Square in front of Supermacs and the Imperial Hotel.
*Corrib Co-op Cabs* and *Galway Taxi Co-op* can supply limousines with drivers for day tours.

## TRAVEL ARRANGEMENTS

Travel bookings to other parts of Ireland, and elsewhere world-wide:
*Aran Travel*, Dominick Street, telephone 091–66574
*Corrib Travel*, Abbeygate Street, telephone 091–64713
*Fahy Travel*, Bridge Street, telephone 091–63055
*John Ryan Travel*, William Street, telephone 091–67375/6/7.
For travel information about other regions and reservations: Tourist Office in Árus Fáilte, Victoria Place, telephone 091–63081. Open all year, Mondays to Saturdays until 5.45 p.m. Closed half-day Saturdays during winter months (November, December, January, February). July and August, open until 7 p.m. and on Sundays from 11 a.m.–4 p.m.
*Aran Islands bookings*, see Aran Islands section, page 82.
For rail information, telephone 091–61444.
*Bus Éireann enquiries* (local and national services and tours to Connemara and the Burren), telephone 091–62000.

# FESTIVALS

### March
17 March is *St Patrick's Day*. Parade through the city. Local holiday, most shops are closed.

### April
*Cuirt Literature Festival*. Festival with readings by Irish and international writers; performances, workshops. Usually held early in the month unless it clashes with Easter.
Contact Galway Arts Centre, telephone 091–65886.

### July
*Salthill Festival*. Show-jumping, street concerts, discos and children's events. Early in the month. Telephone the Tourist Office in Galway 091–63081, or Pat Ivers at 091–24868 for information.

*The Eyre Square Festival.* Open-air shows, fairground. Usually held early in July.
*Galway Arts Festival.* Ten days of theatre, music (all kinds), readings, spectacular street events, children's shows, art exhibitions and comedy. Usually held last week in July. The streets are filled with a cheerful buzz as crowds overflow from the pubs and cafés.
*Galway races.* A week's horse-racing in the week following the Arts Festival. Famous races, celebrated in song. Local holiday, many businesses close on the Wednesday which is the Galway Plate Day. The relaxed Arts Festival mood usually continues.

### August
*Streets Children's Festival.* Weekend of entertainment and special events for children centred around Quay Street/High Street/Cross Street area of the city.

### September
*Oyster Festival.* At the beginning of the month is the Clarinbridge Festival, the original Oyster Festival. Lots of oysters (and smoked salmon) consumed, competitions, music, dancing and drinking.
*The Galway City Oyster Festival* is held at the end of the month. Everyone dresses up and parties for three days, and possibly nights. Lots of oysters and smoked salmon consumed.

# SHOPPING IN GALWAY

Galway is the regional shopping capital with a wide range of shops. Shops are open Mondays to Saturdays, excluding bank holidays, but most of the dedicated craft and gift shops remain open on bank holidays and Sundays. The large shops remain open until 9 p.m. on Thursdays and Fridays. Some small corner grocery shops stay open until very late. See useful information, page 100.

This section of the guide will give an indication of where you may buy quality gifts with particular emphasis on those made in Ireland and Galway. To help you in your search for the perfect gift, a brief outline of products associated specifically with Galway is given first.

Galway has been called the 'The Knitwear Capital of Ireland'. Certainly many of the shops stock beautiful handmade and machined knits in a wide range of styles, from contemporary designer work to more traditional patterns. Many are designed and made in Galway, and the traditional Aran pattern knitwear was brought to the fashion world by the people of the Aran Islands.

Galway is also the home of quality crystal which is similar in style to Waterford Glass. The Galway Crystal Factory, about 3 miles/4.8 km out of the city towards Oranmore, has an elegant showroom with a window on to the factory so visitors may watch the glass being blown and cut. The Clarinbridge Crystal showroom is approximately 10 miles/16 km out of the city on the N18, *en route* to the Burren.

Galway is the location of the Royal Tara China factory (see Royal Tara, page 136). The Irish Porcelain factory is located close to Royal Tara China and also welcomes visitors to the showroom.

You may consider taking home a cassette, compact disc, or record of Galway music. A number of Galway-based bands, groups and solo artists, traditional and contemporary, have established themselves on the national and international circuit. Ask in any of the many record shops for suggestions.

Celtic design jewellery, a lot of which is produced locally, is on sale in most of the gift shops. The Claddagh ring, for men or women, has been selling to visitors for many years, and is offered in both gold and silver. The design is of a type which used to be widespread in Europe, but which in Ireland has become associated with the Claddagh, the village across the river from the city. (See Old Galway Walks, page 122.) In the 17th century Richard Ioyes (Joyce) was captured by Algerian Corsairs while he was on his way to the West Indies. He was sold to an Algerian goldsmith who trained him as a goldsmith and jeweller. In 1689 Richard was released from slavery along with other British subjects, following an appeal by King William. Richard was offered his former master's daughter and half his wealth if he would stay in Algeria, but he chose to sail home. He continued working as a goldsmith and jeweller and introduced the 'Fed' or 'Faith' ring to Galway. The people of the Claddagh fishing village adopted it as their betrothal and wedding ring. It shows two hands clasping a heart surmounted by a crown. When someone is engaged, the ring is worn with the point of the heart facing towards the knuckle. After marriage, the ring is worn facing the other way. A number of Galway jewellers make the Claddagh ring. Look out for Hartmann's, Kinney's and Faller's near Eyre Square.

All the main shopping streets are close together. To help the visitor, the streets have been gathered into four locations:
1. Eyre Square area;
2. Shop Street/Middle Street;
3. High Street/Quay Street/Cross Street;
4. Dominick Street.

This is not a comprehensive list of Galway shops. Only those selling gift items likely to interest visitors are included. (Galway has many fine clothing shops from large stores to small exclusive shops and pocket–money boutiques. These are located throughout the city and you will pass many en route.) Only an indication of the range stocked by the shop is given. Where something is unusual or specifically local it will be highlighted. If you are resident in a country outside the European community look out for shops displaying the 'Cash Back' sign. Under EC regulations, visitors from outside the community may claim a refund of tax on any goods bought. If you complete the appropriate forms this tax will be refunded to you at your point of exit from Ireland. All Galway shop assistants are familiar with major credit cards. You should transact your business with Irish currency or by using an internationally recognised credit card. A number of shops have a bureau de change. Banking hours are given on page 99.

**EYRE SQUARE AREA.**
At the lower end of Eyre Square is the tourist office which has an excellent stock of Irish-interest books.

Archway Crafts and Antiques shop is opposite the tourist office. This is a small but well-stocked shop with beautiful knits, unusual woollen hats, porcelain jewellery, leather work and local rush work.

The Eyre Square Centre is a shopping mall selling mostly clothes and food. (It also has a crèche which will take care of children for up to two hours.) Options, located towards the Corbett Court end, stocks a wide range of goods from crystal and Belleek porcelain to novelty clocks.

Off Eyre Square, past Richardson's Pub and a little way up Prospect Hill is a small leather goods shop and workshop. You can pick up a Galway-made handbag or purse here at a very competitive price.

Roche's Stores stock a small selection of gift-wrapped Irish linen and lace goods.

Faller's, next to the Imperial Hotel, has a good range of contemporary and traditional design knitwear. Look out for the cotton knitwear made in County Mayo. You can also buy your Irish tweed cap here.

Down Williamsgate Street is the distinctively decorated exterior of the 'Treasure Chest'. This large shop stocks an excellent range of quality Irish products: Belleek, Waterford Glass, Royal Tara China, and a wide stock of quality European gifts. Look out for the miniature Irish cottages. Also stocks knitwear and tweeds.

Below the main Post Office in Eglinton Street is the K.W. Shop. It stocks a good range of quality Irish gifts in glassware, china, linen, lace and tweed. Nearby is Mac Sweaters which has a good range of knits. Look out for the cashmere items.

On the opposite side of Williamsgate Street is a lane leading to Meadows and Byrne. This shop stocks a superb range of modern-style quality Irish-made pottery and glassware, hand-turned wooden bowls, and top of the range waterproof clothing. (There is also an excellent coffee shop in the gallery overlooking the shop.)

Next door is Arcadia Antiques selling jewellery, and easily transported antique and reproduction pieces.

## SHOP STREET/MIDDLE STREET.

Return to Shop Street and walk down to Powell's, stockists of Irish music records, musical instruments and sheet music.

(If you are interested in clothing boutiques the only city-centre street not covered by the gifts guide is Abbeygate Street, which is lined with clothing boutiques. The street stretches from the side of Powell's and across the road and down between Lynch's Castle and Grealy's Medical Hall.)

Further down Shop Street from Powell's is Eason's Bookshop with its local and national interest books well displayed inside the entrance. Nearby is Hawkins House, a small but well-stocked bookshop which has a selection of Irish interest books.

Back in Shop Street, walk down Buttermilk Lane, between the sides of Anthony Ryan's shop. Turn right when you reach the bottom. Beside the Brasserie Restaurant, up the stairs, is the Two Lanes Gallery. Linda Keohane is the owner and artist. She does miniature watercolour and ink paintings and also uses leaves and feathers to produce exquisite, original works of art. Every work is beautifully framed.

Further along the street is the Cornstore, a small shopping mall. Here you will find a bookshop, original design T-shirts, a toy shop and Design Ireland Plus, an elegant little shop which is a branch of the Crafts Gallery, Doolin. It stocks a superb range of quality Irish handcrafts: pottery, Batik wallhangings, rugs and jewellery.

Opposite the Cornstore main entrance is the Kenny Gallery, a long-established gallery which sells quality original work. If the work displayed in the gallery doesn't interest you, then have a look upstairs or in Kenny's Bookshop. Kenny's has just the right atmosphee for the browsing book-lover. Second-hand and new books are stocked in a network of rooms with an occasional chair placed at just the right angle if you find yourself getting interested in a first chapter.

Next door is Charlie Byrne's second-hand bookshop which is crammed with gems for book-lovers of all tastes.

## HIGH STREET/QUAY STREET/CROSS STREET.

The front door of Kenny's Bookshop is on High Street. This short narrow street is full of interesting little shops. Kelly's Crafts has a good range of goods including knits and pottery. The Galway Woollen Market stocks an extensive range of sweaters and linen goods.

A left turn at the bottom of High Street brings you to Cross Street and The Silver Lining Gift Shop which sells glassware, china and novelty gift items. Next door Traditions sells Aran and other knitwear.

A right turn at the bottom of High Street brings you to Judy Green's

Pottery Workshop. Judy Green's pretty, hand–thrown pottery is popular with both visitors and locals. Small items are gift-wrapped and Judy is used to packing goods for export. If a large item takes your fancy it can be wrapped and posted home for you.

Next door is The Pewter Shop for figurines and presentation goblets.

Twice As Nice on Quay Street is a treasure store of vintage clothes, lace and linens. It also stocks some superb silver jewellery and handcrafted unusual clothing accessories. If you can't see what you want, do ask, as there is an extensive stock tucked out of sight.

At the bottom of Quay Street, turn left for what is often called 'Galway's prettiest shop', Cobwebs. The range of gifts in the shop delights both adults and children of all ages. You could spend hours in here enthusing over one pretty item after another.

Continue straight on towards the docks for Celticraft selling a variety of Irish gifts.

**DOMINICK STREET.**

To get to O'Máille's and the Bridge Mills, either return to Quay Street and turn left into Cross Street, past Judy Green's Pottery Workshop, then left over O'Brien's Bridge; or cross the Wolfe Tone Bridge in front of Cobwebs and turn first right along the canal.

Turn right into Dominick Street and walk up to O'Máille's, the shop which sold Maureen O'Hara and John Wayne their Irish tweeds and knitwear. Only the best traditional design clothing is stocked here.

At the top of Dominick Street, just around the corner is The Bridge Mills, a converted mill which now houses a number of shops, coffee shop, wine bar and art gallery.

Finally, if you are outside the Bridge Mills you are in the vicinity of the Galway Market which is held every Saturday morning from 9 a.m.–1 p.m. (although in the summer months many stallholders stay around until later). The market is located outside St Nicholas' Church in Market Street. This is predominantly a country market. One can buy free-range eggs, farm–made butter, vegetables (some organically grown), cheese, home-baked cakes and bread and flowers. During the summer months artists and craftspeople join the countrymen and women to sell their work.

**SHOPPING EN–ROUTE TO THE BURREN.**

*Clarenbridge*, about 30 minutes drive from Galway on the N18 Limerick Road, is the home of the Clarenbridge Crystal and Craft shop. Apart from locally produced crystal, you can buy quality Irish clothes, unique hand-painted silk scarves to co-ordinate with fashions on sale as well as other quality gifts. Excellent coffee shop beside garden. Shop and coffee shop open 7 days. Open all year.

Abbey Handcrafts have a large selection of handknits and other Irish–made goods. Tea rooms in old cottage.

*Kilcolgan.* Located on the side of the N18 by the turn for the R477 road to Kinvara are The Woollen Forge and Powers Woollen Mills for knitwear and other quality goods.

# WHERE TO STAY IN AND AROUND GALWAY CITY

## HOTELS

This is a list of Galway City and Salthill hotels. The Irish Tourist Board and the Irish Hotels Federation use a star rating for hotels ranging from 5 stars to indicate international standard luxury, to one star for simple, often family run, hotels. All will have a high standard of cleanliness and hygiene. A rough guide to cost is given based on the price for single overnight accommodation. This is as follows.

Economy: £15 to 25
Budget: £25 to 35
Moderate: £35 to 45
High: £45 and over

When asking the price, check whether a service charge is added.

*American Hotel*, Eyre Square, telephone 091–61300. Old established family hotel. 70 rooms en suite. Located in the city centre at the top of Eyre Square. **. Rating: budget.

*Anno Santo Hotel*, Threadneedle Road, telephone 091–23011. Modern hotel located away from centre of Salthill, but within 15 minutes' stroll down the hill. Close to tennis club. Open all year except Christmas. **. Rating: economy to moderate.

*Ardilaun House Hotel*, telephone 091–21433 and Fax 091–21546. Award winning hotel located in own gardens in secluded position on Taylor's Hill, between the city and Salthill. 95 rooms. ****. Rating: moderate.

*Atlanta Hotel*, Dominick Street, telephone 091–62241. Old established hotel. Family run. Very central. Private car park.**. Rating: budget high season; economy low season.

*Banba Hotel*, Salthill, telephone 091–21944. Overlooking the bay. 30 rooms, not all en suite. *. Rating: economy.

*Brennan's Yard*, Lower Merchants Road, telephone 091–68166. Attractively renovated old building in medieval part of city. **. Rating: budget to moderate.

*Corrib Great Southern*, telephone 091–55281, fax 091–51390. Located on Dublin approach road into city on slightly elevated site which gives views to the bay across the roofs of suburban housing. Luxurious modern hotel with sauna and indoor swimming pool. Rooms en suite. Extensively enlarged in 1991 to incorporate conference centre. ****. Rating: high.

*Eglinton Hotel*, Salthill, telephone 091–26400. Overlooking the bay. All rooms en suite. Nightly entertainment during the season. *. Rating: economy.

*Flannery's Motor Hotel*, telephone 091–55111. Modern hotel at side of Dublin approach road into city. Rooms en suite. ***. Rating: budget.

*Galway Bay Hotel*, Salthill, telephone 091–22494. *. Rating: economy.

*Galway Ryan Hotel*, telephone 091–53181, fax 091–53187. Modern hotel at side of Dublin approach road into city. Rooms en suite. Specialises in family holidays with trained staff to organise children's activities (but not during winter months). ***. Rating: high.

*Glenlo Abbey Hotel*, telephone 091–26666, fax 091–27800. Recently developed from old abbey on shores of Lough Corrib on N59, a few miles out of the city. Golf course in grounds. Awaiting classification. Rating: high.

*Great Southern Hotel*, telephone 091–64041. Modernised 19th century hotel which stands in central location dominating Eyre Square. Excellent restaurants. Live music in the downstairs bar. En suite rooms. ****. Rating: high.

*Holiday Hotel*, Salthill, telephone 091–22518. Close to Seapoint, amusements and beach. Open all year. 10 rooms en suite. Location of 'Cheers' nighclub. *. Rating: budget.

*Imperial Hotel*, Eyre Square, telephone 091–63033, fax 091–68410. Well–established modernised hotel in centre city location. 100 rooms, all en suite. **. Rating: budget.

*Jamesons Hotel*, Salthill, telephone 091–28666, fax 091–28626. New hotel in centre of Salthill. Awaiting classification. Rating: budget.

*Jury's Inn*, Quay Street, telephone 091–66444, fax 091–68415. New hotel bordering Corrib and facing Spanish Arch. Open all year. ***. Rating: budget.

*Lochlurgain Hotel*, Monksfield, Upper Salthill, telephone 091–22122, fax 091–22399. 12 rooms en suite. Located away from the hurly-burly of Salthill centre. Five minutes' walk to beach. Open March to 30 September. **. Rating: budget.

*Monterey Hotel*, Salthill, telephone 091–22563. Centrally located for amusements and beach. 12 rooms. Open summer only. Location of CJ's live music nightclub. *. Rating: economy.

*Rockbarton Park Hotel*, telephone 091–22018, fax 091–61060. Ten rooms en suite. Located in quiet area to the rear of Leisureland. Five minutes' walk from promenade. Open all year except Christmas. **. Rating: budget.

*Rockland Hotel*, the Promenade, Salthill, telephone 091–22354, fax 091– 26577. 14 rooms en suite. Open all year. Centrally located. **. Rating: budget.

*Sacre Coeur Hotel*, Salthill, telephone 091–23635, fax 091–23553. Modern hotel centrally located for amusements and beach. 40 rooms, all en suite. Open all year. **. Rating: budget.

*Salthill Hotel*, telephone 091–22711. Located off the promenade near Leisureland. Open all year. 55 rooms en suite. Piano bar entertainment seven nights a week during summer. ***. Rating: moderate to high.

*Skeffington Arms Hotel*, Eyre Square, telephone 091–63173. Extensively modernised. 27 rooms, all en suite. Popular local meeting place. **. Rating: budget.

*Spinnaker House Hotel*, Knocknacarra, Salthill, telephone 091–26788, fax 091–26650. Located on bayside near golf club and golf range. **. Rating: budget.

## SELF-CATERING APARTMENTS

*Corrib Village*, telephone 091–22989, fax 091–23661. Accommodation during summer in students' village by the side of the River Corrib. 4 and 5 person accommodation. Restaurant, launderette, children's supervised play room and crèche. Tennis courts, pool table, T.V., ground floor or first floor accommodation. Short walk by riverside path into city centre, 5 minutes' drive by road. Open from mid–June until mid–September.

*Salthill Holiday Homes*, telephone 091–24703, fax 091–25017. Beside bay. Fully equipped luxury apartments in block built 1993. Open all year.

*Niland House*, telephone 091–67355. Fully equipped luxury apartments in converted stone warehouse in medieval part of the city. Open all year.

*Galway Town Homes*. Modern luxury town houses in city centre. Open all year. Telephone 091–67477 or write to Trident, Unit 2, Sandymount Centre, Dublin 4.

## GUEST-HOUSES AND BED AND BREAKFAST ACCOMMODATION

You will find guest–houses and bed–and–breakfast accommodation located on, and to the side, of every approach road into the city. In the city you will find them near the University on Newcastle Road, near University College Hospital on St Mary's Road, near O'Brien's Bridge, on Prospect Hill off Eyre Square and on the streets along, and to the side of, routes R336 and R337 to Salthill. They are located throughout Salthill and along the R336 route on the west side of Salthill.

The houses vary from large modern suburban houses to modernised terraced property.

## HOSTEL ACCOMMODATION

Hostel accommodation is becoming increasingly popular in the city and Salthill. Some provide double or family rooms, others 3, 4 or more at busy times, sharing. All provide cheap accommodation with showers and facilities for preparing your own breakfast.
*Gentian Hill*, Knocknacarra, Salthill, telephone 091–25176. Located about 2 miles/3.2 km from city centre on the bay. City transport (bus no. 1) passes the door. Double rooms. T.V. lounge.
*The Grand Hotel Hostel*, Salthill, telephone 091–21150. Old hotel located on the sea front converted into hostel accommodation. Bord Fáilte approved. Family rooms, double rooms, shared rooms. Open all year.
*Archview Hostel*, Dominick Street, telephone 091–66661. Bord Fáilte approved. Located in the heart of Galway near what is often called the 'left bank area'. Early–morning cafés and takeaway food nearby. Open all year. Popular, so advisable to book.
*Woodquay Hostel*, St Anne's, 23/24 Woodquay, telephone 091–62618. Newly opened in former guest–house. Centrally located (Eyre Square end of town) on Woodquay beside pubs and shops. Open all year. Two double rooms.
*Corrib Villa*, Waterside, Woodquay, telephone 091–62892. Open all year. Located on quiet street near the Courthouse and the Salmon Weir Bridge, 20 bedrooms. Two family rooms.
*Galway City Hostel*, Dominick Street, telephone 091–66367, fax 091–66289.
*Salmon Weir Hostel*, Woodquay, telephone 091–61133. Open all year. Next door to new theatre.
*Stella Maris Hostel*, Salthill, telephone 091–21950. In centre of activities. Open all year.
*Kinlay House*, Eyre Square, telephone 091–65244. Open all year. Some private rooms.

## CAMPING AND CARAVAN SITES

*Ballyloughan Caravan and Camping Park*, telephone 091–55338/52029. Open from 1 April to 30 September. Located off the Dublin Road, about 2 miles/3.2 km from the city centre, on the shore, in the suburbs. Turn right by Dawn Dairies (or left if approaching from Oranmore). Washing and drying facilities, showers, T.V. room, motor caravans accepted, dogs on lead allowed, gas mantles available, gas cylinders on sale. Close to suburban shops and only 1 mile/1.6 km from shopping centre. Pre-booking of pitches accepted. Beside Ballyloughane beach. Bord Fáilte approved.
*Barna House Caravan and Camping Park*, telephone 091–92469. Open 1 May to 30 September. Located about 3 miles/4.8 km from the city along the R336 towards Spiddle, on the right just before the Texaco Filling Station. Washing and drying, camp shop, gas mantles available, T.V. room, showers, motor caravans accepted, public telephone, dogs allowed on lead, close to Silver Strand (see guide, page 122), gas cylinders for sale, pre-booking of pitches accepted. Bord Fáilte approved.
*Teresa Condon's site*, Knocknacarra, near Salthill, telephone 091–23316. Open May to September.
*Hunter's Silver Strand Caravan and Camping Park*, telephone 091–93452/92040. Open 1 April to 30 September. Located 3.5 miles/5 km from the city on R336 towards Spiddle. Entrance just after Texaco Filling Station. Washing/drying facilities, shop, gas mantles available, showers, motor caravans accepted, public telephone, dogs on lead, pre-booking of pitches accepted, gas cylinders for sale. Close to Silver Strand beach (see page 122).
*O'Halloran's site*, Knocknacarra, near Salthill. Telephone 091–23416. Open May to September.
*Salthill Caravan Park*. Telephone 091–23972. Near golf course. Open May to September.

# WHERE TO EAT IN GALWAY CITY

In Galway you can eat gourmet food to international standard in elegant surroundings, gourmet food in more informal surroundings, well-cooked Irish traditional, ethnic, vegetarian, coffee shop fare or fast foods. Galway specialises in seafood (including oysters, lobsters and smoked salmon) and excellent brown soda bread. Coffee shops, pubs and take-away outlets have not been indicated unless outstanding, as they are so numerous and highly visible. Coffee shops in Galway offer more than baked snacks; many serve superb salads and light hot meals at economy prices (see below). Pubs offering food also serve good quality food like salads, hot lunches, soup, cold meats at economy prices.

A selection of restaurants in Galway and Salthill offering meals across the indicated price range is given for each area of the city. Where children's menus are listed, enquiries were made about baby-changing facilities. Where they are available, they have been mentioned. Vegetarian food is mentioned where offered (most restaurants will provide a salad or omelette).

This is not a 'good food' guide. The visitor must make up her/his mind about the quality, but because competition is so fierce the standard is generally high. The list is intended to help you to locate a suitable restaurant while you are out sightseeing or shopping, or to help to choose a suitable venue for dinner. During the winter and early spring the restaurants may close an hour earlier than stated here.

All restaurants are required by law to display their menu and prices outside the restaurant. With à la carte menus it is possible to select as little or as much as you wish.

The price range is indicated using the following ranges:

| Economy: | under | £5.00 |
| --- | --- | --- |
| Budget: | under | £10.00 |
| Moderate: | under | £15.00 |
| High: | over | £15.00 |

## EYRE SQUARE AREA

*The Chestnut Restaurant and Bar*, Eyre Square, telephone 091–65800/65575. Upstairs restaurant overlooks Square. Cocktail bar and wine list. Open seating, recently decorated. Quiet. Will do half portions for children. Tourist menu and à la carte. 12.30–10.30 p.m. each day. Rating: budget.
In the bar, salads and fish dishes are available from 12–10 p.m. Rating: economy.
*Eyre House/Park House*, telephone 091–62396/64924. Close to the station on Forster Street. Large establishment, elegantly decorated and carpeted. Booth-style seating. Full licence and wine list. Carvery in the bar. Children's meals with chips or half portions. High chairs available. Lunch 12–3 p.m. Dinner 6–10.30 p.m. Wheelchair access. 1990 Bord Fáilte/Ballygowan award for excellence in 'medium' category. Rating: budget to moderate.

113

*Rabbit's Bar and Restaurant*, telephone 091–66490. On Forster Street near the station. Family run. Soups, hot meals or sandwiches in the bar. Steaks and seafood in restaurant. Good atmosphere. Lunch 12.30–2.30 p.m. Dinner 6.30–10.30 p.m. Rating: budget to moderate.

*Dragon Court*, Forster Street, telephone 091–65388. Chinese and European dishes. Lunch 12.30–2.30 p.m. Dinner 7–10.30 p.m. Sunday 5 p.m. to midnight. High standard of décor. Rating: budget to moderate.

*Great Southern Hotel*, Eyre Square, telephone 091–64041. Open to non-residents for lunch and dinner. Lunch rating: budget to moderate. Dinner with table linen, candlelight, gleaming silver and intimate table arrangements. Extensive menu. Rating: high.

*Skeffington Arms Hotel*, Eyre Square, telephone 091–63173. Open to non-residents. Bar carvery 12.30–3 p.m. Substantial meat and vegetable meals. Dinner in restaurant from 6–10.30 p.m. Sunday 12.30–10.30 p.m. Rating: budget to moderate.

*The Bentley*, telephone 091–55093. Near the top end of Eyre Square on Prospect Hill. Bar with lunchtime carvery. Substantial plain food, children's menu. Rating: economy to budget.

*Kasbah Wine Bar* in Frenchville Lane (runs parallel to Station). Open from early morning to late at night for breakfasts, salads, and a variety of hot dishes. Eclectic decor, candles. Relaxed atmosphere.

*Supermacs*, top of Eyre Square, Galway's answer to McDonald's. Bright, modern interior. Child friendly.

## EGLINTON STREET (NEAR CENTRAL POST OFFICE)

*Conlon's Fish Restaurant*. Upstairs and downstairs. Takeaway style upstairs with seating. Good wheelchair access. Bench–style seating in booths downstairs. Very basic. Specialises in wide range of fish dishes. Oysters all year round. Menu in four European languages. Children's menu with fish fingers made in the restaurant. Open seven days a week and evenings. Rating: economy to budget.

*Oriental House*, near Abbey, telephone 091–62352. Specialises in food from different regions of China, also European food. 12.30–2 p.m. for lunch Mondays to Fridays, 6–12 p.m. for dinner. Seven days. Recently decorated to high standard. Rating: budget to moderate.

*McSwiggan's*, telephone 091–68917. Around the corner from Eglinton Street on Woodquay. Pub downstairs. Restaurant upstairs. Victorian style interior décor with wooden floors and tables. Lots of Victorian bric-à-brac. Convivial atmosphere. Open seven days a week. Last orders 11 p.m. À la carte menu. International cuisine including vegetarian. Rating: budget.

*Maxwell McNamara's Coffee House and Restaurant*. On corner opposite Moon's department store. Polished wooden tables, upholstered booths. Open 9 a.m. until 10 p.m. Sunday from 12 noon. Children welcome. Budget.

*Galway Bakery Company (GBC)*, telephone 091–63087. Opposite Moon's. Coffee shop and self–service snack bar downstairs. Restaurant upstairs. Booths. Well decorated. Children are given crayons and a menu to colour. Good plain food. High chairs, baby changing facility. Open 12–10 p.m. and 11 p.m. at weekends. Coffee shop open from 8.30 a.m. À la carte menu, international cuisine including vegetarian. Rating: budget.

*Elevenses coffee shop* upstairs at 'News at Ten'. Coffee shop with excellent salad bar and confections. Open daily 9 a.m.–9 p.m. Closed on Sundays.

## SHOP STREET

*McDonald's*. Open seven days a week. Cheerful child-friendly interior. Wheelchair access. Has a baby changing facility. Usual McDonald's burgers etc. Rating: budget.

## MARKET STREET/ABBEYGATE STREET

(Located off Shop Street, go down lane to right-hand side of Lynch's Castle.)
*The House of Bards*, telephone 091–66515. Medieval house carefully decorated in keeping with period. Open plan seating. Meat, poultry and fish dishes. Children catered for. Lunch 12–6 p.m., dinner 6–10.30 p.m. Seven days a week, wine licence. Quiet. Elegant. Wheelchair access ground floor. Rating: economy/budget/high.
*Brannigan's*, telephone 091–65974. Stripped pine and brass bric-à-brac Victorian interior. Air conditioned. Full bar. Lively. Menu leans to American ethnic. Open from 12–10.30 p.m. on weekdays. Sundays 6–10 p.m. Rating: budget.

## HIGH STREET

*The Malt House Restaurant*, telephone 091–67886. Located in The Olde Malte Arcade near The King's Head pub. Pub, restaurant. Egon Ronay recommended. Lunch 12.30–2.30 p.m. Dinner 7–11 p.m., Mondays to Saturdays. Rating: budget/moderate/high.
*The Grapevine Restaurant*, telephone 091–62438. Located over 'The Bunch of Grapes' pub. Meat and poultry as well as fish and shellfish. Fully licenced. Wine list.
*Round Table*. Coffee shop and café. Opposite Kenny's. Quiet, well maintained. Medieval fireplace adds comfortable glow. Meat and two veg dishes, salads and snacks. Order meals at counter. Open 9 a.m.–6 p.m. Wheelchair access. Rating: economy.

## CROSS STREET/QUAY STREET

*Seventh Heaven*, telephone 091–63838. Located down side street near Druid Theatre. International gourmet and vegetarian food at economy and budget prices. Wine. Light modern décor. Lots of pine. Open plan and booth seating. Open lunchtime and late (until 10.30 p.m. and sometimes midnight if customers require it). Wheelchair access. Often has a cabaret of poets, comedians or musicians.
*Fat Freddy's*, Quay Street, telephone 091–67279. Fun warehouse décor, wooden tables, candles and checked-cloth atmosphere. Mainly pizza. Open from 12.00–10.30 p.m. Seven days a week. Rating: economy.
*McDonagh's Seafood Bar*, telephone 091–65809. On other side of fish shop. All fish dishes guaranteed fresh. Cheerful bistro-style décor. Open for lunches and all day until 11.30 p.m. (possibly earlier in winter). Bring own wine if you desire; a pint of Guinness or beer will be bought at nearby bar and brought to your table if you wish. Wheelchair access. Rating: economy to budget.
*Tig Neachtain*, telephone 091–66172. Lunches in bar 12.30–2.30 p.m. Rating: economy. Restaurant upstairs is small and intimate. 6.30–10.30 p.m. Specialises in gourmet food. Rating: moderate to high.
*Pierre Victoire's*. Medieval stoned-walled building on one floor. One of a franchise operation managed from the UK by French chef. High standard at affordable prices insisted upon. Rating: budget to moderate. Open from 12.00–3.00 p.m. and 6.00–11.00 p.m.
*The Hungry Grass*. Carvery and good value sandwiches for lunchtime eating. Day time only. Rating: economy.
*Pasta Mista*. Italian restaurant. Open mid-day until late. Rating: budget to moderate.
*La Mezza Luna*. Italian restaurant. Open mid–day until late.

## MIDDLE STREET

*Bewley's.* Self-service hot food, cakes and pastries. High chairs. Baby changing facility in ladies' room. Open from 9 a.m.–5.30 p.m. Wheelchair access. Closed Sundays. Rating: economy.

*The Brasserie.* Next to An Taibhdhearc Theatre. Past winners of International Bar-B-Q championships. Ribs, Mexican food, pizzas, poultry, salads. Cheerful buzz. Wine. À la carte. Open from 12–10 p.m. Wheelchair access. Rating: economy to budget.

*De Burgo's,* St Augustine Street, through lane at side of church, telephone 091–65185. Old wine vaults. Low vaulted ceiling and simple décor in keeping with architecture. Meat and fish dishes. Open mid-day until late. Rating: budget to moderate.

*Aideen's Wine Bar.* Located in lane by side of church. Carpeted, dark polished wood tables, napkins, discreet lighting. Fresh pasta, meat, fish and some health conscious items including gluten-free pasta for coeliacs. Open 7 days mid–day until 11 p.m. Rating: budget.

## SPANISH ARCH AREA

*Shama Restaurant,* telephone 091–66696. Indian cuisine. 12–3 p.m., 6 p.m.– 2.30 a.m., seven days a week. Chef has 25 years' catering experience, including diplomatic service. Restaurant housed on ground floor of medieval building. Old Galway and Indian décor blend perfectly. Wheelchair access. Rating: budget.

*Hooker Jimmy's.* Interior evokes old style cottage with modern comforts. Seafood specialists but all tastes including vegetarian catered for. Open mid–day until late. Rating: budget to moderate.

*Nimmo's Wine Bar.* Upstairs restaurant overlooks river. Wooden floor with theatrical touches in décor. Lunch and dinner menus. Fish, meat and vegetarian.

*Brennan's Yard Hotel Restaurant.* Hotel is a modernised old stone building. Meals in attractive atrium area off main bar. Fish and meat dishes. Rating: budget to moderate.

## BRIDGE STREET

*O'Brien's Bridge Restaurant.* Irish meat and fish dishes. Polished wood tables, cosy

elegance. Linked to Lisheen bar. Lunches and dinners.
*Bridge Mills.* Meals and snacks downstairs. View of river and old mill wheel. Wine.

## SALTHILL

*The Galleon Restaurant,* telephone 091–29863. Plain substantial food. Children are given the menu and crayons to colour it. Has baby changing facilities. Open from lunchtime until midnight in the summer, 10.30 p.m. in winter. Open all week in the summer season. Rating: economy.
*The Spinnaker Bar and Restaurant,* telephone 091–26788. It is along the front near the golf club, on bay side of road. Has a wide menu. Specialises in seafood. Bar menu as well as restaurant. À la carte. Open from 12–3 p.m., 7–10 p.m. Music. Wheelchair access. Rating: economy to moderate.
*The Bay Restaurant,* above Lonergan's Bar, telephone 091–22049. Specialises in seafood. À la carte and table d'hôte. Open from 12.30 p.m. for lunch, from 7 p.m. for dinner. Good décor, comfortable. Rating: budget to moderate.
*Murray's Piano Bar* located in Hotel Salthill. Food from 12–10 p.m. Seafood snacks or choose from à la carte menu. Entertainment while you eat, seven nights a week during high season. Rating: economy to moderate.
*Strawberry Fields.* American-style diner. 1950s décor and music. Steak sandwiches and bagels with cheese. Open from 8 a.m. to midnight seven days a week. Rating: economy.
*Dynasty Chinese Restaurant,* telephone 091–27259. Cantonese and Peking–style food. Wine licence. Open seven days a week. Open for lunch from 12–3 p.m., 7 p.m. to midnight for dinner.
Takeaway and fast food cafés are clearly visible and do not need listing. Central hotels like the Rockland, Hotel Oslo and the Holiday are open to non–residents for à la carte and table d'hôte. See accommodation guide, page 110.

## SUBURBS

*Ty ar Mor,* telephone 091–92223. French-style cuisine. Elegant little dining-room right on sea shore by the pier in Barna. Lunch 12–5 p.m., dinner 7 p.m. Fully licensed. Closed out of season. Open seven days a week, May to September. Rating: moderate to high.
*Donnelly's Seafood Restaurant and Bar,* Barna. Open plan in restaurant, booth seating in bar. À la carte. Open from 12–10 p.m. Rating: economy for lunch, moderate for dinner.
*The Twelve Pins Bar and Restaurant,* Barna, telephone 091–92368/92485. Substantial food. Lunches available in bar from 12.30–2.30 p.m. À la carte dinner from 6.30–10.30 p.m. Rating: economy in bar, budget to moderate/high in restaurant.
*Casey's Westwood Restaurant,* Upper Newcastle. Telephone 091–21442/21645. Attractive country house restaurant on N59. Lunches and dinners. Bar food all day. Full licence. Rating: economy to high.
*Collins' Wayside Inn,* Tuam Road. Telephone 091–757877. Breakfast, lunch and dinner menus. Full licence. Rating: economy to moderate.
*Jacksons Restaurant,* Tuam Road. Telephone 091–756269. Lunch and dinner menu. Seafood, steaks and vegetarian. Full licence.
*The Huntsman.* On College Road near Dublin Road roundabout. Telephone 091–62849. Full licence. Steaks and seafood.

# DAYTIME ACTIVITIES

## SPORTS

### Angling.

### Game Angling.

For licences and booking for River Corrib fishing, contact the Western Regional Fisheries Board at Earl's Island, Galway, telephone 091–63118.

For game and coarse fishing in Connemara see guide, page 22.

*Freeneys Tackle Shop*, High Street, telephone 091–68794, can arrange ghillie for freshwater fishing trip.

### Sea Angling.

Contact Kieran O'Driscoll, telephone 091–67179/57563 or Fax 091–67215 for information and bookings for angling trips.

For sea–fishing in Connemara see Connemara section of guide.

### Aqua Sports.

*Windsurfing and sailing.* Board and boat hire from Galway Sailing Centre at Rinville, Oranmore, telephone 091–94527. Take Dublin road to Oranmore. Drive through the village. Sailing is signposted to the right (if you reach the T–junction to the Limerick road you have gone too far).

*Canoeing and kayaking* hire and courses 12 miles/19 km along the coast at Spiddle. See Connemara section of guide, page 22.

*Canoeing* courses on quiet stretches of river and canal in Galway City are organised every June/July by members of the University Canoeing Club. See local press and posters prominently displayed during June.

*Diving* in Connemara, see Aqua Sports section of Connemara guide, page 22.

### Bowling.

*The Galway Bowl* is located beside the Galway Shopping Centre on the Headford Road. Open 10 a.m. to midnight seven days. Open all year. Crèche from 10 a.m.–1 p.m.

### Gaelic Games.

*Hurling and Gaelic football* are played in Galway. Pearse Stadium is located on Rockbarton Avenue in Salthill. Contact the Galway County G. A. A. at 091–63473 for winter and summer football and hurling programmes.

### Golf.

*The Galway Golf Club*, telephone 091–21827, is located overlooking Galway Bay at Salthill. Visitors welcome Mondays, Wednesdays, Thursdays and Fridays. This is a popular club, so advance booking is advisable. Bar, snacks, lunches and dinners. Club professional. Club hir, caddie car hire.

*Rosshill*, telephone 091–53950. 18–hole par 3 course overlooking bay. Visitors welcome any day. Located off the Galway to Oranmore coast road.

For *Oughterard* and *Ballyconneely* courses see Connemara guide, page 23.

*Tuam Golf Club* is only a 30-minute drive from Galway city. Visitors are welcome any day. It is located a short distance out of Tuam on the Athenry road, the R347. Bar snacks and lunches. No professional. No club or caddie hire. Telephone 093–28693.

### Tours.

Scenic bus trips or walking tours of city may be booked at the Tourist Office in Eyre Square. Taaffe's Bar in Shop Street take bookings for bus tours of Connemara. River walk open from Spanish Arch to Salmon Weir Bridge.

You can walk by the sea only five minutes' stroll from Galway City centre. Cross the Wolfe Tone Bridge at the bottom of Quay Street, turn left and walk towards the ocean.

*High Street*

*Eyre Square*

## Golf Range.

*The golf range* is located at Salthill, near the Galway Golf Club and the Spinnaker Pub. Telephone 091–26737. Clubs and balls provided. Bunker practice, 24 floodlit bays, video lessons, golf simulator, putting and pitching practice. Instruction courses for beginners available. Mondays to Fridays, 10 a.m.–10 p.m., Sundays 8 a.m.–8 p.m. Wholefood snack bar.

## Gymnasium.

*The Galway City Gym,* telephone 091–752666. Located on the Tuam road (near the roundabout at the junction of the N59, the N6 and the road from the city centre via prospect Hill and Bohermore). Has exercise bikes, rowing machines, weights, sunbeds and showers. Open from 10 a.m.–10 p.m. Mondays to Fridays, 10 a.m.–6 p.m. on Saturdays.
*Galway Bowl Gymnasium.* Fully equipped gym, showers, sauna, Turkish bath, beautician. Open from 7 a.m.–11 p.m. Mondays to Fridays, and from 10 a.m.–6 p.m. Saturdays and Sundays.

## Horse Riding.

There is a riding centre at *Salthill/Knocknacarra*. Horses and ponies. One-hour or two-hour treks. Beach riding. Lessons if required. Fully insured. Telephone 091–21285.
*Monard Riding Stables,* Turloughmore, telephone 091–97075. Within easy reach of the city. Instruction and hacking on quiet country lanes and farmland. Cross–country course with 35 obstacles. Riding and jumping in outdoor arena. Open all year, seven days a week. Take the N17 through Claregalway to the N63 (Roscommon) turn–off, and follow the road through Lackagh and into Turloughmore village. Turn left opposite the Jet Petrol Station, then take the first right.
*Glencree Riding Stables,* Lackagh, Turloughmore, telephone 091–97104. All levels catered for. Indoor and outdoor, hacking, trekking, cross–country, forest walks. Open all year, seven days a week. Take the N17 towards Tuam, through Claregalway to the N63 (Roscommon) turn-off. Glencree is clearly visible a short distance along the road.
*Claregalway Riding Centre* is located on the far side of Claregalway on the left. Hacking and trekking. Open all year, seven days a week. No listed telephone number.
*Clonboo Riding School,* Corandulla, off the Headford road, telephone 091– 91362. Approximately 9 miles/15 km from Galway.
*Monivea forest treks.* 15 miles/24 km from Galway. Telephone Reaska Riding Stables, 088–550866.

## Pitch and Putt.

*The Taylor's Hill* 18–hole course is located near the Ardilaun Hotel (on the opposite side of the road). Open from dawn until dusk, spring to late summer. Balls and clubs provided. There is no name on this course, only a sign saying 'pitch and putt'.

## Racquet Sports.

*Galway Lawn Tennis Club,* telephone 091–22353, has indoor and floodlit outdoor hard courts and lawn courts, also badminton courts. Visitors welcome but advised to avoid weekends. (If you have forgotten your racquet there are two excellent sports retailers in Galway: 'The Great Outdoors' near the main post office in Eglinton Street, and Staunton's at the Corbett Court Entrance to the Eyre Square centre.)
*Squash* is available at the Galwegian's Rugby Club, Glenina, Renmore, telephone 091–53484.
*Squash, badminton, tennis and racquet ball* at Árus Bóthar na Trá on Dr Mannix Road, Salthill. Visitors welcome. Open 10 a.m.–11 p.m. daily. Telephone 091–22733.

## Soccer.
The *Galway United* ground is at Terryland, near Galway Shopping Centre on the Headford Road. See local press for details of matches.

## Snooker.
*The Tower Snooker Club*, telephone 091–62324. Located above the Lion's Tower Pub near the main post office in Eglinton Street. Open to visitors.
*The Victoria Snooker Club*, telephone 091–65471. Opposite the Tourist Office in Victoria Place, at the bottom of Eyre Square. Open to visitors.

## Swimming.
Galway beaches provide safe swimming. (See beach guide below.)
*Leisureland*. Indoor heated 25 m pool and children's pool with slide, pirate ship, bubbles and water spouts. Open 7 days all year. Public sessions restricted and vary according to seasons. Telephone 091–21455.

## River Cruise.
*The Corrib Princess* is a purpose–built 150 passenger cruiser which was launched in 1991. Two decks, one covered. There are daily sailings during summer season at 2.30 p.m. and 4.30 p.m. from Woodquay. Bar and snack bar on board. Go to boat or book in advance at Tourist Office, Eyre Square. Telephone 091–68903 or 091–92447 after hours.

## Steam Train Excursions.
*West Rail* (an independent organisation formed and run by steam railway enthusiasts) runs excursions from Tuam, Ballyglunin (location used in 'The Quiet Man' film) and Athenry stations every Saturday during July and August. Telephone Tony Claffey 093–34545, Michael O'Neill 093–24182, or contact Iarnród Éireann at 091–62131.

## Tours.
Scenic bus trips or walking tours of city may be booked at the Tourist Office in Eyre Square. Taaffe's Bar in Shop Street take bookings for bus tours of Connemara. River walk open from Spanish Arch to Salmon Weir Bridge.

## Flying.
Flying lessons are available at the Galway Flying Club, Carnmore. Telephone the Clubhouse at 091–55477 for bookings and information.

## Drama/Painting Classes.
Contact the Arts Centre, telephone 091–65886 for information.

**Bridge Enthusiasts** will be able to get a game at the Galway Bridge Centre on St Mary's Road, telephone 091–62274.

# BEACH GUIDE

You can walk by the sea only five minutes' stroll from Galway City centre. Cross the Wolfe Tone Bridge at the bottom of Quay Street, turn left and walk towards the ocean.

You can walk along by the seashore to the end of Salthill Promenade at Blackrock, a walk of approximately 1.5 miles/2.4 km.

**Grattan Strand.**
Located off Grattan Road before you reach Salthill. Sandy beach. Safe swimming. No amenities.

**Salthill.**
Located about 1 mile/1.6 km from Galway City centre. Popular beach. Promenade with seats and shelters. Amusement arcades, fast food cafés, restaurants, pubs and hotels. Seats, toilets, shelters. Safe swimming. Diving board at western end of the beach. Swim rafts anchored off shore. (Awarded a blue flag 1991.) When a lifeguard is in attendance, a red and yellow flag is flown.

**Silver Strand.**
Located approximately 3 miles/5 km west of Galway City. Follow the coast road R336 through Salthill and watch out for a Texaco Station on your left, and Barna Woods on your right. The beach is signposted. Narrow access road. Good parking. Toilets, picnic tables. Natural history information. Sandy beach. Safe swimming. Rock pools to explore.

**Ballyloughane.**
Located on the south of the City off the N6 Dublin road (soon to become the old Dublin road when the N6 is re-routed). After about 1 mile/1.6 km watch out for the traffic light by Dawn Dairies and turn right. Access road through suburban housing to car park. Sandy gravelly beach. Safe swimming. Good stretch for games when the tide is out. Picnic tables, rudimentary toilet facilities.

# HISTORIC GALWAY: OLD CITY WALK

You may enter or leave this tour at any point. If the whole tour (excluding a diversion to look at St Nicholas' Church) is followed, it is unlikely to take more than two hours taking an easy-going pace. If, however, you decide to stop for refreshments *en route*, the tour will take as long as you desire.

Begin in the Eyre Square Centre beside the restored section of the Old City Wall. (There is a signpost in the Mall leading to 'the medieval street'.) The wall will give you an idea of the size of the medieval city. It extended from here down to the river, across towards the junction of Mary Street and Eglinton Street and down to the river on that side.

Walk through the Bank of Ireland premises off the Mall and take a look at the Sword and Mace housed in a glass case in the bank premises. The sword dates from the 17th century. In 1610 the Mayor of Galway was given permission by King James I of England to have a sword carried before him. The Mace was presented to the city in 1712 by the then Mayor, Edward Eyre. In 1841 the sword and mace were given to the last Mayor of Galway, Edmond Blake, in compensation for his loss of office when the corporation was dissolved in 1841. (The city's charter was not restored until 1937.) Miss Anne Blake sold the sword and mace in 1931, and they were eventually acquired by William Randolph Hearst. They were returned to the City of Galway by the Hearst Foundation in 1960.

The older part of the Bank of Ireland building dates from 1836 and was erected on, or near, the site of the Priory of the Knights Templars which was established in 1312.

Walk into Eyre Square. The Square was originally an open green area beside the city wall and gate known simply as 'the green' or 'fair green'. It was set aside for purposes of recreation and amusement. By 1610 the green had become the possession of the Eyre family and in 1710 Edward Eyre, the Mayor, presented it to the city. It was renamed Eyre Square. Although most people still call it Eyre Square it is now known officially as the John F. Kennedy Memorial Park. Walk to the top of the Square, to the paved area. Over the years this paved area has become a sort of outdoor municipal museum.

The Fountain was commissioned in 1984 to mark the 500th anniversary of the granting of the charter which established the town as a borough with mayoral status. It was designed by Eamon O'Doherty and is intended to evoke the rust coloured sails of the Galway Hooker, a traditional Galway sailing craft.

Close to the fountain is the stone and bronze plinth erected to commemorate the spot where the Freedom of Galway was given to John F. Kennedy in 1963, a few months before his assassination. He was the first American President in office to visit Ireland.

The statue to Padraic Ó Conaire was sculptured by Albert Power R.H.A. (Further information about Padraic in the literary walk, see page 128.)

The two cannon were presented to the Connaught Rangers at the end of the Crimean War. The Rangers were a regiment of the British Army, recruited predominantly from Connaught. In 1920 this regiment was serving in India. At the time, the infamous Black and Tan Regiment was operating in Ireland and some of the men serving in India began to learn what was going on in letters from home. In an attempt to draw attention to the injustices being practised at home, many of the men refused to carry out their duties. Most of the leaders were jailed and one of them was executed. Because of their mutiny, the Connaught Rangers Regiment was disbanded.

The large gateway and door is known as The Browne Doorway. It once stood outside the Browne family house in what is now Lower Abbeygate Street. In 1904 the house was a ruin so the Galway Archaeological Association had the doorway removed to Eyre Square to help preserve some relics of Galway's fine 17th century houses. At the time the Square was surrounded by railings which are now around St Nicholas' Churchyard, and the Browne doorway functioned as an entrance gate to the Square.

Across the road, to the right of the Square, is a statue of Liam Mellowes who led one of the few military engagements outside Dublin in the 1916 Rising. He represented Galway in the first and second Dáil Éireann 1919–22. He was executed during the Irish Civil War in 1922.

Before leaving the Square, notice the fine buildings around it. At the bottom of the Square, the Great Southern Hotel dates from 1854 and was established as the Railway Hotel in 1849 when the Galway to Dublin line was built by the Great Western Railway Company. During the early years of this century the Great Western merged with the Great Southern Railway Company. At the top of the Square, across the road and parking area, is Hibernian House. This building dates from 1842, and until 1973 was the home of the Galway County Club. The Bank of Ireland building dates from 1830.

Turn to your left and walk down Williamsgate Street. This was where the eastern gateway into the city stood. Notice the Imperial Hotel across the road to your right. A stone revealed in the modern plasterwork, shows the Galway coat of arms, predominantly a sailing ship with furled sails. It is possible that this stone was once inserted over the city gate.

Williamsgate Street leads into William Street, then Shop Street.

Notice a clock set high into the wall of Dillon's Shop, on the wall facing down William Street. It bears the legend 'Dublin Time' and it is a relic of the days when Galway time was set 20 minutes later than Dublin, and 45 minutes later than Greenwich Mean Time.

Cross over to the other side of William Street so that you may see the interesting stones set above the modern shop fronts. All are from the late 16th or early 17th centuries. Above H. Samuels' facia board are two stone shields. One bears the arms of the Lynch family and the other is probably a tradesman's stone. Continue down William Street and notice the remains of a finely carved medieval window above the entrance to the Arch Shopping Arcade.

Continue walking down William Street to the narrow crossroads. Stop and look over at Powell's shop. Notice on the side of the building leading down Lower Abbeygate Street a two-light window with beautiful carvings, and down from it two plain hood mouldings for windows now gone. Hood mouldings were incorporated above wooden shuttered windows to act as a run-off for the rain water. Lower Abbeygate Street was formerly Littlegate Street and it led to the smallest of Galway's three town gates.

Cross over to Powell's shop, known as the Four Corners, and look back at Lynch's Castle. A rectangular framed panel on the front of this building contains the arms of Henry VII of England (1485–1509) and it appears to indicate that portions of this castle date from that period. Notice the arms of the Lynch family and the carved window frames. On the wall of the castle in Abbeygate Street are the arms of the Fitzgeralds. The arms may have been inserted following the help received from the Lord Justice, Garrett, son of Thomas of Kildare, during the Battle of Knockdoe against the Clanrickardes in 1504. Around the roof are interesting gargoyles.

The castle passed out of the Lynch family hands in 1654. Robert Lynch had supported the Royalist cause and he was deemed a traitor when

Cromwell's troops took over the city. Accordingly he was stripped of most of his land and possessions. By the 19th century the castle had become a ship's chandlers. In 1918 it was acquired by the Munster and Leinster Bank, later Allied Irish Banks. The castle was restored to something of its former glory in 1930. Inside the entrance porch, around the walls, is the story (probably fanciful) of Mayor Lynch and his son. The son is said to have murdered a rival and was hung by his father. (See St Nicholas section, page 138.)

Across from Lynch's Castle, above Grealy's Medical Hall, are the arms of the Blake and Lynch families.

Continue down Shop Street. Lydon's Bakery and Restaurant contains some interesting stones with family crests carved on them and the restaurant has restored 16th or 17th century windows to give some indication of what it was like to live inside one of these fine Galway houses. The restaurant is through the bakery shop and up the stairs. On the first landing is a fine example of a carved heraldic stone and a beautiful piece of simple stained glass depicting the Galway coat of arms.

Further down Shop Street, next to O'Connors T.V. shop, look out for the small arched doorway. The central piece of the panel above the doorway has the date 1594 and five coats of arms. Two of them may be tradesmen's arms and the others are of the Athys, the Lynchs, and the Penrices; all leading Galway families. The two side pieces form a pair dated 1751. The arms of the Blake family are on one side and the other side shows a diagonal band with three birds swimming on it.

As you walk down the street past Anthony Ryan's shop, glance to your left down Buttermilk Lane. This street used to house the Judges and Council while the courts were in session. Local tradition has it that Daniel O'Connell was often seen sitting in the oriel window while he prepared his court briefs.

On the other side of Shop Street is Eason's shop. Look out for the small conical stone at the corner of the building. These stones are known as jostle stones. They were placed on corners where the hub of a carriage or cart wheel was likely to cut into the building fabric. Look out for jostle stones on the corners of buildings leading to narrow lanes. (There is a modern jostle stone on a corner of an old renovated building on Nuns Island.)

You may wish to go into St Nicholas' Church at this point. (See St Nicholas section, page 138.)

Continue down Shop Street to where the road divides into High Street and Mainguard Street. Notice the Victorian post box. This type of pillar box was designed in 1865 by G.W. Penfold and very few of them remain in Britain or Ireland. High up on the shop on the corner is a carved slab with the arms of the Lynch and Martin families. The date 1562 is carved on it.

Continue down High Street to the King's Head Pub. Inside the pub is a fireplace with the date 1612 carved in it. This pub was built on the site which Cromwell granted to James Gunning, the executioner of King Charles I of England. Folklore has it that the English Parliamentarians thought it improper that an Englishman would execute King Charles I, so word was sent to Scotland and Ireland for a volunteer; an Irishman, James Gunning, was that volunteer.

Further down the street is a 17th century arched doorway with a 1980s version near it. When you reach the junction of the streets, look to your left. The house facing you at the end of the street was built in the 1790s. Opposite is the town house of Richard Martin of Ballynahinch. (See Literary Galway, page 128.)

Cross over to the pub and look at the shop-front opposite. A fine medieval window top without its hood moulding is inserted into the wall. Over the shop doorway is a tile with the letters 'YHS' on it, which means 'the holy name of Jesus'. You will notice these tiles over a number of doorways in Galway. They were inserted during the 1920s for a reason now obscure.

Kirwin's Lane is now a bit ramshackle. It is worth looking at it if you are interested in medieval windows. Walk along it to Quay Street; the old wall on the right-hand corner was part of a castle belonging to the Blake family. Turn left up Quay Street again and look at the traces of medieval windows over the toy shop.

Walk through Courthouse Lane (sometimes called Druid's Lane by the local people because of the theatre established in an old warehouse there by the Druid Theatre Company). In the entrance porch of Thomas McDonagh's modern building opposite, there is a stone from a medieval building which once stood here. It shows the arms of the Brown and Lynch families and a Latin quotation which occurs in the marriage rites, 'Make lasting God what thou hast wrought us'. It is possible that this stone was carved to commemorate the marriage of a Brown and a Lynch.

With your back to Thomas McDonagh's, turn left in the direction of the river and proceed to the Spanish Arch. What we now call the Spanish Arch was one of four arches which formed the base for a fort built to protect the ships unloading at the quays. The old name for the Spanish Arch was Ceann an Bhalla, 'end of the wall'. As the bulk of Galway's imports in the 16th and 17th centuries came from Spain, it is probable that the Spanish Arch was so named because the majority of ships tying up at the quayside were Spanish.

On the opposite side of the river is the village of the Claddagh. The Claddagh was a village of Irish-speaking people who made their living from the sea. The village was in existence before Galway was established in the 13th century. The name comes from the Irish, An Claddach, 'the flat stony shore'.

The Claddagh was ruled by its own elected chief or king; the last of these, Eoin Concannon, died in 1934 aged 90. The King of the Claddagh dispensed justice and settled arguments. He, like his 'subjects' made his living from the sea, except in the case of Father Folan, a popular Dominican priest, who was elected 'King' in the late 19th century. The 'subjects' had brown or black sails on their fishing boats, whereas the 'King's' sail was white.

The Galway merchants permitted the people of the Claddagh to cross over to the area in front of the Spanish Arch to sell fish. The city was so dependent on the Claddagh for its fish supply that Claddagh people were free of all duties imposed on other traders by the Crown.

The small, single-storey cottages used to have mud walls with thatched roofs, and were arranged around cobbled streets and squares. The people of the Claddagh tended to marry within the village and so kept many practices and customs like the election of a king and the use of the Claddagh ring. (See preface to shopping section, page 104.) In 1927 the local authority had the old houses demolished and concrete walled, slate-roofed houses built in their place.

Next to the Dominican Church is a building which was built in 1846 as a 'Piscatorial School'. It was established by the local Dominican Prior, the Reverend Dr Rushe, to teach Claddagh children skills like lace-making, net-making and other skills to help them make a decent living.

The house at the side of the Spanish Arch was once owned by Clare Sheridan. The entrance portals to the house once stood outside Ardfry House, a big house near Oranmore which was burned down. Clare Sheridan had her studio in the house. Upstairs in her paved roof garden over the Arch, she placed part of the façade of a medieval town house which once stood in St Augustine Street. The Madonna and Child were carved by her.

At this point in the walk you may wish to go into the city Museum. The collection is a fascinating mix of items, from fragments of carved

14th century masonry to 19th and 20th century kitchen appliances and vehicles. At the time of writing it is housed in Clare Sheridan's old studio, but will eventually move to more spacious premises. A moderate charge is made for entry.

# LITERARY GALWAY

## A TOUR AROUND THE STREETS

Start in Eyre Square, beside the statue to Padraic Ó Conaire, the author of *Field and Fair, M'asal Beag Dubh* and numerous stories and tales written in Irish.

Ó Conaire was born in Galway in 1882. His father was a Connemara man from Rosmuck. His mother was from Galway City. When he was eleven, Padraic was sent to live with his uncle at Garrafin in Rosmuck. He attended the local national school before being sent to Rockwell, and then to Blackrock College in Dublin. His original intention was to become a priest, but instead he went to London and took a minor clerical position in the civil service. In London he met fellow Irishman and poet Tom Boyd who encouraged him to write. Ó Conaire was a fluent Irish speaker and was active in the Gaelic League as a teacher. He began writing stories in Irish.

With the outbreak of the First World War in 1914, Ó Conaire returned to Ireland, to Galway and Connemara. He bought a small donkey and cart and became a familiar character travelling the roads collecting material for his stories, teaching and telling stories as he did so. Padraic Ó Conaire died in a Dublin hospital in 1928, and this statue was erected to his memory in 1935. Visitors and locals are attracted to sit up beside the statue of the little storyteller to have their photograph taken. Oliver St John Gogarty, who owned a house in Renvyle, Connemara, once remarked that Galway was the gossip capital of the world. He said: 'It is not without significance that the statue in its principal square should be that of a seanachaí or storyteller.'

William Trevor, the novelist and short story writer, lived for a time at 43 Eyre Square. His father was a bank employee.

George Moore, the novelist, wrote in *Hail and Farewell* how he, W.B. Yeats, and Edward Martin of Tullira Castle (the writer and founder with Yeats and Lady Gregory of the Abbey Theatre in Dublin) were standing looking down at the Salmon Weir Bridge after they had accompanied Lady Gregory to the Galway Feis (annual competitive music performance). He wrote, 'My eyes could not distinguish a fish till Yeats told me to look straight down through the brown water and I saw one, and immediately afterwards a second and a third and a fourth and then the great shoal, hundreds, thousands of salmon, each fish keeping its place in the current, a slight movement of the tail being sufficient.' Yeats and Moore then followed Edward Martin 'through some crumbling streets to the town home of the Martins, for in the 18th century the western gentry did not go to Dublin for the season'.

Close to the Salmon Weir Bridge is the Cathedral. It stands on the site of the old Galway Jail. Wilfred Scawen Blunt (1840–1922) was imprisoned here in 1887 after he had organised a mass protest of tenants on the Clanrickarde estate in Portumna. *In Vinculis* (1889) is an account of his experience in jail.

Lady Gregory, dramatist, folklore collector and founder member of the Abbey Theatre, had a brief love affair with Wilfred Blunt. She wrote two plays about jails. In a note to her play *The Rising of the Moon* she said that when she came to Galway as a child she used to look at the jail and wonder how, if a prisoner escaped, he could get to the Quays and hide himself until he could get a boat and escape. The play deals with that very question.

The University is across from the Cathedral. James Hardiman, author of the celebrated *History of Galway*, was an early librarian here.

The Arts Centre, at 47 Dominick Street, was once owned by cousins of Lady Gregory. She used to stay with them when she visited Galway. Call in to the Arts Centre and look at the ceilings and fireplace to get an idea of the style the gentry enjoyed during the 19th century.

Lady Gregory died in 1932 and she is buried beside her sister, Mrs Waithman, in the New Cemetery in Bohermore, north-east of the city centre.

On the corner of St Joseph's Avenue near Sea Road is the house where Walter Macken was born in 1915. He attended the Patrician Brothers' school in the city, and acted with the Abbey Theatre Company, then returned to Galway to manage An Taibhdhearc Theatre Company. He began writing plays, stories and novels. His novels were immensely popular, as they still are today. In *Rain on the Wind* he evokes life in the Claddagh when it was still a thatched village in a way that no other writer has ever done. His trilogy of books, which includes *Seek The Fair Land*, is still a good and exciting way of understanding difficult periods of Irish history. *Flight of the Doves*, a novel he wrote for children, was adapted into a successful film. Tragically, Walter Macken died when he was in his prime in 1967. His books are still in print.

Not far from Sea Road, on the corner of Taylor's Hill, is Scoil Fhursa. Dónal Mac Amhlaigh was born in Knocknacarra in 1926 and attended this school. His family moved to Kilkenny when Dónal was twelve. He returned to Galway to work for a few years in hotels in the city and Salthill. After a spell in the army, in the first Irish-speaking battalion based at Renmore Barracks, he emigrated to England. His account of his life, *Diary of an Irish Navvy,* translated from the Irish by Valentin Iremonger, is a classic work of Irish literature.

*University College Galway*

*The Spanish Arch by moonlight*

Claire Sheridan the sculptress owned the house beside the Spanish Arch. The novelist Anita Leslie, Claire Sheridan's cousin, lived at Oranmore Castle and she wrote a biography of Claire. She was a colourful character who claimed to have had romantic relationships with Leon Trotsky, Mussolini, Kemal Atatürk and Charlie Chaplin.

Across the river is the Claddagh where historian and writer Mary Donovan O'Sullivan was born. Down Long Walk is the birthplace of Father Yorke. He was born here in 1844 and emigrated with his family to America. He became a celebrated theological writer.

On the dock is the house where Padraic Ó Conaire was born; it is marked with a plaque on the wall. These quays must have felt the tread of many famous literary names: Liam O'Flaherty, Mairtín Ó Direáin, Breandán Ó hEithir and Pat Mullen must have passed by when going to and from the boat to Aran. Synge, too, and Patrick Pearse must have made their way past here to the Aran boat.

Tig Neachtain's on the corner of Quay Street is the old town house of Richard Martin, 'Humanity Dick' (so called because when he represented Galway in Parliament during the 18th century, he introduced legislation which led to the setting up of the RSPCA). Richard Martin was a wealthy Connemara landowner. His estate covered at one time most of west Connemara. His wife was an enthusiastic amateur actress and Richard had a 100-seat theatre built for her in 1783, at the back of the house in Kirwin's Lane. Wolfe Tone visited the Martins, and a playbill preserved in University College shows that he acted in a play here. The theatre was also used by Joseph Smithson's Ennis-based theatrical company. (Joseph Smithson was the father of the actress Harriet Smithson who married the French composer Hector Berlioz.) Richard Martin's wife eventually left him and the theatre was closed at the end of 1795.

Mary Letitia Bell Martin, born 1815, expected to inherit the Martin fortune, but all she inherited were 200,000 acres of mortgaged Connemara land. She emigrated to Belgium with her husband and wrote an auto-

131

biographical novel called *Julia Howard*. She died in New York following the birth of her baby on board ship.

It would have been into this part of town that the poet Mairtín Ó Cadhain came when he came from Spiddle into Galway.

Near St Nicholas' Church is Bowling Green where Norah Barnacle's mother lived. (Norah was married to James Joyce.) Joyce visited Norah's mother here in 1909, when he cycled to Oughterard, and in 1912 when he and Norah went to the races. The little house is open during the summer and you may look around at the memorabilia for a small fee.

Close by is the building which now houses Eason's bookshop and the *Galway Advertiser* newspaper. This was once O'Gorman's Print Shop. Norah Barnacle worked there for a time before she went to Dublin. Joyce's strongest literary references to Galway are the poem, 'She weeps over Rahoon' and the story, 'The Dead'. Characters and situations in this story were obviously inspired by events in Norah's life.

Along Market Street are the offices of the *Connacht Tribune*. Tom Kenny was the editor when Ó Conaire was travelling and writing, and the two became friends. Whenever the writer arrived back in Galway, he called at the *Tribune* office where he would be given a room, paper and a typewriter. He would be locked in the room at his own request, until he had finished a story. Then he signalled and the door was opened.

Upstairs in Kenny's shop in High Street are two stained-glass windows which the Kenny family bought and had transferred from 31 Merrion Square, Dublin. They were described in Joyces *Ulysses* as 'Mr Lewis Werner's cheerful windows'.

Opposite the Art Gallery at the rear of Kenny's is An Taibhdhearc, the Irish-language theatre, established in the late 1920s and opened by Hilton Edwards and Micheál Mac Liammóir. Siobhán McKenna started her theatrical career here. Walter Macken's play, *Mungo's Mansions*, which is set in Buttermilk Lane, was performed here.

The Druid Theatre is currently based in the little theatre they developed in a warehouse off Quay Street. The core of the company started out at the university. As well as a policy of staging classic Irish drama, like Synge's *Playboy of the Western World*, the company have sought out the work of local dramatists. They presented the première of Geraldine Aron's play, *A Galway Girl*. They worked with Tuam writer, Tom Murphy, on a couple of productions and revived the work of Milltown writer, M.J. Molloy.

Other writers born in Galway are: Eilis Dillon, the author of novels for adults and children, John Wilson Croker (1780–1857), who was one of the founders of, and a contributor to, *The Quarterly Review*, the once famous London literary publication now defunct. He was also the founder of the famous London Atheneum Club which is still in existence. George Moore and Walter Scott were members. Frank Harris, the author of the infamous *My Life* which was published in 1925, was born in Galway in

1856. His father was a Welsh naval lieutenant. Maurice Semple, the local historian, lives in Taylor's Hill, and children's writer Ré Ó Laighéis teaches at Scoil Iognáid in the city.

You can buy their books and others in all four of Galway's excellent bookshops: Kenny's, Sheela-na-gig, Hawkin's House and Eason's.

Galway has a thriving literary community. Who knows which of the many writers, poets, children's writers, novelists and short story writers currently living and working in the city will be included in a future literary walk?

## CYCLE TOURS FROM GALWAY CITY

Bicycles are a prominent feature of Galway traffic. Cycle lanes are marked on some of the newer roads around the city. If you have arrived on holiday without a bicycle, it is possible to hire one (see page 101).

Here are a few relatively short tours from Galway City:

**Athenry.**
15 miles/24 km from Galway. Main route is via the Dublin road (N6) until Oranmore and then take a left turn on the R348.

A quieter route to follow is the minor road signposted to Galway Airport at Oranmore. Follow this road until the crossroads, then straight over on the road signposted to Athenry. You rejoin the main road just outside the town by a hump-backed bridge. Once you leave the suburbs and the airport behind you, the route takes you past rich pasture land edged by woods and hedgerows. Look out for the esker, a ridge of rubble and stones deposited by a stream flowing under a glacier during the last Ice Age. Where a road sign shows a hump in the road you cross the esker. (Consult guide on what to see in Athenry, page 144.)

On your return journey if you wish to vary the route, cycle past the new church, over the railway line for 4 miles/6.4 km, and turn left (signposted) to Galway. You rejoin the other route a short distance along this road.

**Oranmore/Rinville/Maree and Clarinbridge.**
A round trip of approximately 26 miles/41.6 km from Galway. The full route takes you to a wooded parkland with a castle and picnic area, a picturesque 18th century ruined big house featured in the John Huston film, 'The Mackintosh Man', along winding country roads to inlets of the southern curve of Galway Bay and past traditional thatched cottages to the village of Clarinbridge, south of Galway on the Limerick road.

The route may be shortened by avoiding the trips along the side roads which end at the sea, or you may wish to journey to Rinville Park only, a round trip of approximately 12 miles/19.2 km.

Take the N64 (signposted Dublin) from Galway. Get on to the cycle lane at either the new bridge over the Corrib, or at the roundabout by the Galway Shopping Centre on the Headford Road. Follow the road to the village of Oranmore. Cycle through the village, past the traffic lights and take the right-hand fork. Follow the road around to the gates of Rinville Park. The path into the park connects up with woodland paths which lead to a picnic area with barbecue facilities and an 11th century Norman castle with outbuildings. The ruined 19th century house in the grounds is Rinville Hall. A path will also connect with the road which curves past the Galway Sailing Club and around the headland.

Return to the park gates and turn right. Follow the road past the houses for a short distance to where it meets an inlet of the sea and turn right. This narrow road by the sea brings you to Ardfry House which was used by John Huston in 'The Macintosh Man', a film which starred Paul Newman. The house was damaged in 1920 during the War of Independence and was deliberately set on fire again for the purposes of the film. The house belonged to the Blake family who were the Lord Barons Wallscourts. They also had a 15th century castle here.

This road ends at the sea. Retrace your route back to the T-junction and turn right. At the next T-junction turn right. At the crossroads turn left for Maree. Follow the road through Maree village to the right-hand fork. This is a cul-de-sac but it takes you past traditional cottages and a wonderful view of Galway Bay and the oyster beds. Retrace your route and take the second turn on the right. At the T-junction turn right for Clarinbridge. The road through the village will take you by a direct route back into Galway.

**Spiddle/Moycullen/Galway,** a round trip of 28 miles/44.8 km.

Follow the R336 through Salthill to Spiddle Village. There is a fine beach here (see page 122), craft shops (see page 60) and ample places to eat (see page 63).

St Éanna's Church is a charming example of Celtic Romanesque architecture. It was designed by William A. Scott and completed in 1904. William Scott was the Professor of Architecture at Dublin University and was also responsible for assisting Yeats with his plans for Thoor Ballylee (see page 140) and for the design of the interior of St Brendan's Cathedral, Loughrea (see page 146).

St Éanna's has four windows by the Sarah Purser Studio and stations of the cross by Ethel M. Rhind. In the graveyard are the remains of a medieval parish church.

At this point you may wish to visit the pier. Access to it is a short distance beyond the church and past the crossroads where Moycullen is signposted to the right. The Moycullen road takes you up to the bogland above Spiddle. The views of Galway Bay from this road can be spectacular. As you descend to Moycullen you are rewarded with a wonderful panorama of Lough Corrib and its islands. Moycullen village has gift shops and restaurants (see pages 59, 62). At Moycullen you may turn right and cycle back to Galway via the N59.

If you wish to avoid the traffic, cross over the crossroads, cycle down towards the church and take the first right immediately past the church. Keep to the right. The road takes you by Ballycuirke Lake. At the T-junction turn right and continue on this road to the N59. Turn left turn for Galway. A short distance along is a right turn for Barna. Take this road. Then take the second left, then the first right and continue straight over two sets of crossroads back into Galway by a back road which brings you out on the west side of the city.

If you wish to stay on the N59 you return to Galway by the university.

## Ross Castle.

A round trip of 24 miles/38.4 km.

Cycle past the University on the N59. Turn left at the traffic lights on Seamus Quirke Road. Pass the West Side Centre and turn right off the road just past the flats at the foot of the hill of Bishop O'Donnell Road. The road takes you past Rahoon Cemetery. Follow the road over two crossroads. After the second crossroads, take the next left, then the first right.

This should bring you back on the N59. Turn left for a short distance to the brow of the rise and take the first right. Follow this road and take next left. The road winds along by Ballycuirke Lake on your left.

At the T-junction (Moycullen church is to your left up the road), turn right. Follow this road round and down until you come to the sports pitch and a junction. Turn left. The road you are travelling on is known locally as the Rocks Road for obvious reasons. This is Moycullen's 'Burren'.

At the T-junction turn right. Follow this road over the crossroads to Collinamuck ('Callownamuck' on some signposts and 'Carrowmoreknock' on the Ordnance Survey Map). Turn left. You are now travelling parallel to Lough Corrib.

Follow the road to a T-junction and turn left. This brings you to the N59. Turn left towards Kinneavy's Pub and the entrance to Ross Castle. (See page 32).

The day tours (see page 136) may also be followed by cyclists.

# WHAT TO SEE IN GALWAY CITY AND ENVIRONS

**ROYAL TARA, MERVUE, GALWAY.**

In premises attached to an elegant Georgian house, not far from the city centre, Royal Tara (Ireland) Ltd, the premier Irish manufacturers of fine bone china, have provided visitors with an opportunity to watch their product being made.

The production of fine china still depends on the individual crafts-person. Royal Tara is not a factory of noisy machines and air thick with dust; visitors are escorted by a knowledgeable guide on a tour of a spacious factory, starting with the raw material and ending with the decoration of the finished piece. Each tour takes 15 to 20 minutes. Photography is allowed. The factory is all on one level and so it is accessible to wheelchairs.

The tours take place at 11.00 a.m. and 3.00 p.m. on weekdays, all year round. The factory is open on Saturdays and Sundays, and a video of the production process is shown. Parties of ten or more can be accommodated at 9.10 a.m., 10.15 a.m., 1.30 p.m. and 2.30 p.m. After the tour, visitors may, if they wish, look around the three showrooms. (See shopping section, page 104, for details of product.) The tours are free and there is no compulsion to buy. The tea rooms, in another part of the old house, are open from 9.00 a.m.–5.30 p.m., Mondays to Fridays, all year round. The large car park at the front of the house is flanked by lawns, shrubs and trees. The tea rooms have french windows opening on to the car park and gardens. Patio-style furniture is provided if the day is fine enough to eat outside.

**How to get there.**

Take the Dublin road as far as Flannery's Hotel — a distance of approximately a mile (1.6 km) — and turn right at the traffic lights. The house is clearly visible on the left, a short distance along this road. It is also signposted off the Tuam Road.

**GALWAY CHURCHES.**

**Galway Cathedral.**

The fund for a Galway cathedral was started in 1876 by a substantial bequest from a Mr Murray of Kinvarra. In 1909 Bishop McCormack bought the site of the old barracks at O'Brien's Bridge. However, in 1937 the newly appointed bishop was advised that the site at O'Brien's Bridge was not really big enough for a cathedral; the church would have to be no larger than an average parish church and there would be no space for a car park. Two years later the government decided to close down the city jail which had stood since 1810 just over the river from the courthouse. Ownership of the jail was transferred to the City Council who in turn, in 1941, gave the site to the Bishop of Galway and trustees for the building of a cathedral. Although most of the jail had been demolished by the end of that year, construction of the cathedral did not begin until 1958.

The architect was John J. Robinson of Dublin whose design reflected a number of classic church styles. The main portal arch between the towers was inspired by a church in the Spanish city of Salamanca where there was a college for the education of Irish priests during the Penal times.

The Cathedral was dedicated in 1965 by Cardinal Cushing, the Pontifical Legate, to 'Our Lady Assumed into Heaven and St Nicholas'.

The three entrances have a round arch, with a portland stone carving by Domhnall Ó Murchada in the semicircular space under the arch known as the tympanum.

Irish marble was used where possible throughout the cathedral. The sepia floor marble was quarried in Connemara.

All the windows in the cathedral depict biblical events and figures. The upper storey windows are drawn from the Old Testament, the windows on the ground floor from the New Testament.

Start at the north entrance (facing the University).

To the right is the baptistery with stained-glass windows by Patrick Pollen. The font was carved from a single block of Irish black marble.

Opposite the baptistery the mosaic of St Joseph the Worker was designed by Patrick Pollen. The surrounding panelling is Estromotz marble.

The rose window above the organ in the north gable was designed by George Campbell. The large panels from lower left depict the five Joyful Mysteries.

Moving up the left aisle we reach the mortuary chapel with a mosaic of the Risen Christ. On one side is a small mosaic of Patrick Pearse and on the other a mosaic of John Fitzgerald Kennedy. Patrick Pearse, the nationalist leader, executed for his part in the 1916 Rising, used to spend his summers in Connemara. John Fitzgerald Kennedy was the first serving American President to visit Ireland. He received the freedom of Galway City in June 1963, shortly before his assassination. The windows in the mortuary chapel were designed by Patrick Pollen. Near the mortuary chapel on the aisle wall, the white portland stone carving of the fourth station is by Gabrielle O'Riordan.

The Old Testament theme windows in the east transept were designed by John Murphy of Blackrock. On the large plate glass panel of the east entrance (the one facing the bridge) is an engraving of the Last Judgment by Patrick Heney. Above it the rose window was designed by George Campbell.

Above the altar in the Saint Nicholas chapel (to the left of the east entrance opposite the bridge) is a triptych carved in limestone dating from the 17th century. In an account of his travels around Ireland published in 1752, Bishop Pococke of Meath claims that he saw the triptych in the vestry of St Nicholas Church. The carving was probably commissioned by the Catholic clergy during one of the brief periods when they regained possession of their old church, 1643–52 and 1689–91. Their tenure was so short, however, that either the carving was never erected or was removed. The triptych was found in the parish chapel in Abbeygate Street. This church became the Pro-Cathedral. The smoothness of the stone on the shin of Christ shows where people were wont to touch the statue. The carvings were erected here to give a sense of continuity with Galway's ecclesiastical past. Patrick Pollen also created the windows in this chapel, and the mosaic of the Crucifixion in the retro-choir was also designed and executed by him. To the west of the retro-choir is the chapel of Saint Colman of Kilmacduagha. The fresco was designed and executed by Fr Aengus Buckley O.P. The windows are the work of Patrick Pollen.

The porch entrance on the west was made into a mothers' and babies' chapel with a soundproof glass partition. Over the chapel the window was designed by Manus Walsh.

Over the west entrance are the five Glorious Mysteries designed by George Campbell. The other windows in this transept are the work of Manus Walsh.

St Fachnan's Chapel has a fresco of the saint by Fr Aengus Buckley O.P.

The sanctuary floor is of Portuguese beige marble. The high altar is a single slab of Carrara white marble. It was presented to the cathedral by Lord Hemphill of Tulira in memory of his uncle, Edward Martin, the friend of Yeats and Lady Gregory who agreed to help finance a national theatre (see page 143.) Within the sanctuary are the Bishop's chair and seats for his assistants. Opposite are the seats for the celebrant, deacon and subdeacon. On each side of the Bishop's and celebrants' chairs are twelve seats for the canons of the cathedral chapter.

The shop off the west transept is open from 9.30–5.30 p.m. each weekday (closed for lunch 1–2 p.m.). It stocks a fine collection of crosses, statues, rosaries and books.

## St Nicholas' Collegiate Church.

This church, dedicated to St Nicholas of Myra, was built around 1320 on the site of an earlier church, traces of which may be seen in the chancel wall.

In 1484 the merchants of Galway petitioned the Archbishop of Tuam and the Pope to have the right to elect their own clergy. They represented themselves as 'modest and civil' and claimed that the native Irish were 'A savage race, unpolished and illiterate, who often disturbed them in exercising the divine duties of their religion according to English rite and custom'. The petition was granted and in 1484 St Nicholas' Church became a collegiate church with an elected Warden and eight other Vicars. The Mayor, Bailiffs and Freemen of the city, all members of the leading merchant families, were to be the electors.

After the Reformation the introduction of Protestant services was delayed until 1568. The Catholic clergy took charge for two brief periods 1643–52 and in 1689 until the battle of Aughrim in 1691. Thereafter, the church remained firmly Protestant and is still in regular use by the Church of Ireland community.

Christopher Columbus is said to have prayed here. According to Professor T.P. O'Neill, recent research shows that Columbus was in Galway in 1477. Galway was an important port at that time. Furthermore, St Brendan the Navigator's account of his sea voyage westwards was known throughout Europe, and Saint Brendan had strong associations with Galway — not least through the establishment of a nunnery at Annaghdown for his sister. St Brendan died at this nunnery and until 1477 St Nicholas' Church belonged to the Annaghdown diocese. Perhaps Columbus hoped to find further texts, maps or even oral information regarding the best route to America.

During the turbulent 16th century many of the church's treasures were damaged or lost. The 16th century stoup was discovered in the late 19th century doing 'service as a stand for flowers'.

When Cromwell's army entered the city in 1652, the horses were stabled in the church. You can still see the slabs supposedly damaged by the horses' hooves. The faces were smashed off many of the statues by the iconoclasts in the army.

The church has had bits added to it throughout the centuries: the tower dates from 1500, the large central window from 1583, the spire from 1683 and the parapet is an 1883 restoration.

Visitors are invited to look around. Rubbings of some of the more interesting tombs and details to look out for have been displayed inside. There are many fascinating tomb inscriptions and memorials both inside and outside the church. Look out particularly for the Crusader's tomb, the late 15th or early 16th century Lynch wall tomb in the south transept, the reader's desk from the same period at the entrance to the Blessed Sacrament Chapel, and the floor grave slabs, many with symbols of the trade or profession of the deceased.

At the north-east corner of the churchyard, on Market Street, are the fragments of two 16th or 17th century houses. A 19th century tablet inserted into one of them claims that the window was the one from which Mayor Lynch hung his son. The story is pure 19th century fantasy and the window with its skull must be an early example of a tourist trap. The story of the popular young man, his jealousy and crime of passion and his father's insistence on upholding the law makes a good yarn and it is detailed in the foyer of the bank in Lynch's Castle, Shop Street.

**The Franciscan Abbey.**

Located near the bottom of Eglinton Street. Designed by James Cusack on Greek lines, it was built in the mid 19th century.

The Franciscan Friary was established in 1296 by Sir William Liath de Burgo just outside the town wall on a site near where the present courthouse now stands. It became the principal burial place of the leading merchant families. After 1652, when the Cromwellians sacked the town, the friary was turned into a courthouse and then demolished. With the Restoration of the Monarchy in 1660, the friars returned and built a new friary on a portion of their old land where the present church stands. In 1781 they rebuilt the friary chapel and in 1820 the present building was started. It was finished in 1863.

In the friary are some fragments of 17th century grave slabs and part of an altar tomb. These fragments are all that remained after Cromwell's army sacked the town's churches. The friars will allow visitors through to see these artefacts if asked.

**THOOR BALLYLEE. 20 miles/32 km from Galway.**

The 15th century castle of Ballylee has become famous because it was the home of the poet William Butler Yeats and his family for a time. In 1958 it was almost a ruin. The Kiltartan Society, with the help of Western Tourism and Bord Fáilte, rescued it. It has been fully restored, with a book/craft shop, coffee shop, and video and audio presentations on the life and work of W.B. Yeats.

During August and September 1896, W.B. Yeats and a friend, Arthur Symons, spent a holiday in the west of Ireland. For part of the time they stayed at Tullira Castle as the guests of Edward Martin who introduced Yeats to Lady Gregory. When Arthur Symons returned to London, Yeats was invited to spend a few days at Lady Gregory's home at nearby Coole Park. The Castle of Ballylee is close to Coole Park and Yeats recorded in an essay how he visited a miller who lived near the castle to talk about Biddy Early, the wise old woman of Clare. He also records that Ballylee was associated with Mary Hynes, the beautiful woman who had been celebrated by the poet Raftery (1784–1835).

The old tower among the trees, beside the river, obviously captured the imagination of the young poet. At that time the castle and adjoining cottage were inhabited by the Spellman family. Patrick Spellman was the Master of the Workhouse in Loughrea and he rented the castle from his uncle, James Colgan of Kilcolgan Castle.

Yeats returned many times to stay with Lady Gregory and no doubt visited Ballylee often. In 1902 Mrs Spellman died and the family gave up the castle. It became part of the Gregory estate. In 1916 the castle was put on the market by the Congested Districts Board. At that time the State had been acquiring land to redistribute it to smallholders. The land at Ballylee had been bought, but no one wanted the castle. Yeats bought it. In a letter to his father he called the castle his tower.

At the time Yeats bought it, the castle had four floors with one room on each floor, connected with a spiral stone stairway. There was a cottage attached to the castle by a porch and Yeats had plans drawn up to extend this to form an entrance to a second cottage to be built behind, and parallel to, the first. There was a walled garden and across the road an outhouse which Yeats eventually converted into a garage. Yeats planned to earn the money for the work by giving lectures in Paris and Milan. In Yeats's absence, his good friend Lady Gregory supervised the building and restoration work.

Meanwhile Yeats married Miss George Hyde-Lees in October 1917. He was anxious to move to the castle with his wife, but the work on it was held up by a shortage of materials. Then Yeats contracted influenza. Eventually, in May 1918, Mr and Mrs Yeats went to stay at Ballymantane House which Lady Gregory owned and lent to them while they waited for Ballylee to be made habitable.

Materials were still in short supply, but Yeats was able to buy a derelict mill for its stone and wood. Furniture for the castle was made locally by craftsman joiner Patrick Connolly from William A. Scott's designs. William Scott was the Professor of Architecture at the National University of Ireland and he drew up the plans for the building work. The ironwork was made in Burke's Forge in Gort.

By 1919, Yeats, his wife George and baby daughter, Anne, were able to live in part of Ballylee. Work continued on the castle for the next few years. However, it was often held up because these were the years of the War of Independence, followed by the Irish Civil War. Yeats and George were often away from Ballylee during these unsettled times. They bought a house in Dublin at 82 Merrion Square. Despite all the difficulties and disruptions, by 1922 the family had settled into their castle, although in a letter to Olivia Shakespear, Yeats said that it would be another year before all the work on the castle would be complete. In that letter to Olivia Shakespear, Yeats used the name Thoor Ballylee as his address, saying that Thoor is the Irish for tower and 'it will keep people from suspecting us of modern gothic and a deer park'.

*Lynch's Castle*

During the Civil War the nearby bridge was blown up. Then the builder was shot and hospitalised so that the work was held up yet again. Yeats was elected to the Senate in 1923 and soon afterwards was awarded the Nobel Prize for Literature and so he was often absent from his beloved Ballylee. It was 1926, ten years after he had first set out to buy the castle, before Yeats could move into Thoor Ballylee and live there with his family, even on a semi-permanent footing.

Because of illness Yeats went abroad to live during 1927. In February 1928 he was in Rapallo when his collection *The Tower* was published. Many of the poems were written at or inspired by Thoor Ballylee. Yeats gave full instructions about the cover design for the book. He wanted a golden design and an imaginative impression of his tower, but whatever else was in the design, the magnificence of the walls had to be shown.

When Yeats first bought Ballylee Castle he had talked to friends about how he would grow old there and what a wonderful place it would be for his children to grow up in; but those dreams were not to be. After 1928 Yeats never went to Ballylee again.

In 1932 his great friend Lady Gregory died. The castle once more began to decay into a ruin, a possibility foreshadowed in the last line of Yeats' poem 'To be carved on a stone at Thoor Ballylee.' A stone with the poem carved on it was not placed at Thoor Ballylee until after Yeats's death. The Board of the Abbey Theatre had it carved and erected in 1948.

In 1961 the Kiltartan Society was formed locally to foster interest in local literary history. (Lady Gregory was a translator and dramatist, and together with Edward Martin of Tullira Castle and W.B. Yeats, formed the Irish Literary Theatre which was a forerunner of the Abbey Theatre.) The restoration of Thoor Ballylee was proposed as a project. In 1963 Mrs Yeats and her children, Michael and Anne, placed the property of Thoor Ballylee in the hands of a trust to ensure its restoration and maintenance. Today the castle of Thoor Ballylee is open to the public.

A visit to Thoor Ballylee will introduce you to the history and political background to Yeats's life and his own personal history. You will learn also a little of Yeats's dreams and plans for the old castle of Ballylee. You will be able to climb the spiral stone stairs into each room and hear beautifully read extracts from his poetry and look at some fine first editions of his work.

William A. Scott's plans were found and used for the restoration work, and the thatch was put back as it once had been. Sadly, most of the old oak furniture had disappeared, but some pieces were located in the district and replaced. Other pieces were made by local craftsmen, just as they had been in Yeats's time. The walls were repainted in the colours which George and W.B. had chosen.

Before you enter the tower there are wooden benches in a screening room to sit on and enjoy an excellent video which lasts for 15 minutes. Then in each room there is a tape to listen to while you look at the exhibits.

The audio tapes are synchronised so that in order to get the full benefit of the presentation you should stay in each room until the tape has finished playing.

The coffee shop and bookshop/souvenir shop on the ground floor may be visited without making the tour. There is a good car park and you are allowed to wander along the path which winds around through the wooded grounds surrounding the castle.

Perhaps after visiting Thoor Ballylee you may wish to visit the grounds of Coole Park, which was the home of Lady Gregory. Unfortunately the house was knocked down in the 1950s for its building materials, but the grounds are still there, the lake with its swans and the huge copper beach tree still bearing the initials of the famous writers who visited Lady Gregory. Among them you can see the initials 'W.B.Y.' and 'G.B.S.' (George Bernard Shaw). The Forest and Wildlife Service has made a nature reserve of the grounds and there are picnic tables. There is a well-signposted nature trail which is described in a Wildlife Service Nature Trail booklet available at the car park.

Those interested in literary history may like to know that the blind poet Raftery (1784–1835), who was born in County Mayo and wrote in Irish, is buried in the old graveyard in Killeenan (signposted to the east of the N18 near Kilcolgan). The author of the songs 'The Ould Plaid Shawl' and 'Galway Bay', Francis Fahy (1854–1935), was born in nearby Kinvarra. Tullira Castle, home of Edward Martin, is east of the N18, north of Coole Park near the village of Labane.

**How to get there.**

Take the N18 Galway to Limerick road for approximately 18 miles/28 km and watch out for the signpost to Thoor Ballylee on your left, before you reach Gort. If you want to visit Coole Park after Thoor Ballylee, take a left turn on the N18 for a short distance to the signpost for Coole Park.

As you approach Oranmore you may be interested to know that the castle standing by the shore was built by the Burkes who also built Thoor Ballylee, and that today it is lived in by Commander Bill King who is one of the few men to sail singlehandedly around the world. His late wife was the author Anita Leslie.

### ATHENRY. (Baile Átha an Rí 'Town of the King's Ford').

15 miles/24 km from Galway.

This is a small country town with evidence of its 13th century origins still showing in its winding narrow streets, town walls, castle and Dominican Friary. Athenry is located at the junction of three ancient kingdoms, Hy-Many (O'Kellys), Hy-Briuin Seola (O'Flahertys) and Hy-Fiachrach (O'Hynes). The Anglo-Normans decided to make it their centre of power in this part of the territory.

The **Castle** this was built in the 13th century for Meiler de Bermingham, who was given the land by William de Burgo, the Anglo-Norman conqueror of much of Connaught. It has a three-storied keep, still in a surprisingly good state of repair. In 1991 it was roofed by the Office of Public Works. The ground floor is vaulted on three square pillars. The first floor was the hall or main apartment and was entered through a fine Early Gothic doorway approached through an outside flight of steps. (Notice the lack of a fireplace in this room.) The roof gables were later additions.

The **Dominican Friary** was built within a short walk of the castle. Meiler de Bermingham gave the land to the Dominican Order in 1241 and a small friary dedicated to Saints Peter and Paul was started. Although begun with Anglo-Norman patronage, throughout the 13th century native landowners, specifically Felim O'Connor, Eoghan O'Heyne and Cornelius O'Kelly donated funds for the extension of the friary. In 1424 it was extensively rebuilt following a fire. You can see the difference in the alterations to the aisle and transept arcades.

In 1574 the friary was sacked, as was the town, by Clanrickarde's sons in their rebellion against the English Crown. The priests eventually returned early in the 17th century but were forced to leave in 1652 following Cromwell's victory. Around 1750, parts of the buildings were demolished to make way for a military barracks.

The surrounding graveyard is open all the time but the friary is locked. The key is available on deposit of a returnable fee. (Information about this is clearly displayed on the entrance gate.) At present the key is with Mrs Sheehan, whose address is given as 5 Church Street. However, the street names in Athenry are not clearly displayed. To find Mrs Sheehan, walk up the town, past the square with market cross, past Paddy Burke's bar and look out for 'The Fields of Athenry' gift shop and Kelly's Pharmacy on your right. Mrs Sheehan's house is the fourth door along from the pharmacy entrance.

The **town walls** were built following a battle between the Anglo-Normans of Connaught, led by William Liath de Burgo and Richard de Bermingham, and the followers of King Felim O'Connor (who was an ally of Edward Bruce of Scotland) in 1316. The Irish army was beaten and the money which was made from the sale of the arms and armour taken from the fallen was used to finance the building of the walls. It is chronicled that over 8,000 men were killed in that battle. Most of the original town wall, which was surrounded by a moat, is still standing together with five of its six towers. Of the five gates, only one remains. With the market cross on your right, walk forward then take the first left. The gate can be seen quite clearly straddling the road.

The **Market Cross** is in the town square. It is a 15th century lantern or tabernacle cross of a type more usually found in England than in Ireland. Only the head of the cross is 15th century, the stepped pedestal is from a much later period. This was the spot where financial matters used to be finalised during the weekly market.

The tradition of weekly agricultural trading still continues today at the **Athenry Mart** which is on the Galway road side of the town. Visitors may wander around the pens and listen to the selling if they wish. The pens are covered and the floor is concrete, so special footwear is not necessary. The Mart is held every Monday, Tuesday and Thursday for the sale of sheep and cattle. Children may be interested in visiting the pens where the calves are kept. In the Mart buildings, there is a canteen on the first floor serving hot food, drinks and snacks all day.

Behind the Market Cross are the remains of a 13th century church, **St Mary's**, which some authorities think may have been originally a Franciscan friary. It was destroyed in the Clanrickarde sacking of 1574. Two nave columns are used as gateposts at the entrance to the overgrown graveyard. Fragments of a medieval nave and transepts survive. A Protestant church was built on to what was the chancel of the church. This is now used by the Athenry scout movement as a hall and is not open to the public.

The **Fields of Athenry** heritage cottage is located in North Gate Street. This is a traditional one–bedroomed, stone–flagged cottage with open fire furnished in 19th century style with old farm machinery in the yard. Access is through the gift shop and is free. Tea, coffee and scones are served daily from May to September.

**How to get there.**
Athenry is off the Dublin road. Take the R348 signposted to the left to Athenry. The road takes you through hedgerow-edged pastures studded here and there by mature trees.

The Dublin to Galway train stops at Athenry. The journey takes only 14 minutes from Galway. At present there are trains at 8 a.m., 11.35 a.m. and 15.10 p.m. Return trains at 13.27 p.m., 16.47 p.m. and 20.46 p.m.

**LOUGHREA CATHEDRAL AND THE TUROE STONE.**
Located 22 miles/35 km from Galway on the N6 Dublin road.

St Brendan's Cathedral contains some of the finest examples of Irish church art from 1903–57, and lies off the main street of the town. Outside, the Cathedral looks no more than an example of typical late 19th century Gothic Revival architecture. William Byrne was responsible for the exterior.

The reason the market town of Loughrea became the location for this spectacular collection is because Edward Martin of Tullira Castle, patron of the arts, friend of Lady Gregory and her literary set, decided to commission new windows for his local church in Labane, near Ardrahan. He discovered that he would have to go to England or the Continent of Europe to have work designed and executed. He commissioned the English artist, Christopher Whall, a disciple of William Morris, to furnish the windows for Labane and Loughrea Cathedral but stipulated that the work for Loughrea should be carried out in Ireland.

Whall sent A.E. Child over to Dublin to execute the Loughrea windows. Martin helped Child to be appointed as teacher of stained glass in the Dublin Metropolitan School of Art in 1903. In the same year he also persuaded Sarah Child to found the Túr Gloine (Tower of Glass) Studio which was to have such an important influence on Irish Church art.

The interior, down to every last furnishing detail, was completed under the direction of William A. Scott who was the Professor of Architecture at Dublin University. (See Thoor Ballylee, page 140.) Scott gathered together some of the finest artists and craftspeople working in Ireland for this project. John Hughes crafted the Virgin and Child in the Lady Chapel. A.E. Child, Sarah Purser, Hubert McGoldrick, Michael Healy, Evie Hone and Patrick Pye created the windows. It is a wonderful collection of work from the Dublin School of stained glass illustrating its beginning and development.

The windows in order of date are:

1903: Child: *The Annunciation, The Agony in the Garden, The Resurrection* (all two-light).

1904: Healy: *St Simeon*; Purser: *St Ita* (painted by Catherine O'Brien); Child: *Baptism of Christ* (this is a two-light window).

1907: Healy: *The Holy Family, Virgin and Child with Sts Patrick, Brendan, Colman, Iarlaith, Columcille, Bridget* (in the Lady Chapel).

1908: Healy: *St Anthony*; Purser: *Childhood of Christ, Passion Cycle* (two three-lights in east transept which were painted by Child).

1925: McGoldrick: *The Sacred Heart*.

1927: Healy: *St John the Evangelist*.

1929: Child: *Sts Clare and Francesca* (two-light).

1930: Healy: *Tu Rex Gloriae Christe*.

1933: Healy: *Regina Coeli*.

1934: Child: *Centurion*.

1935: Healy: *St Joseph*.

1936: Healy: *The Ascension* (three-light).

1937: Child: *St Patrick*.

1936 to 1940: Healy: *The Last Judgment* (three-light window beside his *Ascension* on the west transept). These two works are recognised as Healy's finest.

1942: Hone: *St Bridget* (she had to 'sweeten' the features).

1950: Hone: *The Creation* (rose window).

1957: Pye: *St Bridget* (in porch).

Undated: Purser: *St Brendan* (in porch).

The altar rails, font, and all stone carvings are the work of Michael Shortall. William Scott designed the ironwork, wooden furnishings and sanctuary pavement. Note the details on the pew carvings. The stations of the cross are by Ethel Rhind.

Close to the church, in a converted stable, is a museum of church relics and embroidered vestments. If the door is locked, ask either at the presbytery or in the church.

The Carmelite Friary, near the Cathedral, was founded in 1300 by Richard de Burgo. The nave and the tower date from the 15th century.

**THE TUROE STONE.**

This is a granite boulder approximately 3 ft/1.68 m high, which has been hewn into a domed shape and extensively decorated. It is thought to date from the 3rd to 2nd century B.C.

The late Michael Duignan identified that the ornamentation is in four parts and may have been decorated with colour. Similar designs have been found in Brittany and are associated with a people referred to as the La Tène Celts by European archaeologists. The La Tène Celts have been established as living in 500 B.C. and this stone appears to indicate that they, or their influence, reached Ireland.

A Pet Farm and Leisure Park opened here in 1993. There is a duck pond, a nature trail, a playground with swings, picnic and barbeque area, a wishing well and a collection of old farm machinery on site. A coffee shop provides snacks as well as toilets and baby changing facilities. Open April to October seven days from 10 a.m. until 8 p.m. Telephone 0905–42140.

**How to get there.**
The route to Loughrea along the N6 is well signposted.

To get to the Turoe Stone take the R350 north out of Loughrea for approximately 4 miles/6.4 km to Bullaun. Take the road to the west sign-posted to the Turoe Stone. The Stone stands in front of Turoe House.

## ROSS ERRILY, HEADFORD AND TUAM MILL MUSEUM AND 'CASTLE GROUNDS'.

This tour takes in a remarkably well-preserved friary only 15 miles/24 km from Galway City, then a journey cross-country to Tuam with its Mill Museum.

**Ross Errily** was a Franciscan Observantine Friary founded in 1498. It is one of the best preserved sites of its kind west of the Shannon. The church has survived and also a number of conventual buildings. The river, when diverted, supplied water to the mill, the brewery, the kitchen and toilets. There is a stone fish tank in the kitchen and a massive fireplace with oven. Notice, too, the reader's desk by the window in the refectory. Open all year.

**Tuam Mill Museum**, well signposted in the town, is open 10 a.m.– 6 p.m, Mondays to Saturdays. It is housed in an old corn mill and the restored miller's house contains working models of different types of mills. Visitors are shown explanatory slides, then the mill is activated for a short time. Very moderate charge.

In the public **Castle Grounds** the children's playground has swings, see-saws, a roundabout and a climbing frame and caters for a range of ages. There is a crazy golf course which is free but players must provide their own equipment, and a swimming pool with low rates for daytime swimming. At the back of the swimming pool there is a small wildlife display which is interesting for small children.

**How to get there.**
Take the N84 to Headford and turn left in the village, then right at the signpost. Car park. A short walk down the lane and across a field will bring you to the Friary.

From Headford take the R333 to Tuam. Park in town car park. Everything well signposted.

# Rainy Day Activities

Visit Galway's churches, particularly the Cathedral (see page 136) and St Nicholas' church (see page 138).
Visit Galway's art galleries: The Arts Centre at 47 Dominick Street, The Kenny Gallery on Middle Street, The Geoghan Gallery in the Bridge Mills.
The Omniplex 7 screen cinema complex is located on the Headford Road. Booking usually essential. Telephone 091–67800. The Claddagh Palace 2 screen cinema is located at the foot of Taylors Hill near Lower Salthill.
Go shopping. The Corrib Shopping Centre (Roches) and the Eyre Square Centre offer complete cover for parking and shopping. The Galway Shopping Centre has partial cover.
Play snooker. (See page 121.)
Play indoor bowls. (See page 118.)
Visit the amusement arcades in Salthill.
Visit the Royal Tara Chinaware factory. (See page 136.)
Go to the golf range at Salthill for indoor video golf.
Browse through the bookshops, select a good book and retire to a coffee shop, pub, hotel or your accommodation to wait for the rain to stop.
Visit Thoor Ballylee. (See page 140.)
Visit Dunguaire Castle. (See Burren Tours, page 198.)
Visit Aillwee Cave. (See Burren, page 202.)
Visit Aughnanure Castle. (See page 28.)
Go indoor swimming. (See page 121.)
Play badminton or squash. (See page 120.)
Spend an hour in a gymnasium. (See page 120.)
Take a cruise on the Corrib. (See page 121.)
Visit Athenry Mart, Castle and carriage repairers. (See page 144.)
Visit Tuam Mill Museum. (See page 149.)
Battle of Aughrim Interpretative Centre is located just off the N6, 4 miles/6.4 km short of Ballinasloe. Three dimensional and audio/visual displays of the last great battle on Irish soil. Open Easter to September, seven days. Coffee shop.

# Children's Activities

Swimming at the beach or indoors at the Leisureland pool with its water slide.
Visit Leisureland amusement park with its miniature train and rides.

*Nuns Island*

Visit the toyshops located in the Cornstore, on Headford Road, in Roches Stores, and in Quay Street.

All the Galway bookshops have good children's sections.

Contact the Arts Centre, telephone 091–65866 for information about children's dancing/music and painting classes.

Go horse riding. (See page 120.) Stables cater for inexperienced as well as experienced riders.

Hire a rowing boat on the Corrib.

Go cycling. (See page 101 for information on cycle hire.)

Take a trip around the town on the horse bus. (See page 121.)

Take a trip to the Aran Islands. (See page 82.)

Play pitch and putt. (See page 120.)

Book a kayak or canoeing lesson in Spiddle at the Aqua Sports Centre opposite the beach. Children specially catered for. (See page 118.)

Go indoor bowling. (See page 118.)

Take a steam train excursion. (See page 121).

Visit Tuam Mill Museum and children's playground. (See page 149).

Visit Peter Pan Funworld located indoors at the Corbett Commercial Centre close to the junction of the Dublin road, the airport road and College Road. Caters for children up to 13 years old. Open seven days a week, 10 a.m.–7 p.m. Supervised. Soft play area, playhouse, slides, ball pond, punch bags, bouncing castle, scramble nets and café.

Visit Rathbaun Farm to see animals. Covered areas as well as open. Lunch or tea provided. Located near Ardrahan on the N18 18 miles/30 km from Galway.

Visit Turoe Pet Farm. See page 149.

# EVENING ACTIVITIES

Galway City is the entertainment capital of the west. All events, shows and concerts are advertised in two newspapers, the *Galway Advertiser*, out on Thursday, and the *City Tribune*, out on Friday.

Traditional music devotees should seek out the Dominick Street/Sea Road area of the City. The Crane Bar has traditional music without amplification every night during the summer and at the weekend during spring, autumn and winter. Taylor's, Monroe's Tavern, and the Waterfront also have traditional music on various nights. They offer other ethnic music like cajun and blue grass as well. The programme will be advertised outside and inside the pubs.

Further into the centre of town, the Lisheen bar near O'Brien's Bridge, the King's Head and Taaffe's in High Street, O'Malley's off Eyre Square and the Púcán on Forster Street are noted for good traditional sessions.

Many pubs recruit traditional musicians during the summer to play for visitors and they will advertise this outside the pub and in the free newspapers. Traditional music sessions are unpredictable. They can occur in a pub at any time. They will happen when a few musicians gather together and feel like playing.

'Siamsa' is a theatrical display of Irish dancing and music held in the Taibhdhearc Theatre in Middle Street during June, July and August.

Set dancing is available at Árus na Gael in Dominick Street, Árus Bothar na Trá in Salthill, telephone 091–22733, and at Cregg Castle in Corundulla, telephone 091–91434. Cregg Castle also has a resident traditional music teacher during June, July and August.

Many pubs offer more contemporary live music. McSwiggan's on Woodquay and Sally Long's on Abbeygate Street are notable examples.

Disco dancing is available in the night-clubs and some of the pubs. The city centre night-clubs are located at The Bentley on Prospect Hill, Kno Knos in Eglinton Street and the Central Park in Abbeygate Street. Salthill is the favourite night-club/disco location for many Galwegians, particularly the younger ones. All the clubs are close together, and they all advertise.

There is a shortage of venues for popular concerts in Galway City so many are held in Leisureland or Seapoint in Salthill. Leisureland is also the location of orchestral concerts. Small classical concerts and recitals are held in St Nicholas' Church, or in the Aula Maxima at the University.

The new Galway theatre was developed from an existing 18th century theatre and is located near the Town Hall. The Druid Theatre Company uses a small theatre converted from a warehouse. It is located in the lane off Quay Street. Galway Youth Theatre productions are staged in the Arts Centre at Nuns Island. Punchbag Theatre, a new professional company, turned an old garage at the bottom of Quay Street into a theatre and specialises in new Irish plays.

The Arts Centre has regular readings and performances. The programme is advertised. The Arts Centre is at 47 Dominick Street and information is available at the desk in the gallery.

For information about the cinemas see 'rainy day suggestions' (page 150).

The greyhound stadium holds races every Tuesday and Friday evening at 8.15 p.m. Covered stand, bar and full betting facilities. Car park. The stadium is on College Road, a ten-minute walk from Eyre Square. College Road leads off Forster Street. Entrance fee £3.00.

Medieval Banquets are held nightly June to September in Dunguaire Castle (see page 198.)

Floodlit tennis is available at the Galway Tennis Club (see page 120). See also 'day time activities' for information about ten pin bowling, squash and gymnasia.

Many visitors to Galway enjoy sitting in a city pub or wine bar to enjoy the conversation. It is quite in order to ask for a cup of coffee in most pubs, and of course, non-alcoholic drinks are available.

Lastly, on a fine evening consider a stroll around the city. Walk to the Cathedral over the Salmon Weir Bridge. If visiting during September, watch out for the eels in the nets below. Follow the river walk down to O'Brien's Bridge. A leisurely walk down Dominick Street and along Raven's Terrace will bring you to the Wolfe Tone Bridge and Nimmo's Pier.

Another interesting walk is along by the sea from the Claddagh to Salthill Promenade to see the sun set on Galway Bay. Remember, however, that directly opposite is south; the sun sets to your right!

# ECOTOUR

### GALWAY — CORRIB CIRCUIT.

**Stop** Woodquay (M292256), near old railway bridge pillars.

The River Corrib, after its short journey from the lough, flows quietly past the quay towards the weir where man has his greatest, but final, impact on the voluminous Corrib waters. Mallard, coot and moorhens swim and feed in the shallows around Woodquay and roost on the floats which prevent boats drifting over the weir. Black-headed and common gulls are regular visitors to the floats, and occasionally in winter (in recent years) an adult ring-billed gull — a long way from its American home — has joined the local gulls. The reed swamps upstream provide cover for breeding coots, mallard, little grebes and secretive water rails.

The weir, constructed in the mid-1800s, maintains the level of Lough Corrib at its pre-drainage summer level and regulates the rise and fall of the lake to about 5 ft/1.5 m at the maximum. The weir has been designed to ensure that salmon and eels can pass freely up and down the river. Returning adult salmon, easily seen from the Salmon Weir Bridge when the water level is low in summer, pass up a central fish ladder, and young smolts descending to the sea in spring are carried naturally with the higher flow over the weir, as are the eels which descend during the stormy nights of autumn. The ascent of the tiny elvers (young eels) in spring is facilitated by a brush-like ladder through which they can wriggle their way over the weir. Below the bridge, large eel-like sea lampreys can sometimes be seen when the water is shallow. Some of these parasites, which suck the blood of other fish, also ascend into the lake to breed.

The river upstream of the weir is also linked to the sea by a series of canals, once the source of power for numerous mills. Although for a long time the city turned its back on these disused waterways, their potential as amenities is now being recognised and pleasant walks have been developed along their banks. Trout, salmon and roach use the canals and provide food for herons which stalk their prey silently amidst the city bustle. Grey wagtails nest under the bridges and several pairs of dippers, more typically inhabitants of rushing upland streams, live the year round on the canals and along the main river.

**Link** 2.5 miles/4 km.

From the city centre we follow the signposts out of the city towards Oughterard and Clifden (N59). After 2 miles/3 km houses to the east of the road thin out and lower Lough Corrib comes into view.

**Stop** Bushy Park (M272278), at the car park by the church.

Across the road to the north-east is the broad expanse of lower Lough Corrib with, in the foreground, the winding Corrib River and beyond it the man-made Friar's Cut. The lower lake is only 7 to 10 ft/2 to 3 m deep and naturally fairly rich in nutrients. In the summer, dense growths of water plants (e.g. pondweeds) fill the southern part of the basin. These provide food for up to 600 moulting mute swans during July and August and seeds and plant food for many thousands of pochard, tufted duck and coot during autumn and winter.

The extensive reedswamps, particularly along the old river, provide cover for breeding little grebes, water rails, mute swans, coots and moorhens. Hen harriers are sometimes seen quartering the reedswamps in winter. Brown trout, pike, eels, roach and bream are some of the fish which inhabit the lake along with a wide variety of invertebrate animals which serve as their food.

Two large rivers, the Cregg and the Clare, flow into the lower lake from the east. The latter carries with it nutrients which are enriching the

south-eastern part of the basin and, undoubtedly, accelerating the natural evolution of the lake into marsh and eventually dry land.

**Link** 8 miles/13 km.

As we travel north-westwards, the undulating bog-covered hills of Galway granite dominate the western prospect and contrast sharply with the low-lying limestone bordering Lough Corrib. The road follows the boundary between these two rock types and this is sometimes apparent in the rocks which were used to build the walls — granite to the west and limestone to the east of the road. Ballycuirke Lake, to the east, links lower Lough Corrib and the next Stop at Ross Lake. The canal connecting Ballycuirke to Lough Corrib is the haunt of the kingfisher, an uncommon species in west Galway.

**Stop** Ross Lake (M180362), at 'No dumping or overnight parking' sign.

Ross Lake is one of the Corrib family of lakes. It is shallow, served by springs from the limestone and by small rivers and streams from the granite uplands to the west. Originally, it discharged into the lake downstream only through underground passages, but the building of a canal during one of the earlier Corrib drainage schemes has provided surface links which have had serious ecological consequences. Once an excellent trout lake, small trout are caught only rarely these days. Ross Lake is populated mostly with coarse fish — rudd, bream, hybrids of these species, perch, eels and pike which arrived naturally (or with some human assistance) when the canal was opened. Recently, roach were introduced into the Corrib system, apparently by foreign anglers using them as live-bait. This alien species now also occurs in Ross Lake and has spread through much of the rest of the Corrib system with, as yet, unknown consequences for the ecology of the lakes.

The reedswamps on the north-west shore harbour breeding water rails, rarely seen but easily recognised by their evening chorus reminiscent of squealing pigs! Mallard, red-breasted mergansers, coot and moorhens breed on the lake islands as do common gulls, black-headed gulls, the occasional pair of common terns and sometimes great crested grebes. Herons nest high in the coniferous plantation on the east shore of the lake. In winter, a family of whooper swans frequents the low-lying pastures on the west shore and pochard, tufted duck, curlew and cormorants are regular visitors.

Across the lake on the north-east shore stands Ross Castle, the former home of the Martin family. A member of the family, though not a resident of the house, was 'Humanity Dick' Martin who was renowned for steering the first animal protection legislation through the British Parliament in 1822.

**Link** 6 miles/10 km.

The granite hills to the west give way to low-lying scrub and reclaimed pasture. Glacial sand deposits once formed prominent hills to the west of the road, but quarrying is rapidly removing these relics of the Ice Age. To the east, as we approach Oughterard, the manicured golf course, though ecologically uninteresting, does serve as a feeding area for curlew, common gulls and lapwings. Signposted to the right is Aughnanure Castle, a fine 15th century tower house, built in part over the Drimneen River. The road takes us through the village of Oughterard and across the bridge over the Owenriff River.

**Stop** at Owenriff River (M112426), at car park opposite Sweeney's Oughterard House Hotel.

The Owenriff River is the largest river entering Lough Corrib from the west. It is an important salmon river and supports fine trout, too. A trout hatchery, established at the end of the last century and located upstream on the south bank, is said to have been the first commercial hatchery ever built in these islands.

Beneath the overhanging vegetation on the west bank, the work of the river prior to drainage can be seen clearly. The horizontal strata were eroded and, in places, undercut quite dramatically by winter spates.

About 220 yds/200 m upstream there is a little park with magnificent oak, beech and horse-chestnut trees — the latter two being introduced species — and alder typically growing at the water's edge. Across the road, amongst the deciduous trees, is a fine specimen of Scots pine.

The rocks projecting from the water in the middle of the river serve as perches for herons, perky little grey wagtails and dippers of the distinctive Irish race which have darker upper parts and less chestnut-brown colouring on their under parts than their British cousins.

**Walk.**

Continuing up the road about 330 yds/300 m upstream we can take the track marked 'Waterfall' where we may be lucky enough to see a salmon leaping the falls on the way to its spawning grounds upstream.

**Link** 7 miles/11 km.

Leaving Oughterard brings a visual and ecological surprise. The lush wooded landscape at the edge of the town gives way to stark, open moorland broken only by gorse (furze or whin) and willow scrub, young forestry plantations, some reclaimed pastures and the dark banks of peat exposed by traditional turf cutting methods. To the south of the road Lough Bofin sports a prominent wooded island with its Scots pine reminding us of early post-glacial times — before the changing climate, man and his livestock combined to denude the mainland of its tree cover.

**Stop** Loughaunierin, east shore (M017458), at small road running north from main road.

*Salmon Weir Bridge*

All the ingredients of Connemara unfold before us — bogs, lakes, mountains and an ever changing sky. In the foreground is blanket bog with its low vegetation of mosses, sedges, rushes, sparse heather, ling and occasional patches of taller scrub. Loughaunierin is a typical poor, acid lake with a stony shoreline and only small areas of fringing reedswamp in inlets sheltered from the almost incessant wind-whipped waves. Animal life is scarce in these habitats and most is confined to the shelter of the vegetation or the protection of the lakeshore stones. In the summer, shoals of minnows can be seen in the shallows swimming amongst the delicately flowered water lobelia. Birds such as mallard, teal, pochard (in winter) and little grebes occur on the lake in small numbers and only infrequently. Meadow pipits, skylarks, the occasional snipe and red grouse enliven the bogs. More elusive are the merlin and the breeding golden plover. The wetter areas of bog with stands of bog cotton and white beak-sedge attract wintering Greenland white-fronted geese. Unfortunately, several such areas have been destroyed in recent times and others are under imminent threat from extensive commercial peat extraction and afforestation, so the future of this internationally rare sub-species is now in some doubt in Connemara.

Though the lakes are poor, the deeper ones contain non-migratory charr (a species of fish), relics of post-glacial times. Those connected to the sea often support good runs of migratory sea trout. However, at present, the sea trout stocks in some Connemara waters are in decline, for reasons which are being hotly debated. Among the factors alleged to be affecting the stocks are intensive industrial salmon production along the coast, acidification of streams and rivers by commercial forestry, particularly in south Connemara, and adverse weather and water level conditions at critical times of the year. Only time and detailed research will tell if all or any of these factors are affecting the sea trout population — which naturally undergoes periodic declines anyway.

**Link** 6 miles/10 km.

Extensive commercial peat extraction, such as that to the north of the road, is now being carried out in many parts of the west of Ireland. As a result, large tracts of land are taken out of biological production for many decades, whereas the traditional methods of hand-cutting for local domestic supplies — also seen on both sides of the road to Maum — are less damaging to the environment.

Turning northwards at Maam Cross, we take the R336 towards Maum, passing the bright, white quartz intrusions where the bedrock has been exposed and then hummocky glacial moraines as we descend the steep, twisting road into the Maum Valley.

**Stop** Maum (L967527), at the river or at Keane's pub.

Below the bridge, the surprisingly sluggish Bealnabrack River flows towards the deep, steep-sided, glaciated north-western arm of Lough Corrib. In earlier geological times the northern branch of the river (Joyce's River) had its origin in a high corrie on the distant slopes of Mweelrea, but earth movements broke the river with the result that it has no torrent reach and its origin appears to be on the floor of the Maum Valley some 6 miles/10 km to the north-west. Pike lurk in the deep pools, and in autumn they often take brown trout as these move upstream to their spawning grounds. Otters are common in the area and even during the day we could be lucky enough to see them diving for perch and eels in the upper reaches of the lough.

On land, only the shelterbelts around the houses in the valley support appreciable amounts of wildlife, illustrating dramatically the value of such 'oases' for food and cover. In springtime cuckoos are often seen flying between these pockets of woodland. House martins are regular summer visitors to the area, sometimes nesting over the balconies of Keane's pub.

Sheep are the commonest domesticated inhabitants of the Maumturks and the Ordovician and Silurian sedimentary hills of Joyce's Country to the north. Overstocking, encouraged by subsidies which have placed more emphasis on quantity than quality, has led to a serious deterioration in the vegetation and, where the plant cover has been removed, heavy rains have soon caused erosion. This has produced the gullies and bare patches which are particularly evident on some of the hills around the Maum Valley.

To the west are the steep, bare Pre-Cambrian quartzite ridges of the Maumturk Mountains. Harsh, unrelenting and rising to over 2,000 ft/650 m, they are inhospitable for most life except foxes, which forage over most of the range, and ravens whose throaty croaks are often the only sign of living company for the walker in the hills. The gentler lower slopes of peat, blanketing less resistant schists, are scarcely more hospitable except where Silurian limestone outcrops produce richer herbage which is attractive to rabbits, including a relatively large proportion of the black variety.

**Link** 8.75 miles/14 km.

Downstream of Maum, still on the R336, the Bealnabrack River is joined by the Failmore River and together they flow into a rushy bay where whooper swans and other wildfowl feed in winter and where otters may be seen at any time of the year.

Hen's Castle (Caisleán na Circe), recently restored, stands on a small island in the middle of the lake. Once the home of the celebrated 16th century leader, Granuaile (Grace O'Malley), it is now a quiet refuge for nesting mallard, kestrels and sometimes choughs. Beyond the coll the broad expanse of upper Lough Corrib comes into view. On the descent, in the rushy fields beside the road, there are pine stumps (bog deal) some 4,000 years old and relics of a time when much of Ireland was covered with Scots pine.

After Cornamona the road passes beneath the steep slopes of Ben Levy, an isolated, flat-topped mountain which dominates the isthmus between Lough Corrib and Lough Mask to the north and dramatically marks the boundary between the central plain of Ireland and the western uplands.

**Stop** Panorama of upper Lough Corrib (M096535), at lake side of road in bend at road junction south of Clonbur.

Here it is possible to appreciate the beauty and size of the largest lake in the Irish Republic, extending from the rounded, granite hills in the west to the margins of the limestone central plain in the east. The hump-backed islands (drumlins) emerge from a basin which is as deep as 152 ft/46 m in places. The smaller islands are wooded while the larger islands usually have a crown of pasture rimmed with hawthorn and willow.

The largest island on the lake, Inchagoill, approximately 3 miles/5 km to the south-east, is densely wooded and supports a relatively rich flora and fauna — including breeding woodcock. However, like many of the larger islands, it also has a large population of common rats — which are not the most desirable of companions for avian and human visitors to the island. Inchagoill is also of considerable archaeological and historical interest and can be reached by cruiser from Ashford Castle during the summer months.

The richly vegetated islands of the upper lake contrast markedly with those of the middle and lower basins which are mainly limestone with sparse vegetation. The latter, however, provide a nesting habitat for wildfowl, gulls and terns, roosting sites for spring-migrating whimbrel and safe daytime resting places for otters. Some of the limestone islands also have 'Burren type' flora including the spring gentian and a variety of orchids as well as more typical moorland species such as the insectivorous butterwort.

**Link** 3.75 miles/6 km.

Following the road up the hill we take the next right turn signposted to Cong (R345). Rushy fields and coniferous plantations give way to some richer pastures contrasting with those to the west and north of the lake. The acid run-off from the surface soils has dissolved the underlying limestone so this area is rich in caves and underground passages, much like the Burren.

Approximately 1.5 miles/2.5 km along the road there is a Forest Park, Coill Árd na Gaothe (M132540). With picnic tables, panoramic views over the lake and picturesque forest walks, this is an ideal place for a break in the Corrib Country circuit. Returning to the main road, it is a further 1.5 miles/2.5 km to the next stop. Just west of Cong, there is a fine piece of small-scale vernacular architecture in the form of a stone-built forge with a horseshoe-shaped doorway and a decorated 'slit' above it.

**Stop** at The Corrib Rising, Cong (M149554). In Cong.

There is no natural overland connection between Lough Mask and Lough Corrib. Instead, the water from Lough Mask flows through underground passages and rises again at the northern edge of the village of Cong from where it flows into Lough Corrib along the short Cong River. Attempts were made in the 19th century to construct a canal between the two lakes but, for a variety of reasons, the canal was a failure and it was abandoned. The terminus of the canal can be seen on the east side of the village behind the handball court. Had the canal succeeded, salmon, which do not occur in Lough Mask, would undoubtedly have found their way into it and the recently introduced roach would eventually have spread to Lough Mask as well.

**Link** 12 miles/19 km.

When we depart from Cong along the R345 we leave behind the deciduous woodlands of Ashford Castle with their red squirrels, pine martens and woodcock and move into a landscape of low, undulating sheep pastures enclosed by stone walls. Trees and hedgerows are not common and the wildlife interest from the village of Cross to Headford is minimal. Approximately 1 mile/1.5 km north of Headford, to the west of the road, stands Ross Errily Friary, and to the north of that there is a small lake. In winter, Rostaff Lake floods and attracts a variety of water- birds including Greenland white-fronted geese and waders such as lapwing, curlew and golden plover. To the west of the lake, a bird watchers' hide has been constructed in an admirable co-operative effort between the Irish Wildbird Conservancy, the Black River Gun Club and the State Wildlife Service. The hide is open to the public during the autumn and winter. Signposted to the east side of the main road is the recently restored Moyne graveyard and church — a site probably dating back to the 10th century.

**Stop** at Turlough Cor, west of Rafwee (M280450), at the side road to the east of the main road (N84), 1 mile/1.6 km south of Headford.

Mounds of sterile marl (white, limy soil) and a deep drain are the products of a drainage scheme in the 1960s. The depth of marl, which can be seen at the side of the drain, testifies to many centuries of silt deposition during times of flood. At such times many thousands of wildfowl fed and

roosted on the turlough. When the water receded the naturally fertilised pastures provided rich grazing for large numbers of livestock. Today very few wildfowl and waders visit the area in winter and, until recently, relatively few cattle could be supported on the impoverished pasture. However, recent investment in fencing, re-seeding and fertilising appears to have raised the productive capacity of part of the former turlough and many of the unsightly mounds have been removed. The sequence of events which turned this once fertile turlough into relatively unproductive pasture, largely devoid of wildlife interest, has been repeated several times in the west of Ireland and remaining turloughs,

along with many of our other wildfowl wetlands, are in serious need of conservation.

Back to Galway 14.5 miles/23 km.

From an ecological standpoint, Turlough Cor marks the start of a depressing journey to Galway City along the N84. Several drainage schemes, dating back to the middle of the 19th century, have denuded the area of much of its wildlife interest. The Cregg and Clare Rivers have been deepened and canalised leaving sterile banks and uninteresting hinterlands. Otters still use the rivers and artificial re-stocking has helped to maintain trout and salmon stocks to some extent, but other riverine wildlife is scarce. However, for the historian and archaeologist a detour to Annaghdown is a delight.

The Galway dump attracts jackdaws, rooks, hooded crows and gulls — mainly during weekdays when it is open for dumping. Here, the gull enthusiast (for what else could a birdwatcher who spends long periods in such an environment be?) may see rarities such as glaucous, Iceland and ring-billed gulls. In recent years Kumlien's gull, a sub-species of the Iceland gull, has been reported, as has the first probable European sighting of the American Thayer's gull — an event which brought Galway rubbish dump to international prominence! Wintering whooper swans regularly graze the pastures on the other side of the road from the dump, but piecemeal industrial development threatens to drive them even from that haunt.

# THE BURREN

The Burren takes its name from the Irish *boireann*, meaning 'rocky place'. It occupies about 100 square miles of north County Clare. The land is covered by a sheet of bare, porous carboniferous limestone. In the fissures between the rocks, an extraordinary variety of rare plants flourish and it is this combination of landscape and flora which gives the Burren its unique attraction, drawing visitors here from all over the world.

Around the 10th century, the Dal gCais (the sept or tribe of Cas) began to make their way across the Shannon into Clare. The most famous member of the Dal gCais was Brian Boru, who became High King of Ireland in 1012 before losing his life two years later at the Battle of Clontarf.

His descendants became known as the O'Briens, but as he had at least four wives there developed many branches of the O'Brien family. Between them all, they dominated much of Clare's social and political life for centuries.

In 1172 Dónal Mór O'Brien, who had had constant battles with the O'Connors, swore allegiance to Henry II of England and got the assistance of a party of Norman mercenaries. His successor, another Dónal Mór, paid homage to King John of England in Waterford and was rewarded with the Kingship of Thomond, another name for north Munster. This later Dónal Mór O'Brien was forced back towards Ennis by the Normans, and Ennis remained the northern limit of Norman influence in Clare.

Henry VIII made Morrogh O'Brien Earl of Thomond in 1541. Thomond was later detached from Munster and placed in Connacht. North Clare was by now peaceful, settled country. The leading families built tower houses modelled on Norman castles. All over the county you will see the remains of the 16th century tower houses built by the gentry; most are in ruins now, but Doonagore near Doolin was restored beautifully in the 1970s. Another, Dunguaire Castle, on the coast, is open to visitors.

The wars of the 1640s were ruinous. The all-conquering Cromwellian army devastated County Clare, most of whose landowners had been enthusiastic Royalists. Houses and castles were ruined, Catholic landowners were dispossessed and their holdings given to Protestants. As with Connemara, Catholics dispossessed in other areas were sent into the region to make a living the best way they could. Many leading families hoped that the Cromwellian land settlement would be reversed with the Restoration of the Monarchy in the 1660s. It was not so. Thereafter, Catholics had to conform to the Established (Anglican) Church if they wished to retain a secure title to their lands. Many did so. William O'Brien, Earl of Inchiquin, had his lands restored to him by King William, and he and his successors became the backbone of the Protestant ascendancy of Clare.

Clare has been called 'The Banner County' in modern times because when Daniel O'Connell, the champion of Catholic Emancipation, was returned as Member of Parliament for Clare in 1828 he was greeted by an enormous crowd of banner-waving supporters in Ennis. The Famine years of 1845–48 saw a drastic decline in the population of Clare, as with the rest of the western seaboard.

In 1917, Eamon de Valera was elected as the MP for East Clare. He represented the county in Dáil Éireann until 1959 when he became President of Ireland.

You will see churches everywhere: the ruins of tiny early Christian churches, medieval churches, hidden chapels from the Penal times and 19th and 20th century parish churches. Above all the Burren is remarkable for its megalithic tombs and its Iron Age ring forts.

A tour of major archaeological sites is included in this guide (see page 206). A 1961 survey of megalithic tombs listed 66 graves of early settlers. Tim Robinson has mapped 450 ring forts. If you are an explorer it is possible you may come across some unmarked sites. Listed below is a brief outline to give you a rough idea of what you may see as you tour the Burren.

## COURT CAIRNS.

These are thought to be among the earliest of the megalithic monuments. Their possible date is between 3,000 and 2,500 years before the birth of Christ. They consist of a long chamber divided into compartments where the remains were placed. In front of the tomb there was usually a semicircular space flanked by standing stones. This space may have been used for funeral rites. The tomb itself was covered by a mound of stones held in place by kerb stones. The majority of court cairns were thought to be found in the north of the country (north of a line from Westport to Dundalk). Until recently, only ten of these tombs had been located south of this line, but recent work by archaeologists Jim Higgins and Michael Gibbons has revealed more.

## PORTAL TOMBS (OFTEN CALLED DOLMENS).

The name 'dolmen' comes from the Breton for 'table'. Folklorists often described them as Diarmuid and Grainne's bed. They were probably built around 2000 B.C. by the descendants of the people who built the court tombs and some overlap in date with court tombs exists. Dolmens consist of two or three standing stones, covered by a capstone. The capstone was placed in position by being hauled up the side of an earthen mound which was built around the standing stones.

The majority of Irish portal tombs have been found around the east coast and throughout the north, with a few located in the Clare/Galway area.

## WEDGE TOMBS.

These graves get their name from their shape because they are wider at one end than at the other. The long burial chamber was often surrounded by a special setting of stones and would have been covered by a mound of earth and more stones. It is thought that these graves were built shortly after 2000 B.C. The Burren examples are simplified versions of wedge graves which can be found elsewhere. Almost half the wedge tombs in Ireland occur in north County Clare.

## HILLFORTS (PROMONTORY FORTS).

As the name implies, these were built on the top of a hill. They do not seem to have been designed as either living places or defendable forts. It is thought they may have been used as meeting places. Some excavated examples show that they seem to have been used from the late Bronze Age onwards. The Bronze Age commenced around 1750 B.C. and lasted until about 500 B.C. The name comes from the widespread use of copper and bronze used during the period, but gold was also fashioned during this time.

## SHELS AND RATHS (STONE RING FORTS AND EARTHEN RING RTS).

Cashels (stone ring forts) are smaller than the hill forts and were defendable farmsteads. Some cashels had souterrains (underground stone passages) for storage. Built on level ground, the cashels may have had one or more dwelling houses inside the surrounding stone wall. The wall would have kept the livestock in and predators out at night and was a defensive barrier in times of danger.

The raths (earthen forts) are surrounded by one or more earthen banks and ditches and may have had a pallisade on top of the banks. These ring forts came into use during the Iron Age, but in some areas they continued to be used for a number of centuries afterwards. Iron came into use in Ireland around 500 or 300 B.C. Very little is known of the burial habits of the people during this time, but they left evidence of how they lived.

# USEFUL TELEPHONE NUMBERS AND INFORMATION

## BANKS

Hours 10 a.m.–4 p.m. Monday to Friday with some branches closing for lunch 12.30–1.30 p.m.

*Allied Irish Banks*:

**Ennistimon:** Late day, Tuesday. Telephone 065–71018.

**Ennis:** Late day, Thursday. Telephone 065–28777.

*Bank of Ireland*:

**Ennistimon:** Late day, Tuesday. Telephone 065–71036.

**Ennis:** Late day, Thursday. Telephone 065–28615.

**Lisdoonvarna:** Sub-office held in room in the Ritz Hotel in the Square. Every Thursday, 10 a.m.–12 p.m. From 1 July until 1 October, every Tuesday and Thursday 10 a.m.–12 p.m.

## BICYCLE HIRE AND REPAIR

*Doolin*: Telephone 065–74022/74321.

*O'Connor's Pub*, Doolin, Telephone 065–74168.

*Lehinch Launderette*, seven days a week. Telephone 065–81424.

Cycles rented from the following outlets may be rented from one office and returned to another in the list:

*Doolin*: The Hostel, telephone 065–74006.

*Lisdoonvarna*: Burke's Garage, telephone 065–74022/74321 for hire and repairs.

*Lehinch*: The Caravan and Camping Park, telephone 065–81424.

*Milltown Malbay*: Byrne and Sons, telephone 065–84079, or 065–84111 after 6.30 p.m.

Cycle repairs only in Ennis at McMahon's, telephone 065–28035, or Tierney's, telephone 065–29433.

## BUREAUX DE CHANGE

### Ballyvaghan:
*Whitethorn Crafts Visitor Centre.* 1 mile/1.6 km from village towards Kinvarra. Open 10 a.m.–10 p.m. all year. Seven days a week from June until October.
*Cliffs of Moher Visitor Centre*: Open seven days a week from 17 March until October, from 10 a.m.–5.30 p.m. In July and August the Centre is likely to close at 6.30 p.m. or 7 p.m. For information telephone 065–81171.

### Lehinch:
*Sue's Boutique.* Open all day, six days a week, from early April until end of October.

## CAR HIRE

*Johnson and Perrott,* Shannon Airport, telephone 061–61094. See also Galway, page 100.
*Avis,* Shannon, telephone 061–61644. Rest of Ireland, telephone Dublin 01–776971.
*Budget Rent-a-car,* Shannon, telephone 061–61361. See also Galway, page 100.
*Bunratty Car Rentals,* Shannon, telephone 061–362549.
*Murray's, Shannon,* telephone 061–61618. See also Galway, page 100.
*Thrifty Car Rental,* Shannon, telephone 061–53049/62649, Fax 061–53433.
*Tom Mannion,* Ennis, telephone 065–24211, Fax 065–24166.
*O'Connor's Motors,* Milltown Malbay, telephone 065–84072.

## CAR REPAIRS

### Ennistimon:
*O'Dea's,* telephone 065–71021, or 27021 after 6.00 p.m. Petrol and repairs seven days a week.

### Kilfenora:
*Connole's,* telephone 065–88008. Access and Visa accepted. Seven days a week for petrol and repairs. 24-hour breakdown service.

### Lisdoonvarna:
*Burke's Garage,* open seven days a week. Telephone 065–74022/74321.
*Foudy's* at Benn's Cross. Petrol, punctures and tyres. Open seven days a week.
*Flanagan's,* on the Doolin Road, telephone 065–74109. Punctures, petrol and repairs. Access and Visa accepted.

## CHURCH SERVICES

*Mass* is available throughout the region both on Saturday evenings and Sunday mornings.
*Church of Ireland* service at Kilfenora Church at 10 a.m.
Nearest *Methodist Church* is in Galway or Limerick (telephone 061–28929 for times of services).

## GARDAÍ (POLICE)

*Ballyvaghan*: telephone 065–77002
*Ennistimon*: telephone 065–71163
*Lehinch*: telephone 065–81222
*Lisdoonvarna*: telephone 065–74222

## LAUNDERETTES

**Corrofin:**
Main Street. Washing, drying and ironing service, 10 a.m.–7 p.m. Mondays to Saturdays all year.

**Lehinch:**
First turn left on Milltown Road. Open from 1 May to 1 October, seven days a week, 9 a.m.–9 p.m.

**Lisdoonvarna:**
Sulphur Hill. 9.30 a.m.–5 p.m. Mondays to Saturdays.

**Ennistimon:**
Ennis Road. 8.30 a.m.–6 p.m. Mondays to Saturdays. Ironing Service.

## MEDICAL

(N.B. A 999 call from any telephone will connect you with fire, police, ambulance services. There is no charge for this call.)
*Ennis General Hospital*: telephone 065–24464
*Clare Ambulance Services*: telephone 065–22950
*Ennistimon District Hospital*: telephone 065–71622
*Lisdoonvarna Health Centre*: telephone 065–74184.

## PHARMACIES

**Ennistimon:**
McGrotty's Medical Hall, Main Street. Telephone 065–71043.

**Lisdoonvarna:**
The Burren Pharmacy, The Square. Telephone 065–74104.

**Milltown Malbay:**
Marie Kelly, Main Street. Telephone 065–84440.

**Open late and on Sundays:**
*O'Connell's Pharmacy*, Abbey Street, Ennis. Telephone 065–20373. Open Mondays to Saturdays 9 a.m.–6.20 p.m. and Sundays 11 a.m.–1 p.m.
*Duffy's*, Unit 13 Shopping Centre, Ennis, open until 9 p.m Thursdays and Fridays. After hours service, telephone 065–28833.

## TAXIS

**Doolin:**
'*Safe home*' service, telephone 065–74429. 9 a.m.–midnight.
*Tim Murphy*: telephone 065–81463.

**Ennis:**
*Brendan Armstrong*: car phone 088–563667
*Joseph Barry*: telephone 065–24759
*George Browne*: telephone 065–20712
*Martin Casey*: telephone 065–28237
*M.I. Casey*: telephone 065–22230
*Clare Cabs*: telephone 065–28122
*Joseph Cropera*: telephone 065–28259
*Patrick Hayes*: telephone 065–28558
*Patrick Kerin*: telephone 065–24711

*John McInerney*: telephone 065–29878
*Brendan Murphy*: car phone 088–56410
*M. O'Neill*: telephone 065–24354
*James Woods*: telephone 065–28202.

**Ennistimon:**
*Philip Fahy*, Main Street, telephone 065–71450.

**Lehinch:**
For information regarding coach tours of the Burren, telephone Christopher Browne at 065–81168 or Fax 065–81228.

**Lisdoonvarna:**
*Patrick Flaherty*, telephone 065–74117. Also tours of the Burren in 25-seater coach.

## TRAVEL ARRANGEMENTS

Bus information and schedules are available from Bus Éireann, telephone 061–48777 and 091–62131.

## WEATHER FORECAST FOR REGION

Telephone 061–62677.

# FESTIVALS

**June**
The annual *Irish traditional singing festival* is held in Ennistimon during the first week. Competitions and concerts.

**July**
Milltown Malbay is the location for the *Willie Clancy Summer School*. A week in July is dedicated to the memory of Willie Clancy, the legendary Irish piper. There are workshops and sessions, concerts and ceilís all week. For exact dates telephone Shannon Development 061–317522 during January/February.

**August**
*Cruinniú na mBád (Gathering of the boats)* is held at Kinvarra. A weekend of racing with traditional sailing craft and currachs. Traditional singers and musicians also gather in the village and the emphasis in the evening is on fun or 'craic' for all ages. As the date varies, contact the Galway Tourist Office, telephone 091–63081 early in the year.

**September**
*The Harvest or Matchmaking Festival* is held at Lisdoonvarna in early September. It was traditional for farmers to go to Lisdoonvarna, once the hay and crops were in, to take the waters and look around for a wife. That tradition has been incorporated into a week of dances and events at which single people have a chance to meet each other. Afternoon old-time dances are held in the modern hall in the spa gardens and all the hotels and pubs put on special evenings.

The International Bar-B-que Championships are held in the town during September. Teams from all over the world compete. Visitors may watch and sample.

# CYCLE TOURS

**BALLYVAGHAN TOURS.**

**Corcomroe Abbey and the early Christian churches at Oughtmama.**

This is a short tour of approximately 20 miles/32 km from Ballyvaghan. Follow the N67 to Bell Harbour and turn right, then first left for Corcomroe Abbey (see page 191).

Return from the Abbey, turn left at the bottom of the access lane and turn left at the T-junction, then take the third lane on your right for Oughtmama. At the end of the lane, approximately 0.25 mile/0.4 km from the road, follow a track to your right on a south-easterly bearing across two fields for a further 0.5 mile/0.8 km. The three small stone churches should now be visible on your right-hand side.

This was an early monastic site established by 'The Three Colmáns'; now only three buildings remain. The largest is a typically early Christian building with nave, chancel, flat-headed doorway and plain arch. In the corner is a font depicting two animals with entwined necks which was inserted in the 15th century. There is a second structure to the west, and

further west again are the fragments of another building which has a narrow window in the east gable and a doorway in the south wall. Return to the road and turn right down Corker Pass. Take the 'green road' on your left shortly before it meets the N67. Green roads were the thoroughfares in ancient times and are unmetalled tracks nowadays. Look out for a holy well dedicated to St Patrick on your left. Rejoin the N67 at a modern church (also dedicated to St Patrick) and turn left to return to Ballyvaghan.

**Kinvarra and the Martello tower visible from Ballyvaghan.**
This is an easy-going cycle of approximately 32 miles/52 km from Ballyvaghan along the coast towards Kinvarra and out to the Martello tower.

Starting at Ballyvaghan, follow the N67 through Bell Harbour village (Bealaclugga) and continue along this road until it makes a sharp turn to the right. Here an unmarked road joins it from the left near a small lake before the N67 reaches the village of Burren. Follow the unmarked road and continue heading west until you reach the Martello tower commanding the promontory.

You will pass the monument to the Irish poet, Donnachadh Mór Ó Dálaigh, and the site of a 14th or 15th century bardic school. (Poetry was an important skill in Gaelic Ireland and the poet held an honoured position in the community.) Turn left towards the Martello tower. These towers were built all around the coast of Ireland and Scotland during the Napoleonic Wars, as Britain feared an invasion by Napoleon. They were intended primarily as watch towers.

When you leave the tower turn right and travel along by the shore, known as The Flaggy Shore. Mount Vernon Lodge in this area was the summer home of Lady Gregory and here she entertained her friends including W.B. Yeats and George Bernard Shaw.

When the road ends, either turn right and back to the N67 to return to Ballyvaghan, or take the road on the left through New Quay and stop at the harbour and Linanne's excellent seafood pub. George Bernard Shaw set part of *Back to Methuselah* at Burren pier, nowadays known as New Quay.

From New Quay, cycle north to the N67 or continue along the shore eastwards to where the road rejoins the N67. Turn right on the N67 to return to Ballyvaghan.

**This is a tour which is only a 16 miles/26 km round trip from Ballyvaghan,** but one filled with interesting diversions to Iron Age ring forts, neolithic and Bronze Age tombs and a holy well with a toothache cure.

Take the N67 road out of Ballyvaghan in the direction of Lisdoonvarna. Take the R480 signposted to Kilfenora. Immediately on passing the access road for Aillwee Caves, look out for the earthen ring fort, An Rath, on your left. This is located just off the road in the trees.

Return to the road and watch out for the signpost to Cathair Mhór on your left. (See page 187.) Continue on up the R480. Halfway up the hill, to the left and across fields, are wedge tombs dating from the Bronze Age. (See page 169.) A magnificent gold gorget (neck collar) of the late Bronze Age was found here at Gleninsheen in 1932.

A track descends the hill in a southerly direction for 0.75 mile/1.2 km from the main road which you left in order to look at the wedge tombs; this track leads you to a holy well, the waters of which are said to cure toothache.

Retrace the track back up the hill to rejoin the main road. Near the summit, to the left of the road, is the Poulnabrone Dolmen. (See page 187.) This is one of the most famous dolmens in Ireland, and photographs of it usually give the impression that it is easily seen from the road, at the top of a hill, with the skyline behind it. This is not the case. The dolmen can be quite difficult to see from the road (depending on the weather) since it stands in the midst of a stretch of Burren limestone 'pavements'.

Continue on the road to Cathair Chonaill (Caherconnell). (See page 187.) Return to the R480. Take the road directly opposite you and travel across country. At the next major junction turn left and cycle down Corker Pass to the left turn to Bell Harbour.

From Bell Harbour, the route to your left along the N67 takes you back into Ballyvaghan.

### Round trip, Ballyvaghan to Lisdoonvarna with diversions.
Approximately 30 miles/48 km.

From Ballyvaghan follow the road past Newtown Castle. This was built in the 16th century for the O'Briens. If you take the track down to it you will see that although it is cylindrical, it has a square base. The first and third storeys show the impressions of the wickerwork which kept the mortar in place until it dried.

Return to the road and keep cycling up the hill. You are now on Corkscrew Hill. Halfway up, there is a wide space with seats where you can rest to take in the magnificent view.

Cycle into Lisdoonvarna with its genuine mineral water and Victorian pump-room. (See page 200.)

Return to Ballyvaghan back along the same route and take the second turn left which is signposted to Kilmoon Church. The church is an early Christian one with a 15th century chapel referred to as a priest's dwelling.

Cycle on along the quiet forest-edged road. Take the right fork and continue until it joins a 'green road'. (The 'green roads' are ancient roadways, most of them are signposted and none of them have been metalled. The 'green road' was a major highway in the 16th and 17th centuries.)

The castle you see is called Faunarooska. Little is known of it other than that it was first mentioned in 1641 as being the property of a Fernandus MacFelem and was obviously built here because of its commanding location. Sadly the castle must have been built with inferior mortar as it has not lasted as long as the other cylindrical tower houses, Doongore and Newtown.

Shortly before you reach a junction is Formoyle chapel, which was still in use until 1870. Turn right, then left for the climb up to Caherandurrish. This started out as a stone fort, but was obviously adapted for other uses in later times; local tradition says it was a shebeen, an illegal drinking house. Keep on going up over the hill and you will be rewarded with magnificent views. Follow the road to the right.

The cliff fort over to your right is called Lismacsheedy. Cliff forts or promontory forts date from the Bronze and Iron Ages. These forts may have been used on ceremonial occasions only; because they had no water supply they could not have been occupied for long periods. Certain experts contend that they may have been ancient burial sites.

Follow the road downhill. On your left near the bottom is the track to Rathborney Church. This is a medieval church built inside an earthen ring fort or rath. Join the main road and turn left for your return to Ballyvaghan.

**Another round trip of approximately 35 miles/56 km from Ballyvaghan**, taking in spectacular views and interesting historical sites.

Take the R477 coast road towards Lisdoonvarna. On your left you pass what looks like a tiny church. This is a spring well, known as the Pinnacle Well (for obvious reasons). The stone covering was built in the 19th century to protect the village water supply. The water is delicious. When you consider that women had to walk out to here in all weathers for a bucket of water, you can imagine how relieved everyone must have been when the fountain was erected in the village in 1875!

On your right watch out for Gleninagh Castle. The narrow track by the post box takes you to a field. This is the only access to the castle. To the left, in front of the castle, is a 16th century holy well dedicated to the Holy Cross. Notice the relics deposited by past pilgrims. The castle was built in the 16th century for the O'Loughlains, known as 'The Burren Princes' and was inhabited by members of the family until 1840. You will see castles like this all over the region. They were built as grand houses

for the gentry. In earlier centuries the Norman lords built castles, but these were intended as fortifications. By the 16th century such fortified castles were not really needed, but the newly established gentry obviously felt that they too needed a castle to live in.

Gleninagh is an L-shaped castle with the projection housing the spiral staircase. The castle has had some conservation work carried out on it by the Office of Public Works. It is open to visitors from mid-June to the beginning of September, from 10.00 a.m.–4.00 p.m.

To the right of the access lane is an ivy-covered medieval church. Less than 1 mile/1.6 km further on, you will see a signpost to a fulachta fiadh, located to the right of the track. These were cooking sites used by ancient hunter warriors. They heated stones in a fire and tossed them into a trough of water when they were hot enough, along with the animal they had killed. The meat may have been loosely wrapped in straw or twigs beforehand. (Experiments have shown this to be an efficient way to boil meat.) The mound you can see is the debris from the cooking method; the blackened, and sometimes cracked stones and animal bones were thrown away from the fulachta fiadh by the cook. These ancient cooking sites are recognisable by their distinctive horseshoe-shaped mound.

When you reach Black Head, refer to Ecotour Link (page 242), and when you reach Fanore read the Ecotour Stop Fanore on page 24.

At Fanore, turn up by St Patrick's Church into the Caher Valley. This is known locally as the Khyber Pass. There is another fulachta fiadh 1.4 miles/2.25 km further along on this road, to your left over a stone bridge and on a neck of land between the road and the river. Keep climbing. At the junction turn right and then right again by Formoyle Chapel on to the 'green road', an ancient thoroughfare. Follow this as it heads south-west.

When you reach the tarred road turn left; this road brings you close to Kilmoon Church. At the main road turn left for an exhilarating ride down Corkscrew Hill and back into Ballyvaghan.

## LISDOONVARNA TOURS.

### A short ride of 15 miles/24 km from Lisdoonvarna to Doolin and back.

Follow the N67 to Ballyvaghan as far as the left turn signposted to Kilmoon Church. This is an early Christian church with a 15th century 'chapel'.

Follow the road past the church. Cycle past the plantation on to open moorland and take the second turn on the left towards the sea and Ballinalackan Castle. This castle is owned privately, but the owner of the guest-house beside the castle will usually oblige interested visitors with the key during the summer months.

Ballinalackan Castle dates from the 16th century. It was held by the O'Briens until Cromwell's time (17th century), when it was handed over to a Cromwellian officer in 1667. (This seizure and handing over of land and property by Cromwell served two purposes: he rewarded loyalty and he broke up and sometimes impoverished those who might have formed a resistance.) The castle was bought and sold many times in the succeeding years until the 19th century when an O'Brien (who claimed descent from Turlough O'Brien) eventually purchased it.

The bowfronted house was built in the mid-19th century by John O'Brien, a son of Cornelius O'Brien's second wife. (See Cliffs of Moher, page 232.) John's son, Peter, became Lord Peter O'Brien and he was nicknamed 'Peter the Packer' from his habit of packing juries with people he knew would give the 'right' verdict.

Cycle over the crossroads and into Roadford and Doolin. (See page 194.)

Return to Lisdoonvarna by the T-junction at Roadford and turn left past the cemetery (if you reach Aran View Hotel you have gone too far; go back down the road to the junction). The route back to Lisdoonvarna is straightforward from here.

**From Lisdoonvarna, a cross-country route to Kilfenora** then back to Lisdoonvarna by some major Burren antiquities; the distance is approximately 30 miles/48 km.

The road to Kilfenora is well signposted. While there, you may like to call into the Burren Display Centre and the Cathedral. (See page 196.) Follow route R476 signposted from Kilfenora to Corrofin and take the first turn left (approximately 1 mile/1.6 km away) along the minor road.

You pass Cathair Bhaile Cinn Mhargaidh (Caherballykinvarga or simply, Ballykinvarga). (See page 187.)

Another 1 mile/1.6 km further on, the road swings sharply to the right; keep going to the right and this brings you to Noughaval. (See page 198.) Travel along this road until you reach the crossroads then turn left. A short distance along is Cathair Chonaill (See page 187.) Further on again on your right is the signpost to Poulnabrone Dolmen. (See page 187.)

Continue on a short distance to the next turn left. Follow this road for 1.25miles/2 km to a T-junction. Turn right and travel for approximately 1 mile/1.6 km to the next T-junction, then turn left and continue for approximately 0.5 mile/0.8 km to a right -hand turn and take it. After 1.25 miles/2 km, the road swings right and then left again for another 1.25 miles/2 km to another T-junction. Turn left. The prominent hillock a few meters along this road on your right is said to be a fairy hill (i.e. a fairy meeting place).

At the right-hand bend are the remains of what was once intended to be the Burren's finest house. Built by Judge Comyn (see Doolin, page 194), it was finished only shortly before his death in 1952 because additional rooms had to be built as his furniture collection increased. The house was demolished shortly after his death. You come into Lisdoonvarna by St Brendan's well and the bridge over the Gowlaun River.

**A circular route from Lisdoonvarna** taking in Ennistimon, Lehinch, Liscannor, the Cliffs of Moher and some interesting historical sites en route. The distance is 35 miles/56 km.

Take the N67 road south, signposted to Lehinch, and turn left towards Ennistimon. At Kilshanny crossroads (about 4 miles/6 km from the centre of town), a turn to the left, then left again down a narrow track, brings you to the ruined medieval church of Kilshanny. It was founded in early Christian times and was recorded as being an offshoot of Corcomroe Abbey in 1194. By 1302 it seemed to have lost its abbey status and was listed as the parish church for Kilshanny.

Return to the crossroads. Over on the other side, behind the first house on your right, is the huge cairn known as Carn Connachta. Folklore claims that this was the site where the chiefs of the Corcu Modruad were inaugurated. The Corcu Modruad were a Celtic tribe who settled in north and west Clare just before or possibly just after the birth of Christ. Some archaeologists think that the mound may be a neolithic or Bronze Age burial mound dating from 1900 years B.C. A similar cairn at Poulawack near Noughaval was excavated by the 1934 Harvard Archaeological Expedition and 18 burials and some Bronze Age burial goods were found there, but since Carn Connachta has never been excavated, no one knows yet what it contains. It is possible that it is a Bronze Age burial mound which was regarded by local people as a special place, although the reason may have been long forgotten. It would make sense for an incoming tribe trying to establish itself to use a locally significant place for their ceremonies. There are records of a battle here in 1573 between two factions of the O'Briens.

Keep on towards Ennistimon (see page 192). Take the road to Lehinch out over the bridge. Watch out for signs of the West Clare railway. Percy French's song with the wonderful refrain 'Are you right there Michael are you right?' pokes gentle fun at the railway company for being unreliable. They sued Percy as they thought he had made a laughing stock of them. Percy arrived late for the court case in Ennis and when asked by the judge why he was delayed, he replied that he had come by the West Clare railway!

*Clonfert Cathedral*

Cycle into Lehinch and take the coast road towards Liscannor. The castle to your left is another 16th century tower house called Dough Castle.

Before you reach Liscannor, about 2 miles/3.2 km from the golf club is a narrow road turning towards the sea. This will take you to the lovely little ruined medieval church at Kilmacreehy. It has an interesting wall tomb. Notice the strange medieval head-dress. Hugh MacCurtain (1680–1758), who was once a soldier and became a teacher, scholar and writer, is buried here in an unmarked grave. To the north-west of the church lay St MacCrithe's well which was reputed to cure sore eyes.

Cycle into Liscannor (see page 231). Cycle on to the Cliffs of Moher. Refer to Ecotour Stop The Cliffs of Moher, page 232, and follow it as you travel the route back to Lisdoonvarna.

**Follow the Ecotour commencing at the Burren** (page 237) and follow it to Ballyvaghan pier. Return to Lisdoonvarna via the coast road, a distance of 12 miles/19 km.

# DAYTIME ACTIVITIES

## BEACH GUIDE

### Bishop's Quarter Beach.
2 miles/3.2 km east of Ballyvaghan, 14 miles/22.5 km north-east from Lisdoonvarna via Ballyvaghan.
Large car park. Pedestrian access to beach over low narrow bridge. Sandspit encloses small tidal pool useful for supervised rubber dinghy play. Open sea and sand dunes. Faces Galway Bay, safe swimming. No amenities. Wheelchair access. Grassy area for picnics. Sand looks grey because it is made from limestone. Lifeguard at weekends.
**How to get there.**
Located off the coast road to Kinvarra, signposted.

### Tracht Kinvarra.
8 miles/12.8 km east of Ballyvaghan, 20 miles/32 km north-east of Lisdoonvarna via Ballyvaghan.
Car park. Toilets. Lifeguard when flag flying. Picnic tables on raised concrete plinth. Difficult for wheelchair users. Wheelchair access leads to stony edge of beach. Sand looks grey because it is made from limestone. Shops and bars in village on access road.
**How to get there.**
Take the N67 towards Kinvarra. The beach is signposted. Long drive, approximately 2 miles/3.2 km to beach from main road.

### Fanore.
8 miles/12.8 km south-west of Ballyvaghan. 10 miles/16 km north-west of Lisdoonvarna.
Car park. Adequate toilets. Good stretch of golden sand. River enters sea here. Care should be exercised when swimming near river outlet. Grass areas and dunes for picnics. Wheelchair access.
**How to get there.**
From Lisdoonvarna, take the road to Doolin and the R477 around the coast. Beach is clearly visible at side of road. From Ballyvaghan, follow the coast road via Black Head.

## Lehinch.

9 miles/14.4 km south-west of Lisdoonvarna, 21 miles/33.6 km south-west of Ballyvaghan.

Excellent sandy beach. Lifeguard lookout. Open Atlantic, so good surf and strong currents. Picnic area, toilets. Ramp for boats could be used for wheelchairs but looks rather steep. Seaside resort, so plenty of amusements and places to eat. Surfboards for hire.

**How to get there.**

From Lisdoonvarna, take the N67 through Ennistimon then on to Lehinch.

## Spanish Point.

15 miles/24 km south-west of Lisdoonvarna, 27 miles/43 km south-west of Ballyvaghan.

Golden stretch of sand. Toilets. Picnic tables. Lifeguard. No swimming when red flag is flying.

This beach was popular with the Victorian middle classes. The ruin on the cliffs was the Atlantic Hotel which fell down in 1903. Under the cliffs, through the archway, you can see the old stone boxes which used to fill up with sea water when the tide was in. When the tide went out the water was retained in the boxes and the guests would come below and steep themselves in the salt water for a while. At that time salt water was thought to cure many ailments. On the cliffs opposite the site of the old hotel is a Victorian post box in the wall.

**How to get there.**

Take the N67 and join the R482 at Lehinch.

## Quilty Beach.

South of Spanish Point. It is reached through the village around by the pier. It is a favourite spot to drive to, to look at the sea. No amenities. Working pier. Good sandy stretch. Good view across the bay to the cliffs south of the Cliffs of Moher.

**How to get there.**

From Lisdoonvarna, follow the N67 southwards through Ennistimon, Lehinch and Milltown Malbay to Quilty village—a distance of approximately 20 miles/32 km. The beach is south of the village; the unmarked road which leads to the beach hugs the cliff top.

# SURFING AND SAIL BOARDING

From Lehinch. The shop near the promenade hires out surfboards. Telephone 065–81167/81543. Open seven days a week in the summer months.

# ANGLING

## Sea Angling.

The north Clare coast, particularly around Black Head, is good for shore fishing, i.e. casting out a line from the rocks. Contact Dermot Collins (telephone 065–21131) for organised sea angling.

## Game Angling.

You do not need a licence for brown trout fishing. (You do for salmon and sea trout but most of the fishing in north Clare is for brown trout.) The trout season opens on 15 February and closes on 12 October. The salmon season opens 1 February and ends on 30 September. There may be local variations; if in doubt, contact Michael Cleary, the Regional Assistant Inspector for the Fisheries Board, telephone 065–27675. Michael Cleary will be able to give information regarding private fishing areas and whether or not any permit is needed.

*The Aille River* is a small spate river which flows through Lisdoonvarna and enters the sea at Doolin. The best fishing is between Roadford and Lisdoonvarna and the river fishes best after flood. Access to the banks is difficult because they are overgrown. Best methods to use are worm or fly. No permission needed.

*Luogh Lough.* Near Cliffs of Moher (R062935). Holds fair stock of brown trout. Easy access. Signposted. No permission needed.
*Lickeen Lough.* (R170910). Lies about 2 miles/3.2 km south of Kilfenora. Well signposted. Good stock of rainbow trout. May be fished from the shore or from boat. Boats for hire, permission needed and moderate fee payable. Fly fishing only. Contact the Lickeen Trout Anglers' Association, Lickeen, Kilfenora, telephone 065–71069 or 065–81022.
*Inchiquin Lough* near Corrofin (R270900). Excellent stocks of brown trout. Fishes well early in the season. Summer months can be difficult if the water is low. September fishing is good. Access easy, well signposted and there is a car park and pier. Boats available from Burke's shop in Corrofin, telephone 065–27677.

**Coarse Fishing.**
*Lough Cullaun* (R315905) is regarded as a good pike fishery. It lies off the Corrofin/Tubber road. No permission needed but it cannot be fished from the bank. Boats must be hired. Contact Michael Cleary, Corrofin, County Clare, telephone 065–27675.
*Lough Bunny* (R370970). On the Corrofin to Gort road. Pike, perch and rudd. Boat essential (contact Michael Cleary, Corrofin. See above.)
*Lough Atedaun.* (R295880). Rudd, pike, perch, tench. Car parking. Boat useful as only a small area is fishable from the shore. Contact Michael Cleary for boat hire. (See information under Lough Cullaun above.)

# GOLF

*Lehinch championship course* is recognised as one of the world's top courses. This course has two particularly famous holes, the fifth known as the 'Klondyke' and the sixth known as 'The Dell'. Telephone 065–81103 for information regarding green fees.
*Lehinch Castle* course is an 18-hole coastal course. Telephone 065–81103 for information. Modern club facilities and professional shop.
Pitch-and-putt is available in Lisdoonvarna. The course is signposted opposite the Spa Well's gardens.

# HORSE RIDING

*Willie Daly's* horse riding and pony-trekking centre. Lake, beach and mountain trails. Open seven days a week, 9 a.m.–9 p.m. Located off the Ennistimon/Lisdoonvarna road (well signposted). Telephone 065–71385 for information.
*Burren Riding Centre*, Kilmoon Cross, Lisdoonvarna. Telephone 065–74422. Daily trails through the Burren at 11 a.m. and 3 p.m. Instruction available. Different ages and levels are catered for.
*Kinvarra Riding Centre*, telephone 091–37147. Trekking arranged.

# ROCK CLIMBING

Contact *Kilshanny Outdoor Education Centre*, telephone 061–73230. (July and August telephone number: 061–71422.) Bunk house accommodation available.
*Turlough Activity Centre.* Rock climbing and caving instruction. Telephone 065–78119 (dormitory accommodation).

# TENNIS

Public courts available at Lehinch.

## ʌMING

ɔeaches, page 183.

### PAINTING COURSES

*Burren Painting Centre*, O'Neill's Town House, St Brendan's Road, Lisdoonvarna, telephone 065–74208 or fax 065–74435. Daily tuition and weekly courses.

### WALKING

The Burren Way is way marked from Ballybaghan to Liscannor. Green roads –old droving roads–are clearly signposted throughout the Burren.

# EVENING ACTIVITIES

**Liscannor.**
*Burren Castle Hotel* near Liscannor has live music, keyboards and drums, nightly from June to September. Room to dance.

**Ennis.**
*Cois Na hAbhna* near Ennis, open all year for ceilís and set-dancing classes. Telephone 065–28366 for schedule.

**Bunratty.**
*Shannon Ceilí* at Bunratty Folk Park twice nightly from May to September. Irish meal with wine and entertainment in the barn in the folk park. Telephone 061–61788.

**Corrofin.**
*Teach Ceoil* in Corrofin has twice-weekly music sessions (traditional music).

**Lehinch.**
*Lehinch cinema* shows all the general release films. Located near the promenade, open all year.
*Amusement arcades* in Lehinch are open during the summer.
*Dunguaire Castle banquets*, twice nightly, May to September, booking through tourist office, or telephone 061–61788. Lots of wine, lots of food in convivial setting in first floor banqueting hall, entertainment, pageant of words by Raftery, Yeats, Lady Gregory. Harp music.

**TRADITIONAL MUSIC PUBS** (Summer is defined as June to October):

**Ballyvaghan.**
*Ballyvaghan Inn*. Music on Saturdays and Sundays, all year.
*Monk's Pub*. Music on Sundays all year and Saturdays also in the summer.

**Doolin.**
*O'Connor's Pub*, Fisherstreet. Open all year.

**Ennistimon.**
*Phil's Place*, Main Street, music every Friday, all year.
*Nagle's Bar*. Music every night during the summer.
*The Matchmaker's Old Shack*. Music on Fridays, Saturdays and Sundays all year and other nights in the summer.

**Fanore.**
*O'Donoghue's*. Music in the summer on Saturdays and music in July from 4–7 p.m.

**Kilfenora.**
*Nagle's Bar*. Music Fridays, Saturdays and Sundays all year.

*Vaughan's Bar.* Music Mondays and Saturdays all year, music Fridays and Sundays and Wednesdays in summer.

**Kinvarra.**
*Winkles Hotel* for music sessions throughout the year.
*Dunguaire Castle banquets.* See page 198.

**Lehinch.**
*Comber's Bar.* Music in the summer on Mondays and Saturdays.
*Cornerstone Bar.* Music Tuesdays and Sundays in summer.
*The Nineteenth International Bar.* Music all year Fridays and Saturdays and also Thursdays and Sundays in summer.
*Village Inn.* Music Mondays and Wednesdays in summer.

**Lisdoonvarna.**
*The Kincora.* Music all year, every Thursday.
*The Roadside Tavern.* Music every Saturday all year and every night during summer.
*The Irish Arms.* Music July to October on Sundays and every night during summer.

**Roadford.**
McGann's Pub. Open all year for regular sessions.

# WHAT TO SEE IN THE BURREN

### RING FORTS, A WEDGE TOMB, POULNABRONE DOLMEN.

Start at Ballyvaghan and take the R480 towards Corrofin. Just beyond the road signposted to Aillwee Cave, watch out for the signpost to 'An Rath' on your left. This is an Iron Age earthen ring fort. Park at the side of the road. Access is over a stone stile. The fort is clearly visible past the trees.

A short distance further on is the signpost to Cathair Mhór on your right. This is a stone ring fort with obvious gateway. On your left a little further on is a wedge tomb, and approximately 1 mile/1.6 km further on again, nestled against the hill to your left is the Poulnabrone Dolmen, a portal tomb. Access is across a field, a journey of about 0.3 miles/500 meters. Wear flat shoes if you wish to walk to the dolmen.

A very short distance further along on your right is Cathair Chonail (Caherconnel), another stone ring fort. (It lies behind the house on your right.) Walk up the drive and across the yard. The farmer has obligingly placed a marked oil drum to indicate the fort.

Return to the road and turn right along the road to the T-junction at Leamaneh Castle (see page 199) and turn right. Turn right at the next turn, and right again. You pass the signpost to Cathair Bhaile Cinn Mhargaidh (Ballykinvarga) on your left. Parking space is by the side of the road. Access is gained across a stone stile and across land trampled by cattle.

This stone fort has a good example of a cheveaux de frise, an outer circle of pointed stones placed close together. There is one path free of stones into the fort entrance. A stranger would find it difficult to approach the fort by night without being in danger of tripping or possibly breaking an ankle. Even in daylight, an approach without care would have been difficult.

Follow the road around to the left and into Kilfenora (see page 196). From Kilfenora take the road to Lisdoonvarna and from there back to Ballyvaghan by Corkscrew Hill.

## TEAMPALL CHRÓNÁIN (ST CRONAN'S CHURCH).

This is a small 12th century church tucked into a secluded corner near Carran village. It is a simple, single-chamber stone building, now roofless. There is a small window in one gable and a blocked up narrow stone doorway in the other. The doorway cut into the side wall is wider and taller than the original door and dates from the 15th century. The only decoration on the church is a series of quaint heads jutting out from the walls on the outside which indicate that the church was built in the 12th century. Nearby is a small pyramid-shaped stone structure said to be where St Cronan was buried.

### How to get there.

If approaching Carran from Bell Harbour (Bealaclugga) and the N67, look out for the signpost indicating the narrow road on the left just before Carran village. The road ends by the entrance to a farm a short distance along. Climb the stone stile into the field. Please remember that you are walking over land used to rear cattle. Don't frighten the livestock and shut all gates behind you. Leave no litter. Cross the field towards another stone stile. Turn sharp right and head down to another stile and the church.

## COOLE PARK.

9 miles/14.4 km from Kinvarra, and 24 miles/38.4 km from Ballyvaghan, Coole Park was the home of Lady Augusta Gregory, dramatist, co–founder of the Abbey Theatre and friend of many writers, notably W. B. Yeats.

She was the second wife of Sir William Gregory, former governor of Ceylon and a director of the British National Gallery at the time of their marriage in 1880. Through Sir Robert, Lady Gregory met Count Florimond de Basterot, who introduced her to French literature, and Sir Edward Martyn who, although a landowner, was a nationalist.

When Sir William died in 1892, Lady Gregory renewed her interest in Irish folklore and began to learn the Irish language. She joined the Gaelic League and the Irish Agricultural Organisation Society which aimed to help Irish farmers through mutual self–help. She organised meetings for the IAOS and negotiated on its behalf with the British government. Gradually she became a fervent nationalist.

*Lady Gregory in the grounds of Coole Park*

*Coole Park Visitors' Centre*

In 1896 she met W.B. Yeats at Edward Martyn's home. The two became firm friends. Yeats talked to Lady Gregory about his ambition to open in London a theatre where he could put on verse plays. Lady Gregory persuaded him to produce the plays in Dublin. And together they convinced Edward Martyn to give up a German production of his play *Heather Field* to join Yeats in Dublin.

Discussions between Lady Gregory, Yeats and Edward Martyn led eventually to firm plans for a national theatre in Dublin.

The proposed theatre and W.B. Yeats became Lady Gregory's main interests. Yeats often stayed at Coole Park where the peace and beauty of the grounds helped him relax and think. He befriended Lady Gregory's son Robert, who died in 1918, and wrote for him 'An Irish Airman Foresees His Death' and other poems. 'Wild Swans at Coole' is one of Yeats's most popular poems.

Because of her knowledge of folklore and peasant dialect, Lady Gregory was able to help Yeats with his plays, help which he acknowledged. Lady Gregory herself began to write plays for the new national theatre.

Eventually a permanent home and company for the national theatre, now called the Abbey Theatre, was established in 1904.

Coole Park became a refuge and weekend retreat for writers and artists. O'Casey, G.B. Shaw, John Millington Synge, John Masefield and Jack Yeats were among the many visitors who signed the bark of the copper beech in the grounds. This tree is known as the Autograph Tree and may still be seen together with an explanatory diagram.

The great house at Coole no longer stands but the grounds and lake which Yeats and others so enjoyed are still there.

An Interpretative Centre has been established near the old stable block (now a café) and visitors can learn about the natural history of the parkland before taking one of the well signposted nature trails through the grounds.

The centre is open from April to September but the grounds never close.

**How to get there.**
From Ballyvaghan take the R477 to Kinvarra, then the R347 to Ardrahan. Turn left in Ardrahan for the N18 to Gort and watch out for a signpost to the right.

**CORCOMROE ABBEY.**
This is located 4 miles/6.4 km from Ballyvaghan. The name originally given to the Abbey was 'Sancta Maria de Petra Fertili' (St Mary of the fertile rock). The Abbey was a Cistercian foundation established in 1195 and after the Dissolution of the Monasteries in the 16th century, the Abbey was handed over to the first Earl of Thomond. The domestic buildings have vanished, but the church remains. It is cruciform with a chapel in each transept.

The capitals in the choir are decorated with plants and leaves and date from 1205–10. They are carved in a naturalistic way, a style which did not come into vogue in the rest of Europe until later in the 13th century. Several capitals have conventional foliage designs. A group of five depict what have been identified as harebells, a flower which grows in profusion on the hillsides above the Abbey.

Charles Nelson of the National Botanic Gardens has identified other plants: lily-of-the-valley, poppy, deadly nightshade (probably), Solomon's seal, and foxglove. The Cistercians were noted for their gardens and cultivation of medicinal plants. Charles Nelson and Roger Stalley argue that the stone carver at Corcomroe carved from direct observation of the flowers. The carvings would have been coloured and must have looked quite beautiful.

In a low tomb-niche in the north wall is an effigy of Conor O'Brien who died in 1267, and the wall screen across the middle of the nave was built in the 15th century.

It is interesting to note that W.B. Yeats set his verse play, *The Dreaming of the Bones*, in the hills above Corcomroe.

**How to get there.**
Take the N67 from Ballyvaghan to Bell Harbour. Turn right, then left up a lane. There is car parking space nearby. The cemetery around the Abbey is still used, so please show respect as you traverse the grounds.

**KILLINABOY CHURCH.**
10 miles/16 km from Lisdoonvarna, 11.5 miles/19 km from Ballyvaghan.
This is an 11th or possibly a 12th century church with later work, which remained in use until the 18th century. (See Corrofin Heritage Centre, page 208.) The church was built on an earlier monastic site founded by the daughter of Baoithe (St Iníon Bhaoithe).

There is a car park beside the road. Access is up steep stone steps. The church is surrounded by a graveyard which contains the stump of a medieval round tower, which indicates the presence of a monastic settlement.

On the gable wall facing the entrance gate you will see a double-armed cross. This style of cross became popular during the Crusades and was known as the Cross of Lorraine. It was usually placed on churches which held a relic of the true cross. Over the doorway on the right-hand side (the south wall) is a fierce looking sheela-na-gig. Sheela (sometimes written sheelah)-na-gigs are stone carvings of figures displaying female genitalia found on the exterior of medieval buildings, particularly churches, throughout Ireland and western Europe. They are associated with the Celts and early Christians. They may have been connected with fertility rites or erected to ward off evil.

There is a holy well near the church. When leaving the church, turn left. A short distance down the road, a signpost to the right indicates the holy well. Cross the field, keeping to the right of the track which leads to the silage pit. Enter a small wood. The well is straight ahead over two small stone walls and is entirely surrounded by trees. A rough carved cross stands on the well's perimeter.

The track through the wood is only suitable for those who like clambering through fallen twigs and briars. It is interesting to speculate about the life of this early female saint, who must have walked across the fields to reach this spot to pray.

**How to get there.**

From Lisdoonvarna, take the R476 to Kilfenora, then continue on the R476.

From Ballyvaghan, follow the N67 out of the town, then take a left turn on the R480 until you reach Leamaneh Castle and a T-junction. Turn left towards Corrofin.

**ENNISTIMON.**

The town was described by Banim, an early 19th century novelist, as 'The Town of the Cascades.' It is a small market town and the cascades are behind the main street; the River Cullenagh tumbles picturesquely over a waterfall. A signposted path leads down a lane to the backs of the houses where you can stand close to the waterfall. A riverside walk is being developed.

The Falls Hotel was once the home of Francis McNamara, sometimes described as 'minor thinker and poet'. McNamara's chief claim to literary history is his appearance in his daughter Nicolette Devas' book *Two Flamboyant Fathers* and his other daughter Caitlín's marriage to Dylan Thomas. Thomas visited the house in Ennistimon. The Falls Hotel was built in the 18th century and incorporated an earlier fortified dwelling.

Brian Merriman, the author of 'The Midnight Court', a hilarious and irreverent long poem originally written in Irish, was born in the town in the early 18th century. At first, apart from the dwelling where the Falls Hotel is now, the rest of the town was little more than a river crossing. In 1775 there were three houses, and by 1810 the town had grown to 120 houses, seventy of which were slated. (This would indicate a certain level of prosperity.) The ruined church on the hill which dominates the town was a Protestant church built in 1778. The other Protestant church with the octagonal tower surmounted by pinnacles was built in 1830. The Catholic church was built in 1954 and has striking stations of the cross by Father Aengus Buckley, who created two of the frescos in Galway Cathedral.

The West Clare railway was routed through the town in 1887 and sometimes it seems as if the town has remained in that period. The main street is a treasure store of 19th century vernacular touches which may

disappear soon; few towns still have old lace curtains and geraniums in their shop windows. The two old-style shop fronts, which featured on a popular postcard a few years ago, are located at the side of the bridge.

**How to get there.**
Take the N67 southwest from Ballyvaghan and Lisdoonvarna. A journey of approximately 20 miles/32 km.

**DOOLIN.**
This coastal area is located 5 miles/8 km from Lisdoonvarna. During the late 1960s the growing interest in Irish traditional music led enthusiasts to seek out the Russell brothers (Miko, Pakie and Gussie) who lived in the area of Doolin. The brothers often played in their local pub, O'Connor's. Anyone with any interest in Irish music, either as performer or audience, sooner or later headed down to Doolin to hear the Russell family play. Recordings were made of the brothers playing and a tour of folk clubs was organised, but the brothers remained what they were, west of Ireland men who played traditional music because they enjoyed it. O'Connor's Pub is still a mecca for traditional music fans and a session of players or singers can probably be heard there any time of the year. The pub is actually located in a village called Fisherstreet. Another nearby village is Roadford; Doolin is the name given to the area.

The main quay to Inisheer (the smallest of the Aran Islands) is at the end of Fisherstreet and the village becomes very busy during the summer with people heading to the ferry and those who have come to visit O'Connor's Bar. Consequently, a number of craft shops, cafés and restaurants have been opened.

The cylindrical castle with the fairy-tale tower is Doonagore, a 16th century tower house, which was carefully restored in the 1970s, and is now a private residence. Another castle, now a mere stump near Fisherstreet, was once an O'Brien stronghold.

Francis McNamara had a summer residence here, Doolin House, in the early 20th century. He was visited by his friends Augustus John and George Bernard Shaw. Augustus John's 'Lonely figure of a woman keeping watch over an empty land' was apparently inspired by seeing the women who acted as lookouts while the poitín stills were working. Augustus John also painted the sea and the shore with its currachs and you can still see currachs here. Doolin House was destroyed by fire in the 1920s and the stone was used in other buildings. Near Doolin school is a disused phosphate mine. A local landowner, Judge Comyn, owned a few mines here which were worked during the 1930s and 1940s.

Near Roadford is a 16th century church. Travel down the track opposite the post office. The cut stone monument outside the graveyard is an unused MacNamara vault. A stone head with a biretta (a priest's hat) was

*Dungaire Castle*

removed from this church but it was relocated and it is now on display in the Burren Centre at Kilfenora. The church was extensively damaged during a storm in 1903.

At the end of the lane, about 1 mile/1.6 km from the post office, veer to the west, and keep Inisheer to your left. On the crags you will find the remains of a court tomb (see page 169). From here to the Ballinalackan crossroads there are numerous forts with souterrains. Like the rest of the region, much lies undiscovered here.

A grassy mound to the side of the road leading east from the Church of the Holy Rosary (dating from 1830 with modern alterations) leads past a grassy mound. Under the mound lie the bodies of the Spanish Armada survivors who were hanged on the order of the High Sheriff of the County, Boetius MacClancy. He was from a family of hereditary Brehons (lawyers) to the O'Briens and the family had a law school near the Holy Rosary Church which flourished until the collapse of the Gaelic Order in the 16th century. Boetius quickly adapted to the new order and sat in Parliament in 1585.

Near the Ballinalackan crossroads, in a cliff face off the road, is the entrance to Pol an Ionain, a cave with the longest stalactite in Europe. The cave is in pristine condition and should be entered only by experienced and properly equipped cavers.

**How to get there.**
From Ballyvaghan, take the R477 via Black Head and join the R479 at Ballynalackan Castle.

From Lisdoonvarna, take the R478 then the R479, or the R477 and then the R479.

**KILFENORA.**
5 miles/8 km from Lisdoonvarna, 10 miles/16 km from Ballyvaghan.

Although it is only a small village, Kilfenora is the home of the Burren Display Centre, Kilfenora Cathedral and High Crosses.

**Burren Display Centre.**
Housed in a small building, the centre contains a small gift shop and two audio-visual display rooms. Visitors are first shown a short film of the Burren and what they might see while travelling around. In another smaller room they are shown a large model of typical Burren terrain with its megalithic remains, raths, stone forts, and caves; models of the flowers you will see and the animals you might encounter are also shown. A commentary available in most European languages is played as the lights are dimmed. Parts of the display are lit by spotlight as the appropriate section of the taped commentary is heard.

As the centre is on the ground floor, wheelchairs can be admitted although the model room is quite small and it might be too difficult for wheelchairs to manoeuvre if the room is crowded. However, the staff are most helpful and will oblige where possible. There are toilets in the centre, and a coffee shop a little further along the street. The centre is run by a local community-based organisation and it is open all week. It closes for lunch from 1–2 p.m. It is open from early spring until the end of September. There is a moderate entry charge.

**Kilfenora Cathedral.**
This is tucked in behind the Display Centre. The original church founded on this site was dedicated to St Fachtna in the 6th century. In 1152, at the Synod of Kells, the church was changed from monastic to diocesan status.

On either side of the 12th century three-light window are two grave slabs. One of the figures is clearly a bishop but the other may be a simple but important cleric, holding what looks like a book. Possibly the figure represented some important patron. If you look carefully at the window you will see that there are heads of a group of clerics worked into the right-hand capital. The transitional chancel dates from about 1200. In the 19th century the nave was taken over and altered for Protestant worship. It is still used today when Morning Service takes place at 10 a.m. every Sunday.

Notice the sedilia (seat) in the north wall. It dates from the 15th century, and another slab showing a bishop holding a crosier dates from the 14th century. The grave slab of John Neylon who died in 1718 is interesting as it shows his head pointing towards the altar which would indicate that he was a priest, but the slab does not say so.

Outside in the graveyard are the treasures of Kilfenora, its High Crosses. High crosses have been claimed as the finest achievements of the crafts-man/artist of the Celtic Church. Originally there were seven High Crosses at Kilfenora: one was removed in 1821 to Killaloe Cathedral, where it can be seen; only three of the remaining six can be seen today in Kilfenora. Of the three, the most famous is the Doorty Cross. (The Ó Dúghartaigh family were from Tipperary who had hereditary rights to the bishopric. Doorty is the English version of their name.) It was found in fragments and reassembled in the 1950s by the Office of Public Works. The east face commemorates the elevation of St Fachtna's Church to diocesan status in 1152. It shows a bishop, possibly St Peter, standing above two smaller figures. The one on the left holding an Irish crosier is the new bishop. The other figure holding a T-shaped crosier is the abbot. The other side of the cross has suffered from weathering and is not so clear. Another cross which does not have the distinctive 'ring' of the High Crosses stands at the northern end of the churchyard. Outside the graveyard, through the gate, a short distance down a lane and across a field, is another fine High Cross. On the east face is a figure of Christ standing above what appears to be two rope-like strands which end in an unfinished triangle. Some authorities claim this depicts the Crucifixion and others have suggested that a house-

shaped shrine stood against the triangular shape. The cross is probably standing on what was the western boundary of the church land.
**How to get there.**
From Lisdoonvarna, take the R476 to Kilfenora. From Ballyvaghan follow the N67 to Lisdoonvarna then turn left on the R480 (signposted to Corrofin) to the T-junction at Leamaneh Castle and turn right on the R476 for Kilfenora. Before returning you might like to make a detour for a short distance towards the north-east to look at Ballykinvarga (3 miles/ 4.8 km) (see page 187) and Noughaval (5 miles/8 km) where there is a little 10th century church and an interesting old market cross.

**DUNGUAIRE CASTLE.**
Medieval castle set picturesquely on the shores of Galway Bay, 15 miles/24 km from Ballyvaghan.
Open to the public from 1 May until 30 September, 9.30 a.m.–5.30 p.m. Moderate entrance charge. There is a gift shop on the ground floor, and a car park opposite the castle.
Each of the three floors is furnished differently, to show the style of the castle in the different centuries of its occupation. The basement is furnished in the style of the 16th century. The top floor represents the style of furnishing earlier this century when Lady Ampthill lived in the castle.
Tour guides give very informed and articulate talks about the history of the castle and the region. Painted wall panels give excellent graphic illustrations of the castle's role in the economy of the region in each century.
Banquets take place in the hall during the season. Guests are met at the door of the castle by a host and hostess in medieval costume. Mead is handed out and a harpist plays. Guests then follow the 'Lord' and 'Lady' upstairs to the Banqueting Hall. There they sit on upholstered bench seats at long, polished tables. Simple food with medieval names is served with generous helpings of wine.
While guests eat they are entertained with poems and stories by Yeats, Raftery, Lady Gregory and others.
For bookings telephone 091–37108 or call at the Galway Tourist Office in Eyre Square, Galway.
**How to get there.**
Dunguaire Castle is on the N67 near Kinvarra, between the villages of Burren and Kilcolgan. (Unfortunately, two villages in County Galway are called Kinvarra; Dunguaire Castle is near the Kinvarra which is south of Galway City, close to the border between County Galway and County Clare.)

## LEAMANEH CASTLE.

8 miles/13 km from Lisdoonvarna, 11 miles/17 km from Ballyvaghan. This is a ruined 15th century O'Brien castle with a later manor house addition. The original castle was a typical 15th century tower house and you can still climb up inside today to see the magnificent view of the surrounding countryside. (However, as the castle is in ruins, take care with children.) Turlough Donn, one of the last kings of the ancient kingdom of Thomond, built the castle. In 1543 his son Murrough surrendered his title as King when he acknowledged English rule and was created First Earl of Thomond. He gave Leamaneh to his third son Donagh who was later hanged as a rebel in Limerick in 1582.

The manor house extension to the castle was added on in the 17th century by Conor O'Brien, the grandson of Donagh the rebel. Conor was the second husband of Máire Rua of whom many tales are told.

She was born Máire Rua MacMahon in 1615. (The 'Rua' was probably because of her red hair.) In 1634 she married Daniel Neylon of Dysert O'Dea. (His family had been granted the castle because the O'Deas, the Chiefs of Dysert, had supported the northern chiefs in the Nine Years' War of 1594–1603.) Daniel died five years later, leaving Máire with three sons, William, Daniel and Michael. Six months after her husband's death, Máire married Conor O'Brien who built the manor house extension for Máire and himself.

The O'Briens lived in a manner befitting well-to-do landowners; they had fishponds, a kitchen and ornamental gardens, a summer house, stables and cottages for staff, all enclosed by a wall with defensive turrets. Beyond the wall to the north-east was a deerpark. The fishponds were situated southeast of the castle (now fields on the other side of the road from the castle). The well was there too, just beside the junction of the roads. The archway entrance to the castle is now at Dromoland Castle Hotel and a fireplace is in the Leamaneh Room of the Old Ground Hotel in Ennis. Conor O'Brien was a royalist and he was injured in 1651 by Cromwellian soldiers. When he was brought back home, Máire Rua thought Conor was dead and is alleged to have shouted from the top window that she wanted 'no dead men here'. Once she realised he was still alive, she is said to have rushed to his side and nursed him tenderly until he eventually died of his wounds. Once again Máire was widowed, this time with another eight children to support. Two years after Conor's death, Máire married a Cromwellian officer, Cornet John Cooper. They had a son and possibly a daughter. Cornet John proved useful to Máire. He was able to secure her children's claims to both the Neylon and O'Brien estates, but he was an unsuccessful financial speculator and his financial dealings led to the break-up of his marriage to Máire. It was alleged that she threw him out of the top storey of Leamaneh! Certainly she stood trial for his murder in Dublin and would have been found guilty but for the intervention of Charles II. Later, as Máire lay dying, she expressed her wish to be buried beside her beloved Conor and was accordingly laid to rest in the O'Brien tomb in Ennis Friary. Máire's son Donat lived at Leamaneh for another 25 years until he moved to Dromoland Castle. Thereafter, Leamaneh was allowed to fall into disrepair.

It is possible to get into the shell of the house and climb the ruined tower. Parking is restricted to the side of the road and you have to clamber over stone stiles to get into the castle approach and castle shell.

**How to get there.**
Leamaneh Castle stands on a knoll overlooking the junction of the R476 from Lisdoonvarna and the R480 from Ballyvaghan. It does not take long to explore, so you may wish to visit Kilfenora and/or Killinaboy church after visiting Leamaneh as they are only a short distance away. (See page 196.)

### LISDOONVARNA.
Located in west County Clare, inland from the Cliffs of Moher and Doolin.

The town grew from a village in the 19th century with the development of its mineral water supply. Although the official date for the 'birth' of the spa is 1845, there are records to show that the beneficial effects of the waters were known long before that date.

The sulphur spring was accidentally discovered by a man in the early 18th century and by 1713 a local doctor had had the water analysed.

Hely Dutton in his Clare Survey (1808) writes of the waters and how 'Some find it beneficial after a winter's drinking of bad whiskey from private stills', but bemoaned the absence of good accommodation. By 1888 a traveller to the town wrote, 'The hotels vie with each other contributing to the comforts of their patrons and the United Kingdom does not possess a health resort so well favoured in this regard.'

The wells were owned by the Guthrie family and a character called 'Biddy the Sulphur' dispensed the waters from a pump-house. A Dr Westropp bought the wells and built baths and his own house overlooked the pump-house gardens. It had an outside spiral staircase so he could get a good view of the sea.

The pump-house in the spa gardens was built in 1860. It has the original tiled floor, marble counter top and dispensing pump. The well has been glassed over and illuminated so visitors may look down at their own reflection in the water far below.

To enter the spa gardens and to walk down the slope to the little victorian pump-house is to step back in time. The gardens are laid out with formal beds and old style-seats which are evocative of another age. Inside the pump-room, you pay at the counter for a glass of the sulphur water which is pumped up from the well for you. If you can overcome the sulphur smell and drink it (it smells worse than it tastes), you are rewarded with a certificate to hang on your wall at home.

The pump-house in the gardens is open from 10 a.m.–6 p.m. seven days a week, from June to October. During the summer months a sing-song around a piano in the pump-house is held every day from 12–1 p.m.

The spa developed a reputation for matchmaking, as bachelor farmers used to visit the town after the harvest to take the waters and find a wife. During the Matchmaking Festival in September, the ballroom in the modern building (which also houses the tea shop and café) has a dance from 12–2 p.m. every day.

The building close to the Victorian pump-house dates from the late 1930s, early 1940s. It has been modernised inside and houses a sauna and sulphur baths, and patrons can have a massage, wax treatment, or aromatherapy treatment.

There is another small pump-house in a garden close to the Salmon Smokery on Cannon's Hill. Two waters are dispensed here, iron and magnesia. There is another twin well of iron and sulphur at the rear of the pitch-and-putt course. The other wells in the town are open 10 a.m.–6 p.m., six days a week, from June to October.

**How to get there.**
From Ballyvaghan, take the N67 south-west to Lisdoonvarna. The N67 passes through the village and meets the N85 south of Ennistimon. The N85 later joins the N18, which is the road between Galway and Limerick.

## AILLWEE CAVE.

The Burren is rich in limestone caves. However, for the non-specialist the easiest and most entertaining way to go deep underground is to take one of the Aillwee Cave tours.

The centre at the cave entrance won an award for architectural excellence; certainly it blends in beautifully with the surrounding scenery and cannot be detected in the face of the limestone hillside until you are almost there.

Eloquent and courteous guides take small parties into the caves at frequent intervals during the day. While you wait, you can browse in the well-stocked craft shop or have tea or coffee and a home-baked snack in the adjoining coffee shop. (The view of Galway Bay from the upstairs terrace is magnificent.)

The caves were discovered by a local farmer, Mr McGann, in 1944, when his dog entered a small crack in the rocks. Experienced cavers visited and explored the caves; large caverns were found and mapped. Bones of bears (extinct in Ireland for over 1,000 years) were found. There is evidence that they used the caves for hibernation (their pug marks were found), hence the use of a bear silhouette as the Aillwee Cave logo.

The McGann family decided to open the Aillwee Caves to the public in 1976. The first 300 ft (100 m) of passage was deepened as the original passage was a crawl over mud and rocks. Other caverns were excavated. As you walk along the surprisingly wide and well-lit passages, the guide will point out natural phenomena and answer questions. You will pass from the Bear Haven — scene of the bear pug marks — past the cascade, through the Midsummer Cavern, along the Highway and into the Canyon. Spectacular stalactites and stalagmites have been given special names too. Each tour takes about half an hour. Here and there in the entrance passage, tall people have to lower their heads a little. The temperature in the caves remains constantly cool, winter or summer. Wheelchair users can be accommodated for a short distance. The caves are being explored all the time and the guides will have news of other caverns and passages which might in time be opened to public view.

This is a good visit on a rainy day, as the only evidence of rain in the caves is an increase in the river and stream sounds. This is not suitable for anyone who finds walking difficult, as the route is over a mile/1.6 km long, and the ground slopes slightly in places and can be slippery for those unsteady on their feet. Flat shoes with good soles should be worn.

Outside the cave entrance, a telescope has been mounted on a platform for visitors to look through at a small charge.

### How to get there.

Located in the hills outside Ballyvaghan, well signposted from there and from all over the region.

## BALLYVAGHAN.

Ballyvaghan is situated on the north coast of County Clare, facing across Galway Bay to Barna. The village grew in the 19th century when a quay was built. It was used to export grain, bacon and vegetables, while turf for fuel was brought across the bay from Connemara. The village was developed as an administrative centre for north Clare with police barracks, coastguard station and workhouse.

The fountain was erected in 1875. The stonemasons were the Coyne brothers from Connemara who used to bring turf to the quay. On one occasion their boat sank and they stayed in Ballyvaghan, and eventually became stonemasons.

Just outside the village (3 miles/5.3 km from the centre) is Gregan's Castle Hotel. Across the road from it is the original Gragan Castle, a 16th century tower house. The hotel was the 19th century home of the Martin family, descendants of George Óg Martyn, a 17th century Cromwellian who was rewarded with the castle and land.

### How to get there.

The N67, the R480 and the R477 meet at Ballyvaghan.

### KILMACDUAGH CHURCHES AND ROUND TOWER.

Located near Gort, approximately 17 miles/27 km from Ballyvaghan. Kilmacduagh has one of the finest collections of churches in Ireland and a leaning round tower. The monastery was founded early in the 7th century by St Colman MacDuagh. He was a member of King Guaire's family and it is said that the King was so impressed by the saint's sanctity when he found Colman living in a cave, that he gave him the land to build a monastery.

The western part of the cathedral is a small 10th or 11th century structure which was lengthened in the 12th century, acquired a north transept in the 14th or 15th century, a Lady Chapel, a new chancel and a sacristy in the 15th century.

The round tower may date from as late as the 11th or 12th century. The tower would have been used as a belfry but also as a watch tower and a place of refuge if raiders attacked. Note how high from the ground the door is. The monks would have used a ladder to get into the tower and then pulled it up behind them.

The saint's grave is said to be marked beside the grave of Bishop French (1852). Templemurry, St Mary's Church, is a small early 11th century ruin north-east of the cathedral; the Glebe House (Abbot's house) is a 14th or 15th century tower house. O'Heyne's Church lies north-west of the Glebe House. It is a late 12th or early 13th century establishment of Augustinian Canons.

The monastery and churches were extensively plundered during the 13th century. After the Reformation, the monastery was handed over to Richard, the Second Earl of Clanrickarde.

The graveyard around the monastery is still clearly in use. The recent floral tributes are a gentle link back over hundreds of years to when monks walked quietly between the churches and buildings on their way to and from saying their prayers.

**How to get there.**

Take the N67 to Kinvarra then a cross-country minor road to Gort. Kilmacduagh lies off the Corrofin road about 2 miles/3.2 km from Gort Square. It is signposted at the turn. Follow the road for approximately 2 miles/3.2 km. The leaning round tower ought to be clearly visible as you approach. The key is obtainable from the house opposite when a returnable deposit of £5 is given.

Access to the site is over a stone stile and the paths between the churches and the Glebe House are gravelled.

**DYSERT O'DEA CASTLE AND ARCHAEOLOGY TRAIL.**

16 miles/26 km from Lisdoonvarna, 26 miles/41 km from Ballyvaghan.

The 15th century Dysert O'Dea Castle was badly damaged by Cromwellian soldiers in the 17th century. John O'Day of Wisconsin (a descendant of the O'Deas who built the castle) bought the ruin in 1970 and had it restored to its original condition.

The castle has been leased for a peppercorn rent to the Dysert Development Association who have installed a coffee shop, an audio-visual room and exhibits of historic interest. In addition, there is a clear trail in an area roughly 4 miles/6 km radius of the castle leading to interesting historical sites. These may be reached by car, by bicycle or on foot. All are well signposted. An inexpensive and clear map is available from the castle coffee shop.

**The Castle.**

Outside the castle is a board showing what is to be seen on every floor. A small entrance fee is paid in the coffee shop on the ground floor. The castle was built between 1470 and 1490 for the local Chief, Diarmuid O'Dea. It is a typical 15th century castle of the type you see all around Clare and Galway. Above the front door is the murder hole which could be used to defend the entrance. A small room off the staircase would have been used to defend an angle loop in the staircase. The ceiling in the first floor room shows the marks of the rushes used to hold the mortar in place when the castle was being built, and a model in the room demonstrates how that was done.

One room contains old pews, an old-fashioned school desk and a modern television and video. Colour slides with evocative music give a simple and interesting history of the district around the castle. Particular attention is given to the buildings and remains which can be seen on the archaeology trail. The description uses drawings of how an ancient cooking place (fulachta fiadh) worked and is very good indeed. It will be easily understood and appreciated by school-going children. To start the audio-visual presentation, press 'play' on the video machine housed in the wooden casing below the T.V. If you are last to leave, press 'rewind' on the machine.

The collection of exhibits, all clearly marked and displayed, in the other rooms of the castle give a fascinating glimpse into past times in the area. The period covers the neolithic period almost to the present day. There are ancient weapons and tools; there is a chest which was washed ashore from the wrecked Spanish Armada; there are old irons and cooking pots, coins and cigarette packets, extracts from records and memorabilia relating to the First World War and its effect on local inhabitants.

The O'Deas lost control of the castle to the Earls of Thomond a hundred years after they built it, but they regained it in 1584. Unfortunately, they lost control again because they supported the northern chiefs in the Nine Years War of 1594–1603. The castle was given to the Protestant Bishop of Kildare, Daniel Neylon. The O'Deas got the castle back again only to lose it once more after the Siege of Limerick in 1691.

After the Siege of Limerick the triumphant Cromwellian General Ludlow stationed some of his troops in the castle. Just before the soldiers left they badly damaged the roof, the battlements and staircase to prevent the castle being used as a stronghold of Irish rebellion ever again. They also demolished the nearby round tower and broke up the now restored High Cross, an act of malicious damage which did not have any military purpose.

During the reign of Charles II the O'Deas regained possession of the castle, but they supported the claim of James II to the throne of England and when he lost, the O'Deas also lost. The Synge family, a local Protestant landowning family, took over the O'Dea estate but they did not live in the castle. The castle fell into ruin until it was bought by a descendant of the O'Deas, John O'Day, in 1970.

Traces of the 15th century banqueting hall can still be seen outside the castle. You can also see the corbels which supported a corner bartizan or turret, a slop stone where the dishwater was thrown out and a stone chute which channelled well water through the wall into a stone trough. Near the car park are the remains of an old medieval house which may be the house referred to in 1318 as the dwelling place of the O'Dea Chief.

**The Archaeology Trail.**
This trail takes in all sorts of interesting places, from a Stone Age cooking site to buildings associated with periods of history up to the 1940s. Each site is well signposted.

Below Dysert O'Dea Castle on the north side are the remains of a fulachta fiadh (an ancient cooking place) where a stone trough filled with water would be heated to boiling point by dropping hot stones into it. Meat would probably have been wrapped in straw and cooked in the boiling water. (Experiments have shown that a 50 gallon/c.230 litre trough can be brought to the boil in 20 minutes by this method.)

St Tola's is a simple 12th century church with a superb 13th century Romanesque doorway. It can be reached from the castle by a path across the fields, or around by road following the signpost. The church and round tower stump and nearby High Cross are now national monuments in the care of the Office of Public Works. Near the magnificent Romanesque entrance to the church, notice the fragment of the effigy of a knight showing his legs and feet only; the big toes are on the wrong side!

The presence of the round tower which Cromwell's soldiers demolished with cannon shot indicates that this was the site of a monastery. The tower dates from the 11th century, but there is evidence that there was a monastic settlement here in the 8th century. The graveyard is still used and fresh tributes can be seen on graves indicating that the practice of visiting the grave of loved ones on the anniversary of their death is still practised locally.

A stone stile at the rear of the church leads into a field where the High Cross stands. High Crosses of the 12th century represented the pinnacle of Celtic Church art and this cross is one of the finest examples in the country. Sadly, it was twice damaged but was restored and re-erected each time, each restorer adding his mark in an inscription on the base. When the cross was carefully dismantled in 1960 for an exhibition of Irish Church art in Spain, it was discovered that it was made in three sections with stone mortice and tenon joints. The head of Christ was once removable and was used by local people to cure toothache; they placed it against their cheek. The head has now been cemented into place to prevent theft.

Across the field from the cross are the remains of Mollaneen House. This was the home of the land agent for the Synge family who took over Dysert O'Dea from the O'Dea family. In front of the house, towards the road, with the boundary wall on the left, is a holy well dedicated to St Tola. This was visited annually by local people on the saint's day, until 1830 when Edward Synge had it blocked up. (It was reopened in 1986).

Nicholas Synge was the Bishop of Killaloe from 1746–71. He got the lease on 2,920 acres/1,183 hectares of church land and his grandson, Edward, took over the running of Dysert in 1823. Edward was a fundamental Protestant with a passion for trying to convert his tenants from Catholicism to Protestantism. He built schools and bribed the parents with food or threatened them in order to get their children into these schools. The Dysert School can still be seen near Carhue House which was his home. Local resistance fighters set fire to the school and shots were fired at Edward as he returned from a neighbour's house on Ash Wednesday, 1831. A bullet killed his driver but another bullet aimed at Edward lodged in a bible in his breast pocket and saved his life. (The bullet-damaged bible can be seen in the Clare Heritage Centre in Corrofin.) Edward seems to have lost his enthusiasm for proselytising after the attempt on his life. The Synge family had the High Cross repaired in 1871. Francis Hutchinson Synge's grave is on the north side of the church. Even though he was the landowner, he could not be buried within the church walls because he was a Protestant.

Carhue House, the Synge family home, is now in private hands. Near the road which leads to St Tola's church are the ruins of the lodge they built for guests. It was built in a rustic Georgian style and had a coat of arms above the door. The motto reads 'Caelesta Canimes' ('We will sing in heaven'). Tradition has it that the family was given the name Synge when Henry VIII heard an ancestor sing in the church choir. There used to be landscaped gardens around the house with a ha-ha (a step down with retaining stone wall which kept cattle off the lawn without the use of a wall to disrupt the view). The course of a stream was altered so that it ran behind the house and it is possible to see the remains of a summer house.

Near the house are the remains of a medieval road, earthen ring forts and stone forts; this is the site of the Battle of Dysert O'Dea which took place in 1318 when Norman interests were defeated and the future of Clare as a county of Irish interest and law was secured, at least until the Reformation. The old church of Rath with its two sheela-na-gig figures can also be found here.

All the sites can be reached from tarred roads although you will have to approach some sites on foot across fields. The medieval road is suitable for pedestrians only. Alternative cross-field paths are shown for those who want fresh air and exercise through the woods and meadows fringed with hedgerows. Please remember, take your litter home with you (or for disposal in a litter bin) and shut any gates you open.

**How to get there.**

From Ballyvaghan take the Lisdoonvarna road, then turn left on the R480 for Corrofin. At Leamaneh Castle T-junction, turn left on the R476 for Corrofin. In Corrofin continue on the R476 towards Ennis and watch out for the right turn signposted to Dysert O'Dea. From Lisdoonvarna, follow the R476 to Corrofin then continue towards Ennis and watch out for the signpost directing you to Dysert O'Dea which lies to the west of the R476.

## CLARE HERITAGE CENTRE, CORROFIN.

10 miles/16 km from Lisdoonvarna, 14 miles/22 km from Ballyvaghan.

The centre was developed to help people gain some insight into what life was like for those living in Clare from 1800 to 1860. This period covered a particularly traumatic time in Clare's history — the Famine, mass emigration and transportation. However, during this period there was also family life,

farming, fishing, manufacturing, education and recreation. The local organisation which started and still runs the centre has gathered together an impressive collection of artefacts, documents and memorabilia.

The collection is housed in what was once a small Protestant church. The church, St Catherine's, was originally a barn which was converted into a church between 1715 and 1729 on the instructions of Catherine O'Brien, neé Keightley, who lived at Corrofin House. Apparently the church at Killinaboy was falling into disrepair and perhaps it was cheaper or more convenient to build a new church in Corrofin. Catherine was the daughter of Lord Clarendon, Lord Chancellor of England and was a first cousin of Queen Anne. Her husband was the grandson of the notorious Máire Rua of Leamaneh (see section on Leamaneh, page 199).

Apart from removing the pews to house the display cases, the church remains as it was when it was used in the early 1970s. There is an extensive collection of 19th century memorabilia covering life at home, in church, at school, at war and, of course, during the harrowing famine years. There is even a bible with a bullet hole which saved a man's life (see page 207).

There are displays of important archaeological finds like arrow heads, coins, weapons, and copies of treasures found in Clare but now housed in the National Museum in Dublin. There is also information on the flora, fauna and geology of the Clare region. The stump of an oak tree, which was planted in 1691 and blown down in 1974, has been labelled to indicate when in the tree's life major events in Irish history occurred.

Of interest to art historians is the case with memorabilia, including sketches, of Sir William Burton who was born at Clifden House near Corrofin in 1816. Sir William was an eminent 19th century watercolourist and in 1874 was appointed by William Gladstone to be the Director of the English National Gallery. Reproductions of two of Burton's most famous works, 'The Meeting on the Turret Stairs' and 'The Aran Fisherman's Drowned Child' are displayed.

The Clare Heritage Centre houses all available pre-1900 Church records, land records, details from passenger ship lists and workhouse records. A professional genealogical service is offered to those who wish to trace their Clare roots. Staff claim that 80 per cent of enquiries can now be dealt with successfully and they are continually adding to their records. There is of course a charge for this service, but all fees are clearly indicated and agreed upon before any research is undertaken.

All the exhibits are clearly labelled, but a moderately priced information booklet is available, and well worth buying. Access is probably difficult for wheelchairs. Toilets are provided.

**How to get to Corrofin.**
From Ballyvaghan, take the N67 south and then take the left turn for the R480. At Leamaneh Castle T-junction, turn left on to the R476 for Corrofin. From Lisdoonvarna, take the R476 south, signposted to Kilfenora. At the major T-junction, turn left for Corrofin.

**How to get to the Heritage Centre.**
Drive through the village and turn left on the R460 signposted to Gort. The centre is located a short distance along this road on the left-hand side.

After visiting the centre, you may wish to picnic by the River Fergus. Walk down the street past the coffee shop and pottery shop. The picnic site is clearly indicated by a sign over the archway between the buildings. A short gravelled path leads to a grassy riverside place and a picnic table by the slow-moving river. A stone stile gives access to the riverside meadows. As this site is in the heart of the village, the view across the river is slightly marred by farm buildings.

A picnic site with more picturesque views can be found at Lough Inchiquin which is a short drive, walk or cycle out of the village on the Kilfenora road. At the edge of the village take the first left (signposted to the Rent-a-Cottage scheme), then the first right. This road leads to the lakeshore car park, a grassy area and a small stone pier. The lake is popular with anglers. The two ruined castles you can see were O'Brien strongholds.

While in the vicinity why not call at Killinaboy Church and Leamaneh Castle, both on the road to Lisdoonvarna and Ballyvaghan? Killinaboy is 2 miles/3.5 km away and Leamaneh Castle 4.5 miles/7 km away from Corrofin. (See pages 191, 199.)

## BUNRATTY CASTLE AND FOLK PARK.

Located 32 miles/51 km from Lisdoonvarna, and 34 miles/54.4 km from Ballyvaghan, Bunratty Castle has become one of Ireland's most popular attractions for visitors.

The castle was built in the 15th century, on a spot commanding the Ratty River crossing. It was owned by the O'Briens, who became Earls of Thomond, until 1712. For two brief periods during the 17th century, 1642 and 1645, it was occupied by Cromwell's parliamentarian troops. One of the commanders during the later period was Admiral Penn, father of William Penn of Pennsylvania.

In its heyday the castle and gardens were much admired. In 1646 the Papal Nuncio wrote: 'In Italy there is nothing like the palace and grounds of the Lord Thomond, nothing like its ponds and park with its three thousand deer.' The ruined keep was bought by Viscount Gort in 1954, and was carefully restored. The castle now houses Lord Gort's collection of medieval furniture, paintings, tapestries and glass.

Outside the castle a folk park has been created. The park is an attempt to re-create life in rural Ireland, in the vicinity of Bunratty, during the late 19th century. There are eight farmhouses, a watermill, a forge, post office, doctor's surgery, hardware store, drapery store, pawn shop, printers, and even a hotel where you can enjoy a pint. All have been carefully furnished in period, and all represent a cross-section of society; there is a poor labourer's cottage and a rich farmer's house.

Visitors can wander at will around the farmhouses spaciously laid out with their surrounding yards or gardens. They may wander down the old street and enjoy the atmosphere: watching people weave or knit, make bread, candles, pottery, or watch photographers working as they did in those days. If you are interested in agricultural machinery, the Talbot Collection is housed in the house overlooking the park. The collection of implements has an audio-visual explanatory video.

Bunratty House was built in 1804 by the family who lived in the castle then. It has been furnished in typical Victorian style with all the fussy lace and antimacassars — even the drawing-room is set for afternoon tea!

There is a tea shop and craft shop for souvenir hunters in the park.

### How to get there.

From Lisdoonvarna, take the N85 to Ennis and the N18 to Limerick. Bunratty Folk Park is clearly visible off the main road. From Ballyvaghan, take the R480 road to Corrofin, then join the N85 to Ennis and as above.

Open daily from 9.30 a.m.–5 p.m. (last admission is 4.15 p.m.). During
June, July and August, the Folk Park remains open until 7 p.m. (last
admission 6 p.m.). There is an admission charge.

**CRAGGAUNOWEN PROJECT AND KNAPPOGUE CASTLE.**
Located 36 miles/58 km from Lisdoonvarna, 48 miles/77 km from
Ballyvaghan.
This park has a reconstructed ring fort and crannóg. You may already
have looked at the stone and earth ring forts in the Burren (see page 187),
but you will not have seen a crannóg there. Crannógs were small artificial
islands in the middle, or at the edge, of a lake and were probably surrounded by wooden pallisades. They date from the Iron Age, just before
and just after the birth of Christ. Like the promontory or cliff forts, they
were often occupied well into medieval times.

The leather boat Tim Severin used to cross the Atlantic is also displayed
here. Severin's crossing, called the 'Brendan Voyage', demonstrated that
St Brendan could well have crossed the Atlantic and landed on American
shores long before Columbus.

If you have been looking at the derelict raths in the Burren, Craggaunowen will give you the opportunity to see the dimensions and scope of
these early Irish dwellings. There is also a reconstruction of a 4th or 5th century farmer's dwelling, an Iron Age 'roadway' and an outdoor cooking site.

After all the looking and marvelling there is a tea shop for refreshments.

Craggaunowen is open every day from March to October, 10 a.m.–
6 p.m. (last admission 5 p.m.). There is an admission charge.

Knappogue was one of 42 castles built by the MacNamara tribe. This
was their finest. It was built in 1467 and was carefully restored by the
historian John Hunt. It houses a selection of his medieval art collection
and furnishings of the period. Open daily, from May to October, 9.30
a.m.–5.30 p.m. (last admission 4.45 p.m.). There is an admission charge.

**How to get there.**
From Lisdoonvarna, take the N85 to Ennis and then the R469 to Quinn.
Craggaunowen is signposted 3 miles/4.8 km away in an east-south-east
direction. From Ballyvaghan, take the R480/R476 to Corrofin and link up
with the N85 to Ennis, then as above. Knappogue Castle is signposted
from Quin.

**ENNIS.**
Ennis is a lively town with its ancient origins very evident in its winding
narrow streets. It seems to have been established in the middle of the
13th century by the O'Brien family. They built their principal residence
at nearby Clonroad and invited the Franciscans to settle on a piece of
land beside the river. When Clare became a county during the reign of
Elizabeth I, it was natural that Ennis would be chosen as the county

*Two views of the Poulnabrone Dolmen*

capital; the O'Briens had become the Earls of Thomond, the town had an important religious building in its friary, it was centrally placed and it was a trading port. A grant to hold fairs and markets was given in 1610 and two years later James I gave it a charter and it became a town with a Corporation, a Provost, Burgesses and a Town Clerk.

There are good shops and restaurants, an excellent museum and ancient buildings of historic significance to visit. As you stroll about the town watch out for the following details:

The large column in the centre was erected to Daniel O'Connell by public subscription in 1867. It was built on the site where Daniel O'Connell was declared MP for Clare in 1828.

Leading off O'Connell Square is O'Connell Street, a narrow shopping thoroughfare. Off this street is a narrow lane which leads to the girls' primary school. This was once the site of the first theatre in the town which was run by the actor-manager, Walter Smithson. His daughter, Harriet, was adopted and reared by Dr James Barrett, the Rector of Ennis. Harriet followed her father into the acting profession and in 1833 she married the composer Hector Berlioz. He called her 'La Belle Smithson, dont tous Paris delirait'. She died of a stroke at the age of 54 and is buried in Montmartre.

Further up the street is *The Old Ground Hotel*. The hotel premises include the old Town Hall which was built on the site of the jail. The jail was built in 1880 and the prisoners exercised on the other side of the street. The archway through which the prisoners walked to their exercise can still be seen. Inside the foyer of the hotel is a sketch of Ennis made by an Englishman who toured Ireland in 1675. He depicts Ennis at that time as having only four substantial buildings. All the rest were thatched cottages. Upstairs in the hotel is the Leamaneh function room, which has the original Leamaneh Castle fireplace in it. Ask at the reception desk if you wish to see it. If it is not occupied, the courteous staff will be happy to show it to you.

Opposite the hotel is the Pro-Cathedral, dedicated to Saints Peter and Paul. It was built in 1842 at a cost of £5,000. It was later improved in 1911 and again in 1973. The interior is a good example of 'Carpenter's Gothick'. It is interesting that wood and not stone was used so extensively in a church built so close to excellent sources of stone. There is a doric memorial to the Reverend Barrett who was Harriet Smithson's guardian.

A right turn after the Pro-Cathedral along Old Barrack Street will take you to the Market Place. From 1800 an important butter market was held here; now there is a Saturday market for the sale of vegetables, lambs, calves and poultry.

The large John Behan sculpture entitled 'A moment of flight' was erected to commemorate the 750th anniversary of the establishment of Ennis.

Turn right into Market Street and look out for Chapel Lane on your left. This is an old pedestrian way, and if you look up as you walk along you will see 17th century chimney stacks.

A right turn at the end of the lane brings you through High Street and back to O'Connell Square and the monument. (A left turn brings you to Parnell Street, a narrow shopping thoroughfare with some interesting historical details. See below.)

At O'Connell Square you can either go straight across it and down Abbey Street to the Friary (see below), or turn left into Bank Place and take a route to the Friary which includes some interesting sights.

In Bank Place, so called because of the number of bank premises, look at the columns with their lovely carved foliate capitals on the Bank of Ireland.

Cross over the bridge. Until fairly recently, the site occupied by the car parks was covered with tenement buildings. Small lighters were once berthed here in the days when the river was tidal. The importance of the river to the town can be gathered when you see that the town's coat of arms depicts three sailing ships: 'three ships with sails sable'.

On your left is the Protestant Church which was built in 1871. The pyramid-shaped memorial in the ground is to General Bindon Blood who introduced reforms into the British Army early this century.

Turn right into Bindon Street, a fine terrace of red brick mid-19th century Georgian houses. Notice the high fanlights and doric doorcases. The street was named after the Bindons, a prominent Clare family. David Bindon was an MP for Ennis for many years and so were his sons Francis and David at different times. Francis was a portrait painter and is best remembered for his portraits of Jonathan Swift, Lionel Sackville (the Viceroy of Ireland at one time) and Hugh Boulter who was the Arch-bishop of Armagh. Later, Francis collaborated with the architect Richard Castle in the design of some of Ireland's grand houses: Westport, Powers-court, Castletown and Russborough.

At the end of this short street a right turn will bring you to the *de Valera museum*. The building was originally a Presbyterian church built in 1853. The church has been delightfully restored and converted into a simple museum. Behind it, the modern library blends in beautifully with the Victorian structure. The museum is on two levels and entrance is free. Exhibits are in glass cases and on the walls. The collection is a delightful assortment of memorabilia of de Valera and other people and events which shaped the history of Clare and Ireland. There you will find the letter de Valera wrote to the principal teacher of the school he had been working in up until the 1916 Rising, to explain why he would not be returning to his teaching duties. He wrote from Kilmainham Jail in Dublin and expected to be shot like the other leaders the following day. His American citizenship saved him from execution and the telegrams he received when he came out of Pentonville Prison can be seen. Among the exhibits there are old pipes and revolvers, the barrow and spade used by Charles Stewart Parnell to turn the first sod on the laying of the West Clare railway and a cabin door from a ship of the wrecked Spanish Armada. There is a permanent collection of paintings, including English and European landscapes, and a set of eight small Flemish paintings on the life of Christ and a painting attributed to the Dutch artist Philip Wouverman (1619–88).

The building opposite the museum is Coláiste Mhuire. The main building was erected in 1778 as a school endowed by Erasmus Smith. At one time the great-grandfather of Cecil King, the British newspaper magnate, was a headmaster of the school.

Walk along Harmony Row to the New Bridge. At this point if you wish to see a fine example of mid-19th century architecture, turn left and walk along New Bridge Road, over the junction to the Courthouse which has a much admired ionic portico. In the Courthouse grounds there is a monument to Eamon de Valera. (If not, then continue over the bridge to Abbey Street and the Friary. See below.)

If you return to the town centre on the river side of the road and stop opposite the premises of John Costelloe and Sons Ltd, you will see Steele's Rock, three irregular blocks of limestone decorated with a shield on the top of one, and on the south face of another. The rock is a memorial to 'Honest' Tom Steele who was a tireless campaigner and supporter of O'Connell and the cause of Catholic Emancipation.It is said that Tom Steele, a close friend of Daniel O'Connell, used to sit for hours on this rock hoping to get a glimpse of Miss Crowe who lived in the house opposite. Tom was a gentleman farmer and engineer and was apparently not encouraged as a suitor for their daughter by Miss Crowe's parents.

Walk along the footpath and over the bridge. On the right-hand side of the bridge you will see the 1916 memorial. The boulder is quartzite conglomerate. An English translation of the Irish reads 'In memory of the heroes of 1916 who fought and died for Ireland.'

From here you can see the *Friary*. This historic building was built for the Franciscans by the O'Brien family in 1240. The O'Briens were the leading Clare landowners at that time, but it was not until 1300 that the Friary began to take the shape it still retains today.

Turlough O'Brien became King of Thomond in 1277, and he had a new church built on the site of the old one for the friars; the five-light east window was filled with blue and other coloured glass and it was apparently a most magnificent building. The monastery was so beautiful that a eulogy in a medieval tale called 'The triumphs of Turlough' described it in the following terms: 'The Monastery of Ennis; diversely beautiful, delectable; washed by a fish-giving stream; having lofty arches; walls lime-whited; with its order of chastity and their golden books, its sweet religious bells, its well kept graves, homes of the noble dead, with furniture of both crucifixion and illuminated tomes, both Friars' cowl and broidered vestment; with windows glazed, with chalice of rare work-manship a blessed and enduring monument which for all time shall stand a legacy and memorial to the prince that raised it.'

Turlough died in 1306 and the magnificent friary became his resting place. His descendants continued to support the friary and it was to remain the principle burial place of the O'Brien family for centuries. During the 15th century the friary was enlarged. The convent was completed to form three rows of buildings gathered around a cloister walk and garth to the north of the Church. The eastern side housed the sacristy and refectory with dormitories overhead. The northern side would have housed the kitchen with dormitories above it and the western side would have been the reception area, stores and workshops. The main tombs were constructed or rebuilt during this period of expansion. The tombs of the MacMahons and Turlough O'Brien were probably against the wall of the choir of the Earls of Thomond. The art work dating from this period shows that the friar craftsmen were superb artists, but unfortunately their work has been scattered into fragments here and there. Look for the fragments of altar pieces and plaques re-set into the Creagh tomb, the screen with the Archbishop, Virgin and Child, the 'Ecce Homo' and the St Francis carvings. The community must have been thriving at this time, as there are traces of three or four altars in the transept chapel in addition to the high altar and possibly other altars by the major tombs.

The Reformation reached Ennis in 1543 and the friary was suppressed, but the friars were allowed to continue living in the friary well into the reign of Elizabeth I. Donough, the Fourth Earl of Thomond, had been reared at Elizabeth's court as a Protestant and he hired out parts of the friary for use as a courthouse, a hospice and an inn.

The friary then fell into neglect and eventually in 1780 the Church authorities spent money refurbishing it. The nave of the old church was roofed again, and a window inserted in the east end of the tower. The walls were plastered and a vestry was added in the cloister just off the tower. The tower was restored and the spiky pinnacles were added to the top. The friary remained more or less in this state until the 19th century when the Church authorities decided to build a new Protestant church in Bindon Street, and the friary was left to decay once more. In 1893 the Church authorities handed the building over to the Office of Public Works and it became a national monument. Repair work took place immediately, and again in 1952. The medieval windows were restored, the debris was cleared away, plaster was stripped off to reveal the 'Ecce Homo' and the St Francis carvings. Part of the cloister arcade was re-erected. Legal ownership of the friary was handed back to the Franciscans by the Church of Ireland authorities in 1969. The building is now in the hands of the Office of Public Works who have again undertaken improvements and restorations.

The Friary is open from mid-June until September. At one time it was possible to obtain a key when one wanted to visit out of season, but this practice seems to have been discontinued. There is an entrance fee.

Following the Act of Banishment and the penal days until Catholic Emancipation in 1829, the friars went into hiding in the town. In Lysaght Lane, off Parnell Street is a tablet commemorating their sojourn. The junction of Parnell Street and Old Mill Street was where the stone celebrated in the ballad 'The Stone outside Dan Murphy's Door' stood. In Lysaght Lane the stone set into a wall reads 'Offer a prayer for the souls of the poor friars of St Francis who exercised the Sacred Ministry in this house. A place where they found refuge in penal times.' Lysaght Lane was the last refuge of the friars before the reform of the Penal Laws. There are records of them being in numerous houses inside and outside the town during the penal times.

Notice the jostle stones at the entrance to Lysaght Lane and other narrow lanes off Parnell Street. These stones were to prevent the hub of carriage wheels from coming in too far to the corner and damaging the structure of the building.

**How to get there.**

From Ballyvaghan, take the N67 southwards, then take the left turn (R480) signposted to Corrofin and Kilfenora. At the T-junction at Leamaneh Castle, take the left turn (R476) to Corrofin. Continue through Corrofin on the R476 until you reach the left turn on to the N85 for Ennis. From Lisdoonvarna, take the N85 south through Ennistimon for Ennis.

# WHERE TO STAY IN THE BURREN

## HOTELS

This is a list of hotels in, and close to, the Burren. The Irish Tourist Board and Irish Hotels Federation use a star rating for hotels ranging from 5 stars to indicate international standard luxury to 1 star for simple, often family–owned hotels. All will have a high standard of cleanliness and hygiene. As inflation may alter the accommodation rates, a rough indication of the single overnight accommodation is as follows:

Rating:
Economy: £15 to £25
Budget: £25 to £35
Moderate: £35 to £45
High: £45 and over

**Ballyvaghan.**
*Gregan's Castle Hotel.* ****. 16 rooms en suite. Telephone 065–77005, fax 065–77111.

Stately 19th century residence in own grounds 2 miles/3.5 km from Ballyvaghan, at the foot of Corkscrew Hill. Commanding position with superb view of sea. Open from the end of March until late October. Rating: high.

*Hyland's Hotel*, **. 12 rooms, 11 en suite. Telephone 065–77037 or 065–77016, fax 065–77131.

Right in the heart of the village, the house dates from the early 18th century. Family owned, busy establishment. Lots of singing, dancing and special 'Irish nights' during summer. Open from the end of March to the end of September. Rating: economy.

## Doolin.

*Aran View House*. **. 11 rooms, all en suite. Telephone 065–74061.

Splendid 18th century house at the side of the approach road 3 miles/ 2 km from Doolin. Family owned. Superb views all round. Gardens. Traditional music sessions. Open from early March to November. Rating: economy.

### Ennistimon.
*Falls Hotel.* ***.
22 rooms en suite. Telephone 065–71004, Fax 065–71367.
Elegant old country house in beautifully landscaped gardens and woodland overlooking the river with its waterfall, and the town. Once owned by Francis MacNamara whose daughter Caitlín married the poet Dylan Thomas. (The bar is named after Dylan.) Wonderful mural/cartoon of poitín-making on one wall has been preserved by owners. Open January to end of September. Rating: economy.

## Gort.

*Sullivan's Royal Hotel.* *. 10 rooms, five en suite. Telephone 091–31401, fax 091–31916. Old hotel, modernised, on the town square. Open all year. Car park. Rating: economy.

**Lehinch.**

(For those interested in golf, a discount on green fees at both golf courses has been arranged with Lehinch hotels.)

*Aberdeen Arms Hotel.* \*\*\*. 55 rooms en suite. Telephone 065–81100, fax 065–81228. Centrally located, 19th century hotel extensively refurbished to high standard. Open all year. Rating: moderate to high.

*Atlantic Hotel.* \*\*. 15 rooms, all en suite. Telephone 065–81049, fax 065–81029. On main street, family owned and run. Manager was the first person to paddle on a surfboard between England and France. Open from (approximately) Easter to November. Rating: moderate.

*Claremont Hotel.* \*. 14 rooms, nine en suite. Telephone 065–81007. Centrally located. Modernised old hotel. Open all year. Rating: economy.

*Sancta Maria Hotel.* \*\*. 18 rooms, 12 en suite. Telephone 065–81041. Centrally located near the heart of the town. Own garden. Open from March to October. Rating: economy.

**Liscannor.**

*Liscannor Hotel.* \*. 25 rooms en suite. Telephone 065–81186/81187. Telex 91297, fax 065–608697. Located in village, about 5 miles/8 km from Lehinch. Sea views. Open from April to October. Rating: economy.

**Lisdoonvarna.**

Four hotels in this area share a single Fax number: the Imperial, the Hydro, the King Thomond, and Burren Castle. Be clear which hotel you wish to contact when you are sending your Fax.

*Imperial Hotel.* \*\*\*. 84 rooms en suite. Telephone 065–74042/74015, fax 065–74406. Centrally located on main street. A White Group hotel. Excellent standard of décor. Open March to end of October. Rating: economy to budget.

*Sheedy's Spa View Hotel.* \*\*. 11 rooms en suite. Telephone 065–74026. 17th century farmhouse excellently refurbished as a hotel. Centrally located. Family owned and run. Hotel stands above the street surrounded by pretty gardens. Tennis court. Open from March to end of September. Rating: budget.

*King Thomond Hotel.* \*\*\*. 50 rooms en suite. Telephone 065–74444, fax 065–74406. A White Group hotel. Emphasis is on service. Excellent décor. Tennis court. Open April to October. Rating: budget.

*Hydro Hotel.* \*\*\*. 84 rooms en suite. Telephone 065–74005/74027, fax 065–74406. A White Group hotel. Has sauna, sunbed, gymnasium and own sulphur baths. Children's play area with swings and crazy golf. Tennis court. Open from early March to late October. Rating: economy to budget.

*Burren Castle Hotel.* \*\*\*. 30 rooms en suite. Telephone 065–74344, fax 065–74406. Member of the White Group. Recently built 'castle'. Lots of stuffed deer and fake medieval décor. Regular dances, sing–along sessions and 'Irish nights'.

Children catered for with playground and pool room. Emphasis is on fun. Located outside Lisdoonvarna on road to Doolin. Open January to October. Rating: economy to budget.

*Carrigan Hotel.* **. 14 rooms en suite. Telephone 065–74036/74411. Family owned and run. Open from March to end of October. Rating: economy.

*Savoy Hotel.* **. 14 rooms en suite. Telephone 065–74009. Centrally located near town square. Parking on street. 19th century hotel recently refurbished. Open from June to September. Music nightly. Rating: economy.

*Lynch's Hotel.* *. 15 rooms en suite. Telephone 065–74010. Centrally located on town square. Parking on street. Family run. Open June to October. Rating: economy.

*Ravine Hotel.* *. 11 rooms, six en suite. Relephone 065–74043. Centrally located. Open June to end of September. Rating: economy.

*Ballinalackan Castle Hotel.* ***. Telephone 065–74344. Outside town en route to Black Head. Ruined castle in grounds. Building has interesting history. Open April to October. Close to Burren Way walking route. Rating: moderate.

# BED AND BREAKFAST

As in other areas of the region, there are many homes offering bed and breakfast to visitors. Accommodation is particularly plentiful in and around the following places: Ballyvaghan, Burren, Corrofin, Doolin, Ennistimon, Fanore, Kilfenora, Killinaboy (sometimes spelt Kilnaboy), Kinvarra, Lehinch, Lisdoonvarna and Milltown Malbay.

# HOSTELS

**Corrofin**. Telephone 065–27683, Fax 065–24783. Purpose-built hostel on main street in village. Family rooms available. Lake boats for hire.

**Doolin** Hostel. Telephone 065–74006, Fax 065–74421. Modern rooms. I.T.B. registered. Group rates. Open all year. Two buildings, one old, one new. Located on a dairy farm, overlooking the village.

## Kinvarra.

*Johnston's Hostel* on the main street. Open all year.

## Lehinch.

*Hostel.* Telephone 065–81040. 60 beds. Family rooms and dormitory. Open all year. I.T.B. registered. Very central, coffee shop.

## Liscannor.

*Village Hostel.* Telephone 065–81385. Next door to Captain's Deck restaurant (same owners). Close to pubs. Open all year. I.T.B. registered. Ten rooms, no dormitories. 25% reduction for children.

*The Old Hostel,* St Bridget's Well. Telephone 065–84107. Halfway between Liscannor and the Cliffs of Moher. Converted old school. Open all year.

## Lisdoonvarna.

*The Burren Tourist Hostel,* Kincora House. Telephone 065–74300. Large, modernised old building. Licensed bar attached. Set dancing and music sessions. Open all year. I.T.B. registered.

## Spanish Point.

*The People's Hostel.* Telephone 065–84107. On the side of road across from cliff top with path down to the beach. Open all year. I.T.B. registered. 50% reduction for children. Dormitory accommodation.

# SELF-CATERING

### Ballyvaghan.

*Ballyvaghan Holiday Cottages.* Eight modern cottages arranged in a small estate about ten minutes' walk from the village. Excellent views of the Burren. Babysitting arranged, cots and high chairs on request. T.V., no pets. Open all year. For further information and booking, telephone 061–330289, or 065–77086. Fax 061–320855.

*Thatched cottages* (newly built) close to the small harbour. Superb view of bay. Flagged floor, open fireplace as well as central heating and traditional 'half door'. For information, telephone 061–61588 or Fax 061–61988.

*Village and country homes.* Just off the main street, through an archway, small modern houses set in a walled garden. Beautifully laid out and very private. Further information, telephone 065–51977.

*Whitethorn apartments.* Cottages overlooking sea about 20 minutes' walk from Ballyvaghan. Each cottage is very private. Meals available next door at the Whitethorn Restaurant. Contact the Whitethorn Visitor Centre, Ballyvaghan or telephone 065–77044, Fax 065–77155.

*Ballyvaghan Rental Company* has a number of cottages and apartments in the area. Telephone 065–77029 for information.

### Bell Harbour.

*Bell Harbour Holiday Cottages.* Located on coast road towards Kinvarra, approximately 5 miles/8 km from Ballyvaghan. Traditional looking modern cottages in a cluster. Pets welcome, T.V., babysitting arranged. 15 minute drive to supermarkets, pubs and restaurants. Easy walking access to quiet Burren uplands. Further information from Trident Holiday Homes, Unit 2, Sandymount Village Centre, Dublin 4, or telephone 01–683534, Fax 01–606465.

### Corrofin.

Small group of traditional looking thatched cottages set spaciously on mowed grass plateau among trees overlooking Lough Inchiquin. Magnificent views. Flagged floor, open fireplace as well as central heating, and traditional 'half door'. T.V., no pets. 10 minute drive to village.

Another group of cottages is located right in the heart of the village. For information on both sets of cottages telephone 061–61588 or Fax 061–61988.

### Ennistimon.

*Falls Hotel Chalets*, in self-catering section of the Falls Hotel. Four chalets in the landscaped gardens. Babysitting service. Pets allowed. Open all year. Telephone 065–71004 or write to The Falls Hotel, Ennistimon, County Clare.

### Kinvarra.

Thatched cottages near Dunguaire Castle. Five minutes' walk from village. Telephone 099–37247 or 091–37293.

### Lehinch.

*Fairways Holiday Homes*, Lehinch. 12 purpose-built houses furnished with dishwasher, dryer and microwave. Babysitting service, no pets, T.V. For further information telephone 061–330289 or Fax 061–320855, or write to Catherine Carey, 7 Sorbonne Green, College Court, Castletroy, Limerick.

### Liscannor.

Holiday cottages located in the heart of the village near pubs, restaurant and supermarket. 3 miles/5 km from the Cliffs of Moher. 10 minute drive from Lehinch with its beach and golf courses. For information write to Trident Holiday Homes, Unit 2, Sandymount Village Centre, Dublin 4 or telephone 01–683534 or Fax 01–606465.

*Thatching beside Thoor Ballylee*

*Mute swans at Coole*

**Quilty.**
Small estate of modern traditional looking cottages on a cliff top across the bay from Spanish Point. Children catered for with playground, tennis court and babysitting service. T.V. may be hired. Safe beaches 15 minutes' walk away. 10 minute drive to supermarket. Telephone 065–87095 or write to Danny or Geraldine Mungovan, Caharush, Quilty, County Clare.

**Spanish Point.**
*Armada Holiday Cottages.* Small group of traditional style slate-roofed cottages overlooking the beach. T.V. on request. Cots available. Private access to beach. 10 minute walk to shops. Telephone 065–84110.

## CARAVAN AND CAMPING

**Doolin.**
*Camping and caravan park.* 10 caravan pitches, 30 tent pitches. Close to quay and ferry service to Aran. Open Easter to end of September. Pets allowed. Showers, washing/drying facilities. Pubs and restaurants nearby. Supermarkets in Lisdoonvarna, about 15 minutes' drive away. Bus service. Telephone 065–74127.

**Lehinch.**
*Caravan and camping park.* Telephone 065–81424. Open May to September. 62 caravan pitches, 50 tent pitches. Pets allowed. Showers, washing/drying facilities. Children's play area. Camp shop. Short distance from village centre on Milltown Malbay road, N67.

**Spanish Point.**
*Lahiff's caravan and camping park.* Open April to September. Within 400 yds/360 m of beach. 45 caravan pitches, 12 tent pitches. Pets allowed. Showers, washing/drying facilities. Camp shop. Children's play area. Telephone 065–84006.

# SHOPPING FOR GIFTS AND SOUVENIRS

There are craft shops and craft workshops in and around the Burren and in towns and routes mentioned on tours. Only those shops which sell quality Irish gifts and souvenirs are included.

**Ballyvaghan.**
*The Whitethorn.* Just outside Ballyvaghan on the road to Kinvarra. Shop, restaurant and apartments overlooking the sea in a building well camouflaged by good use of local stone. The shop is an elegantly laid out showroom selling tweeds, Aran knits and crystal ware.
*Claire's Restaurant and Craft Shop.* In the heart of Ballyvaghan, on the street leading from the Kinvarra road. A small shop in the cottage at the front of the restaurant sells beautiful enamel jewellery designed by local resident artist, Manus Walshe. Also, a small selection of Irish literary books and children's story tapes by Eddie Lenihan from Clare. Open April until September, 10 a.m. until evening. Open during restaurant hours also.
*Scythian Fleece.* This is the workshop of textile artist Kaethe Burt O'Dea and is located in a small, prettily landscaped, industrial park on the outskirts of the village on the road towards Lisdoonvarna. Kaethe's garments have been described as 'wearable art'. She uses virgin wool which she dyes in rich shades and then beats into felt. This richly coloured felt is then combined with silks and leather to produce original and exotic looking fabrics. These are made up into waistcoats, coats and wraps, or

knitted into jackets. Each garment is an original one and can take up to two months to complete. Open all year from 9 a.m.–5 p.m. Mondays to Fridays.

*Dallán Gallery*. This is next door to Scythian Fleece in the industrial park. Seamus McGuinness is also a textile artist. He embroiders fabrics together to produce unusual pieces which are similar to patchwork and abstract collage. They are colourful and very striking, and each piece is an original. He sells large and small framed pieces. From May until September Seamus will also stock 'one-off' art/craft pieces in other media by other Irish artists. Open seven days a week during the summer, from 9 a.m.–5 p.m.

*Farm Shop*. Located at the foot of the road leading to Aillwee Cave. Large car park opposite. Although food shops have not been included in the guide to craft shops/workshops, this shop has been included because Burren Gold cheese, using milk from cows grazing on the Burren, is made on the premises. From mid-June to early July, during the morning, visitors have the opportunity to watch Burren Gold being made. It is a Gouda-type cheese and is made in three flavours. Bottles of chilled wine and crackers are sold if customers wish to use the stone tables and seats outside for an impromptu picnic. The shop also stocks quality jams, chutneys, honeys and produce from other regions.

*Aillwee Cave Gift Shop*. Located at the entrance to the cave, the shop stocks an amazing variety of quality goods to suit all pockets and tastes. There are tweeds, pottery, glassware, books and small items for children to buy.

## Carran.

*Vincent Fragrances*. Signposts throughout the Burren direct you to this perfumery which is the only working one in Ireland. Vincent trained with European perfumers before a sojourn on Aran persuaded him to set up a perfumery in this flower-rich region of Ireland. His workshop, built on to the rear of his house, is well hidden by trees in the heart of the limestone crags. When you visit the workshop you will be told something of the art and craft of perfume-making and will be invited to sample one of the four different perfumes. Gift packs can be bought.

**How to get there.**

From Ballyvaghan, take the T69 Lisdoonvarna road then turn left on the R348 past the turn to the Aillwee Caves. Keep going to the top until you reach the first major crossroads. Turn left. The road is narrow and makes steep ascents and descents. At the T-junction, turn left, then first right past the UCG research station. Take the left fork. Along this road you will see a small painted stone indicating a route along a track to your right leading into trees. The brightly painted house and workshop are well hidden. The perfumery is in the flat-topped building adjoining the house. Knock on the door if it is closed.

From Lisdoonvarna area, take the road signposted to Kilfenora and Corrofin. Take a left turn on to the R348 to Ballyvaghan and the right turn at the first crossroads. Follow directions as for Ballyvaghan route.

From Kinvarra and the coast road, the perfumery is signposted up through Corker Pass to Carran. The turn to the perfumery is before you reach Carran village.

## Cliffs of Moher.

Visitor Centre and O'Briens Tower. Wide range of inexpensive to moderately priced gifts.

## Corrofin.

*The Pot Shop*. (Near the Heritage Centre.) This sells hand-thrown pottery (the wheel is in the shop) in a range from pocket-money gifts to expensive ones.

## Doolin.

*Crafts Gallery, Doolin*. Exquisite range of quality craftwork: sweaters, pottery, glass, leather, pictures. There is a craft workshop to visit and a showroom and garden coffee shop. Open from 8.30 a.m.–8 p.m., high season. Open from 9 a.m.–5 p.m. out of season.

*R.F.B. Silversmith.* Handcrafted jewellery. Open from 10.30 a.m.–6 p.m. Closed out of season. Specialises in a small but exclusive range of ear-rings and small pieces.

*Celtic Music shop* is near R.F.B. Silversmith premises. It stocks an excellent range of traditional music tapes, CDs and traditional instruments. If customer demand is sufficient, the shop will remain open all year, from 10 a.m.–6 p.m. daily.

### Ennis.

*The Belleek Shop*, Abbey Street. Stocks Belleek china, Waterford crystal.

*A. Honan*, Abbey Street. Antique shop specialises in clocks, although stocks a good range of quality antique furniture including small pieces.

*Upstairs Downstairs Gift Shop.* Near Daniel O'Connell statue. Stocks cold cast wall plaques, old silver figures, bronze chess sets, Irish dolls. Has locally made dried flowers and Shannon pottery. Also stocks pocket-money gifts for children to buy. Currently developing an information centre for tourists. Open from 9 a.m.–9 p.m. from 1 May until the end of September, seven days a week.

*Carraig Donn.* Elegantly laid out shop in O'Connell Street. Stocks quality tweeds, knitwear, Irish produced jams and shortbread.

*Griffin's shop* stocks bric-à-brac ornaments and antique furniture.

### Ennistimon.

*Kilshanny Leather.* Handcrafted decorated purses and other good value items. Interesting shop with old clock. Open Mondays to Saturdays 9 a.m.–6 p.m, all year round.

*Crosbie's.* Good range of quality gifts. Owner makes decorative but useful wooden items. Open during the summer months from 10 a.m.–7.30 p.m.

### Gort.

*The Spinning Wheel.* Small shop in the market place run by Angela Coen the weaver. Stocks her own rugs and wall hangings and original landscapes at very reasonable prices. Also has original handpainted stones which are unique to her shop. Stocks handknits and Aran knits.

### Kilfenora.

*The Dolmen Gallery.* Opposite the Burren Display Centre. Stocks a wide range of pretty gifts of the sort found in good gift shops elsewhere. Local interest gifts to look out for are the models of the Doorty High Cross and decorated clay pipes. Also stocks a small selection of tweed ties and caps.

*Burren Display Centre Gift Shop.* Has a small selection of quality gifts, books and tapes of local and general Irish interest. Also stocks the locally produced jams which can be sampled at the tea shop.

*Máire Rua.* Gift shop opened on the 300th anniversary of the death of Máire Rua of Leamaneh Castle (see page 199). A brief history of Maire's life is written around the walls of the shop. Shannon pottery is a big seller in this shop. Also stocks the Burren jam, jewellery, tapes, tweed caps and ties.

### Kinvarra.

Village Crafts in the main street near the post office. Small shop, but well stocked with good variety of gifts from tweed hats and ties to Celtic design cards. Look out for Celtic design transfer kits.

### Lehinch.

*Kenny Woollen Mills.* Manufacturers of knitwear; shop also stocks crystal, Belleek china ware, jewellery, tweeds, menswear. Open all year, seven days a week in summer.

*Design Ireland.* Branch of Doolin Crafts Gallery. Open 9.30 a.m.–7.30 p.m. in the summer. Earlier closing out of season.

## Lisdoonvarna.

*The Lavender Pot.* This is a counter in the Victorian pump-room at the spa. Low-priced to average-priced souvenirs.

# WHERE TO EAT IN THE BURREN

The price rating is only a rough guide, but is useful as a rule-of-thumb:

| | | |
|---|---|---|
| Economy: | under | £5 |
| Budget: | under | £10 |
| Moderate: | under | £15 |
| High: | over | £15 |

## Ballyvaghan.

*Claire's Restaurant*, telephone 065–77029. Open 7–10 p.m. daily. Weekends only November–March. Country cottage setting with lots of flowers and candlelight. Relaxed informality and good food. Rating: economy to budget.

*O'Brien's Bar and restaurant.* In the heart of the village. Large restaurant with thick carpet, table linen, silver service. Set dinner menu. Open for lunch 12.30–2.30 p.m. Dinner, 6.30–10 p.m. Rate: moderate to high. Bar menu available from 12–6.30 p.m. Soups and traditional plain food. Rating: economy to budget.

*Hyland's Hotel* in Ballyvaghan is open to non-residents. Seafood and meat menu. Rating: moderate to high.

*The tea rooms* in the old coastguard station beside the quay serves superb cakes, sandwiches and salads daily. Furnished like a comfortable country house with a garden room extension beside an attractive secluded garden. Rating: economy.

*Ailwee Caves* coffee shop serves salads, quiche, snacks. Outside the entrance to the cave during the summer, burgers and chips are sold from a stall. Rating: budget.

*Whitehorn.* Located a short distance outside Ballyvaghan on the road towards Kinvarra. Coffee shop with self-service open all day. Small restaurant with table linen. Both overlook the sea. Smart décor and furnishings. Rating: economy to moderate.

*Monks Bar and Seafood Restaurant.* Outside village on quay. Low beams and huge open fireplaces crackling during winter. Lots of wood and atmosphere. Specialises in seafood dishes from full meals to crab sandwiches. Rating: economy to budget.

## Cliffs of Moher.

Visitor Centre serves snacks and meals. Rating: economy to budget.

## Corrofin.

*The coffee shop* beside the Heritage Centre serves snacks and a limited range of hot dishes. Village Pubs advertise soups and snacks.

## Doolin.

*Ilsa's Kitchen*, telephone 065–74244. Very pretty room in flower-covered cottage. Seafood and wholefoods. Dinner only. Rating: budget.

*Lazy Lobster,* telephone 065–74390. Country house dining room, husband of cook fishes for the lobsters which are served that evening. Simple but imaginative. Wine licence. Dinner only. Rating: budget to moderate.

*Bruach na Haille*, telephone 065–74120. Seafood restaurant. Dinner only. Pretty country house décor. Rating: moderate.

*O'Connor's Pub.* Open from 12–8 p.m. Last orders for eating in the restaurant, 8.45 p.m. Hot meals. Specialities: Irish stew, local salmon, and mussels.

## Ennis.

The town is full of restaurants, coffee shops and takeaways which are all highly visible. Visitors will have no difficulty locating a suitable place to eat.

**Ennistimon.**

*The Falls Hotel restaurant* is open to non-residents. See 'where to stay', page 218).

**Fanore.**

*Admiral's Restaurant.* Located on the side of the road. Seafood a speciality. Proprietor has own sea tanks. Rustic elegance and décor. Rating: budget to moderate.

**Kilfenora.**

*The Visitor Centre coffee shop* serves home-baked snacks, soups and limited range of hot meals. Flagged floor, pine tables, flowers. Rating: economy.

*Vaughan's Pub.* Serves smoked salmon snacks. Rating: economy.

**Kinvarra.**

*Partner's Restaurant.* Old shop on the main street. Open 10 a.m.–9 p.m. Mondays to Saturdays and 6–9 p.m. on Sundays. Seafoods, salads, home-baking (own chocolate éclairs). Two high chairs. Clean and cheerful décor with polished wooden tables. Rating: economy to budget.

*Sayre's Restaurant.* On the main street. Established restaurant. First floor loft-like room with assorted wooden tables. Up-market bohemian décor. Wine list. Steaks, duck and interesting sauces. 8–10 p.m. Lunch 12–3 p.m. Easter to October. Rating: budget to moderate.

*The coffee shop* overlooking the harbour sells home-baked snacks, soups, salads, seafood. Small selection of low priced hot meals. Open 9 a.m.–9 p.m. during spring and summer only. Country cottage style décor. Space in ladies' room to change a baby's nappy. Rating: economy.

**Lehinch.**

*The Lehinch hotels* are open to non-residents. See 'where to stay', page 219.

*Eamonn's Restaurant*, telephone 065–81050, on Main Street serves gourmet food in a pretty country house dining-room. Dinner only. Rating: moderate to high.

*Nick's steak and seafood restaurant.* Main Street. Located in a pub. Rating: budget.

**Liscannor.**

*Captain's Deck*, telephone 065–81385. Everything shipshape. Fresh seafood. Vegetarian dishes. Large wine list. Full licence. Open in the evenings from 6 p.m. Rating: budget to moderate.

*Joe's Clifftop Tea Rooms.* Open March to September, 9 a.m.–9 p.m. Substantial meals and snacks. Rating: economy to budget.

**Lisdoonvarna.**

*The Royal Spa Restaurant*, telephone 065–74288. Open all day from 9 a.m.–9 p.m., June to October. Rating: economy to budget.

*Imperial and Hydro Hotels* offer bar food and full à la carte from 12–10 p.m. Rating: budget to moderate.

**Milltown Malbay.**

*Ocean View Restaurant*, telephone 065–84249. Licensed. Open all year. À la carte lunches and dinner. Rating: moderate.

**Newquay, Burren.**

*Linnane's Bar.* Located overlooking the water at the quay. Locally caught fish and shellfish used in simple, excellent dishes. Basic bar décor, not tricked out for tourists. Rating: economy to budget.

*Rose Cottage Restaurant* is located along a winding road overlooking the bay. Dining-room attached to a modern bungalow. 12 tables. Wine. Dinner only. Rating: budget.

# RAINY DAY ACTIVITIES

Aillwee Caves are a good place to visit on a rainy day. (See page 202.) However, although you will be dry in the caves, the passageways may be damp and may tend to be slightly slippery underfoot. Good soled shoes are advisable. The torrents observed from the viewing platforms are more spectacular when it has been raining.
Visit Dunguaire Castle (see page 198).
Visit Thoor Ballylee (see day tours from Galway, page 140).
Visit the spa wells at Lisdoonvarna. During the morning a sing-along session is held in the pump- house. Take a sulphur bath, a sauna, an aromatherapy session or wax treatment.
Take a tour of craft shops. (See page 223.)
Visit Ennis Abbey (see page 215), the de Valera Museum (see page 214).
Visit the Burren Display Centre at Kilfenora (see page 196).
Visit the Clare Heritage Centre, Corrofin (see page 208).
Visit Dysert O'Dea Castle (see page 204). After touring the castle, you can wait in the coffee shop for the rain to stop!
Visit Bunratty Castle and Folk Park (see page 210).
Visit Knappogue Castle (see page 211).
Take a ferry from Doolin to the Aran Islands; the weather may be dry out there.
Visit the Lehinch amusement arcade with its slot machines and video games.
Stay indoors and read a good book.
Wrap up well, ignore the rain and set out on a tour, the rain may stop before you get there.
Visit Coole Park Visitor Centre and tea rooms (see page 188)

# CHILDREN'S ACTIVITIES

Visit Aillwee Cave (see page 202), Dunguaire Castle (see page 198), Craggaunowen (see page 211), Dysert O'Dea Castle (see page 204), Bunratty Folk Park (see page 210) or O'Brien's Tower with its telescope at the Cliffs of Moher.
Pitch and putt is available at Lisdoonvarna opposite the spa well centre.
The Burren Castle Hotel has a children's playground.
Take a ferry trip to Inisheer. The ferries depart from Doolin. (See page 92.)
Go horse riding. Nearly all the stables cater for inexperienced as well as experienced riders. (See page 185.)
Take a trip in a jaunting car hired from The Burren Riding Centre (see page 185).
The cinema in Ennis, telephone 065–21742, may be showing a children's film during the summer season. There is also a cinema on the promenade at Lehinch.
There are slot machines, video games and a few roundabouts on the promenade at Lehinch.
Hire a cycle (see page 170).
Go to the beach (see page 183).
Go into Galway or Ennis and visit the bookshops and toy shops (see pages 104, 225).

# ECOTOUR

**Link** River Shannon To Cliffs of Moher, 80 miles/128 km.

The wide, slow-flowing Shannon River, with its source 210 miles/336 km to the north in the Shannon Pot, with its extensive loughs and bordering callows, at once delimits and confines a distinct and special part of Ireland. The Shannon estuary, flowing westwards from Limerick, is broad and fertile — and deep enough to attract heavy shipping to service the growing industrial complex along its banks. Its rich, muddy bays serve tens of thousands of wintering and migrating wildfowl and waders and are vital refuelling stops for birds travelling between places as far apart as Arctic Canada and southern Africa.

The estuary of the River Fergus is especially important for wintering birds, but its extensive mudflats are difficult to see from the land and it is only at Clarecastle that we get a glimpse of this haven of mud, with its abundance of worms, shrimps and snails.

Travelling south-westwards between high hedgerows along the R473 (L51) from Clarecastle towards Killadysert (also spelt Kildysert sometimes) we get occasional glimpses of the Shannon and some of the islands which grace the outer reaches of the Fergus estuary. The road crosses the occasional quiet, muddy, reed-fringed creek and passes a welcome hillside of deciduous woodland beyond Ballynacally before the countryside opens up to wide expanses of undulating, often rushy fields. We have moved from the fertile limestone lowlands on to the inhospitable Namurian shales and sandstones which are well exposed in roadside quarries along the way. The idyllic scenery is brutally punctured by the belching stacks of the Aughinish alumina plant on the south shore of the Shannon, visible from the road as we approach Killadysert. The natural innocence of this mighty estuary has been stolen. Its waters and the winds that blow over it will never be as pure again.

The change in geology brings a narrowing in the estuary between Killadysert and Foynes on the south shore. At Ailleroe (or 'Red Cliff' — R193530) there is a fine exposure of the local rocks. The seashore is stony and covered with a tangle of brown seaweeds. The road swings north through the tidy village of Labasheeda with its attractive display of old farm machinery.

As we continue westwards, the twin stacks of the coal-fired Moneypoint power station come into view and soon the all-pervasive impact of this installation on the landscape becomes apparent as we meet the legion of marauding pylons which march north-eastwards across a defenceless countryside. Moneypoint, in unison with its counterpart at Tarbert on the south shore, emits thousands of tonnes of sulphur dioxide each year. The significance of its location on the west coast in an area of prevailing south-westerly winds will be obvious to the environmentally concerned observer.

The influence of the salt-laden winds blowing in off the Atlantic becomes increasingly evident as we travel westwards. Trees become scarce and those which do remain to fight the elements are low, stunted and inclined to the east. Gorse holds out the longest, but eventually it gives way to flagstone walls which are in turn replaced on the Loop Head peninsula by earth banks where suitable flagstones are not available.

The main road takes us through Kilrush, past the muddy shallows of Poulnasherry ('Oyster Hole') Bay and across the narrow peninsula to Kilkee with its sprawl of houses and caravans. An excursion to the Bridges of Ross and to Loop Head is well worthwhile for the geologist and general naturalist. The peace and quiet of the countryside — and the state of the roads — makes cycling the preferable mode of travel.

Taking the main road south-westwards we follow the signposts to Loop Head, by-passing Carrigaholt to the south. A detour to the north coast of Loop Head, taking in the shore southwards from Fooagh Point (Q858590) to Trusklieve (Q798548), will be of interest to serious geologists keen to find excellent exposures of Namurian sediments and impressive sand volcanoes — up to 16.5 ft/5 m high and 6.25 ft/2.5 m across at Goleen Bay (Q823560). For the general naturalist, a visit to the Bridges of Ross (Q732500) will satisfy geological curiosity. Here, the sea has created two spectacular arches, rendered more so when the Atlantic gales whip up the surf and force it landward through the constricting gorge. Inland, rushy pastures and stone walls look like unpromising habitat for birds. However, the increasingly rare tree sparrow breeds near Loop Head and a surprising number of rare passage migrants has been recorded here in recent years. On the rocky coast, purple sandpipers and snow buntings can be seen on passage and, beyond the lighthouse on Loop Head itself, wheatears are regular summer inhabitants of the maritime heath while choughs are present all year round. The maritime heath is short and prickly with western gorse and heather, producing a beautiful yellow and purple mosaic in July.

Fulmars, kittiwakes and guillemots are the commonest seabirds nesting on the cliff ledges below. For those with time to spare and a good pair of binoculars or a telescope, the head is an excellent vantage point for observing passing dolphins and porpoises and (if you are prepared to get up early in the morning) migrating seabirds in spring and autumn. (The Bridges of Ross are even better for this activity because they protrude further beyond the general line of the coast than Loop Head and sea-watching can be carried out from a more convenient height.)

Returning by the southern route through Kilbaha, we can visit the small bay (Q835493) to the east of Rinevella Bay to see the 'submerged forest'. Here, pine stumps, some of impressive dimensions, are buried in peat which now extends below the low-water mark, indicating that the sea-level was considerably lower when these trees were growing 4,000 to 5,000 years ago. In Carrigaholt we can take the main road northwards or continue closer to the south shore of Loop Head via Querrin back to Kilkee.

North of Kilkee the cliffs become progressively lower, giving way to a series of sandy beaches separated by rocky headlands. Inland, there are open pastures enclosed by earth banks. At Quilty a visit to the beach is worthwhile at any time of the year. Wading birds such as sanderling and purple sandpipers, seldom seen on less exposed coasts, are commonly recorded on the beaches around Lurga Point. Offshore is Mutton Island, a major wintering haunt for barnacle geese which breed in north-eastern Greenland. The rocky seashore from Lurga Point to Spanish Point is particularly rich, with colonies of the small sea urchin, *Paracentrotus*, and a variety of red seaweeds growing around the low-water mark. There is an impressive storm beach at the point, but the sand dunes are in bad condition and are eroding rapidly.

As we approach Liscannor Bay the bare, grey terraces of the Burren begin to come into focus. The Burren (Boireann means 'a rocky place') is 100 square miles/260 square km of Carboniferous limestone which was laid down under a tropical sea about 300 million years ago. It has been moulded by ice and water and, in more recent times, denuded of much of its soil and vegetation by man and his animals. It is a landscape of contrasts and conundrums, a habitat in which Arctic, alpine and Mediterranean plants live side by side, an environment widely inhabited by people 4,000 to 5,000 years ago but almost empty today. It is a peaceful and calming place, a place where we must slow down, relax and absorb its timeless tale.

However, the Burren proper is still some way away. First let us go through Lehinch, with its broad, surf-washed beach and Liscannor, with its tiny fishing harbour, to the Cliffs of Moher.

**Stop** The Cliffs of Moher (R040919). Park at visitors' car park.

The Cliffs of Moher are one of the most spectacular sights in Ireland. They rise vertically from the sea to nearly 600 ft/200 m at their highest point to the north of O'Brien's Tower and extend northwards from Cancregga Point 6 miles/10 km to Fisherstreet. The history of the cliffs is written in the layers of rocks which were laid down during the late Carboniferous Period, about 300 million years ago. Repeated cycles of sediment deposition formed a delta at the mouth of a large river in the way that the Mississippi delta is being formed today.

Looking southwards from the rock platform below the car park, we can examine the profile of the cliffs. At sea-level there are beds of black

*Oysters at Moran's of the Weir*

shale alternating with thin bands of lighter coloured sandstones and flagstones. Immediately above, stratified beds of flagstones rise over 300 ft/100 m to the thick band of yellow sandstone which forms the prominent ledge on which we are standing. The crumbly, black rock above the platform is Moher shale.

The cliff face is continually under attack from the sea at its base and from the wind, rain and water seeping between the rock strata above and along vertical fractures. Evidence of the continuing retreat of the cliffs can be seen along the path to the south of the car park where recent collapses have been fenced off.

A wide variety of plants grows along the cliff top, creating a colourful ribbon in spring and summer which contrasts with the intensively managed pastures inland. The white flowers of scurvy-grass are some of

the first to appear, both on the cliff top and on the buttresses which project from the cliff face. Sea pink (thrift), sea campion and birds-foot trefoil produce a dazzling mosaic of pink, white and yellow on the rich green background of the cliff-top slopes. On cliff ledges and buttresses, where other plants would be hard-pressed to survive, roseroot, a relic of cold, post-glacial times, thrives in the face of adversity.

The cliff ledges and crevices offer safe, sheltered nesting sites for ravens, choughs, jackdaws, rock pipits, rock doves, peregrines and several kinds of seabirds. Fulmars occupy the uppermost ledges, each female laying a single white egg directly on to the bare rock. Razorbills, which are becoming scarce at the Cliffs of Moher, usually nest below the fulmars. Then come the squabbling guillemots on their crowded ledges, and the kittiwakes with their well-built nests. Puffins nest in burrows in the grassy slopes of Goat Island, the green promontory below the sandstone slab, while shags and great black-backed gulls nest on the top of it. Herring gulls used to be common around the cliffs but have become scarce, as elsewhere, for reasons which are not yet clear but which probably include botulism, a lethal condition contracted at rubbish dumps. The *Pocket Guide to the Cliffs of Moher* by Tony Whilde provides a comprehensive account of the geology, natural history and history of the cliffs.

**Walk.**

The cliffs offer spectacular walks for those with a head for heights and the good sense to stay away from the edge. Using the visitors' car park as a base, it is possible to walk north or south, returning by the same route or by road where it is easily accessible from the cliff top. For the energetic and properly equipped, though, a day spent walking the full length of the cliffs in good weather is hard to beat.

Starting at Fisherstreet in the north, we can join the cliff top track near Castleview guest-house. Doonagore Castle, first built in the 1500s and restored in the 1970s, pierces the sky to the left while Crab Island, off Doolin pier, appears to the right with Inisheer (Inis Oírr) in the background. The ascent is easy but it does involve crossing several streams, walls and electric fences. Near the renovated cottage a detour to the cliff edge reveals the 'text book' stratification and folding of the rock below. To the north of Luogh, hidden by an earth bank topped by a barbed wire fence, is a deep chasm — Poulnagavaul (Pol na Gabhal, 'crooked inlet'). Here the sea has attacked a weakness in the cliff and carved out a deep inlet bounded by vertical iron-stained rock faces with steep grassy slopes above. Southwards, beyond Luogh, the track passes closer to the cliff which, during the breeding season, is occupied by fulmars, kittiwakes, guillemots, razorbills and, on top of some of the lower buttresses with their growth of natural vegetation, puffins — a taste of some of the ornithological delights to come.

Leaving the track where it turns south-eastwards, we head for the cliff edge and climb the steep track to the highest point of the cliffs between Aillenasharragh ('cliff of the foals') and O'Brien's Tower. Care must be taken along this section of the cliff and we should keep well away from the edge which, in places, is falling away.

Aillenasharragh is linked to the Cave of the Wild Horses at Kilcorney (see later) in one legend concerning the ancient Tuatha Dé Danaan. After St Patrick had introduced Christianity to Ireland, the old rituals of sorcery and Druidism were slowly abandoned. In protest, the Tuatha Dé Danaan used their magic power to turn themselves into horses and galloped to Kilcorney where they hid for centuries in the caves. Time passed and the horses were forgotten until one day seven foals emerged from the caves. They were frightened by the bright daylight and bolted, galloping all the way to Aillenasharragh where they plunged over the cliff.

The story of Cornelius O'Brien, who built the tower and several other edifices, is presented in several publications available at the Visitor Centre at the east end of the car park. He was a Member of Parliament for the area and became a legend in his own time.

With a little acceleration it is possible to move out of earshot of the car park in a few minutes and resume walking in the true ambience of the cliffs. The rhythm of the cliff top is broken in places by old quarry workings, reminders of a flourishing industry which employed more than 500 men in the last century. Otherwise, it is easy going to Hag's Head with its early 19th century signal tower. This was erected on the site of an Iron Age promontory fort, built about 2,000 years ago.

Northwards from Hag's Head the graceful sweep of the cliffs carries your eye to the bare, limestone terraces of the Burren. To the south you can see Mutton Island, Loop Head and the mountains of Kerry on a clear day. From here we can move southwards along the cliff to the first quarry where a track will take us back to a minor road and a route parallel with the cliffs either towards the car park or eastwards to Liscannor. Alternatively, we can continue along the top of the cliff, towards Cancregga and the road to Liscannor.

**Link** Cliffs of Moher to Lisdoonvarna. 7 miles/11 km.

The road northwards leads us towards Lisdoonvarna and offers a magnificent panorama of the Burren, the Aran Islands and the Atlantic Ocean which opens out ahead of us. The 'castle' we pass on our left is of very recent construction!

## THE BURREN.

Lisdoonvarna is an ideal base for exploring the Burren; even within the town there is interest for the naturalist. On calm, spring evenings the scrub which clothes the steep banks of the Aille River valley is alive with grasshopper warblers — imitating, as their name suggests, lowly grass-hoppers. Dippers flit along the canalised stream flowing through the spa and foxes have been seen in daylight around the spa, too. A warm spring evening brings bats out to feed on insects along the river and at that time of year the cuckoo is rarely silent.

Taking the Ballyvaghan road, we first pass through wet moorland pastures before reaching limestone countryside again. About 2 miles/3 km outside the town we can take a left turn towards the partly forested slopes of Slieve Elva (a route recommended for cyclists and walkers rather than motorists).

**Stop** Killeany Rising (M163005) at gateway to west of bridge.

After about 500 yds/0.5 km we cross a channel bounded by moss-covered boulders. In spring the channel is usually dry but after rain it floods from the Killeany Rising about 500 yds/0.5 km upstream, not far from the 15th century Killeany church. Upstream from the bridge is a low dam and a pump-house serving a local water supply scheme. Behind the low concrete wall, in early summer, the stream bed is covered with tiny, pebble-cased insects. These are larvae of the caddis fly (*Agapetus*) which is typically found in springs and well adapted to the inevitable drying out which it will suffer before it emerges as an adult fly later in the summer. The Rising is the resurgence of water from the Poulnagollum-Pollelva cave system — the longest in Ireland with 7.5 miles/12 km of passages — which has its source on the side of Slieve Elva.

**Link** 2.5 miles/4 km.

Continuing northwards along the flanks of Slieve Elva, we pass a junction to the left and come to a marker pole on the left about 100 m beyond the junction.

**Stop** Poulnagollum Pothole (M162032), at the lay-by a few metres before the pole.

The pothole is about 100 yds/100 m up the hill and surrounded by a fence on the top of a stone wall. Care should be taken when examining the pothole, especially in damp conditions. It should be entered only by experienced and properly equipped potholers. It is a fossil sink hole left dry as the shales and flagstones of Slieve Elva receded and created active sink holes upstream and closer to the limestone/shale boundary. Usually water can be heard flowing, south-eastwards, along the main streamway about 80 ft/25 m below. In contrast, down in the valley on the other side of the road, the Caher River flows north-westwards to Fanore.

**Link** 4 miles/6.5 km.

Now we descend the valley to Fanore, crossing the 'green road'* at the first road junction, into the confines of Glen Curraun (the 'hooked glen') which is bounded by steep rocky terraces on the left and steep, glacial drift banks on the right.

Alternatively we can return to the Lisdoonvarna-Ballyvaghan road and continue north-eastwards across the moorland slopes of Poulacapple, through the modern conifer plantation and then down onto the limestone to Corkscrew Hill where a new lay-by will serve as a useful vantage point.

* A map of the 'green road' walking tour from Ballyvaghan to Bally-nalackan is available locally.

**Stop** Corkscrew Hill (M204028), at the lay-by part of the way down the hill.

The simple terracing of the Burren limestone is easy to see in the hills above Ballyvaghan, but the origins of the bedding planes which separate the beds and which have been instrumental in the formation of the terraces are uncertain. The limestone, made up mainly of the calcareous skeletons

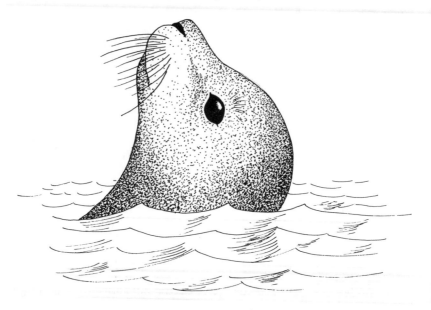

of seabed animals, was laid down under a tropical sea during the Carboniferous Period about 300 million years ago, when the area which was to become Ireland lay close to the equator. The bedding planes may have resulted from temporary cessations in deposition, the emergence of the seabed above sea-level or some form of sub-marine erosion at intervals. Whatever their origin, their relative vulnerability to erosion has contributed to the terracing which is so characteristic of the Burren.

The limestone has had a very stable history. Over most of the region it tilts southwards only a few degrees and no faulting has been reported. This is probably because it is underlain by a very stable formation of older granite. Its marine origin is indicated by the fossil corals, crinoids and brachiopods (lamp-shells) which are widely exposed and evident in walls and buildings wherever limestone is used.

**Link** 4 miles/6.5 km.

A slow descent of Corkscrew Hill brings us into a lush valley and on towards Ballyvaghan, passing the northern end of the 'green road' on our left after about 1 mile/1.6 km.

**Stop** at Ballyvaghan Pier (M228087).

On reaching Ballyvaghan we turn left between the shallow alga-enriched harbour and the thatched cottages. From the pier there is a clear eastward view of a low island where common seals haul out. In winter light-bellied brent geese feed in the shallows and along the shore and also to the west of the harbour. It was here that a family party of six birds, all banded on Bathhurst Island in Arctic Canada in the summer of 1985, spent the later winter and early spring of 1986. Five of the geese retained their lettered yellow bands and metal bands while the sixth carried only a metal band. Have they returned to the same place in recent years?

Other birds, more at home over the sea, can sometimes be seen from the vicinity of Ballyvaghan during the summer months. Razorbills, guillemots and puffins, which breed at the Cliffs of Moher 16 miles/25 km to the south-west, feed off the coast. So do gannets, diving for fish which also attract schools of harbour porpoises to the outer reaches of Galway Bay.

**Link** 4 miles/6.5 km Lisdoonvarna to Poulsallagh.

Taking the R477 westwards from Lisdoonvarna we head towards the sea. Familiar limestone scenery greets us as we approach Ballynalackan Castle. To the left (beside the road to Dublin) there is a vertical crag. At its base is the entrance to Pol an Ionain, a cave which contains the largest stalactite in Europe and possibly the largest free-hanging stalactite in the world. This awe-inspiring feature can, at the time of writing, be seen only by those willing to undertake a fairly rigorous underground expedition with proper caving equipment.

The road continues downhill between hazel scrub and short-cropped craggy pastures almost to the edge of the sea.

**Stop** Poulsallagh (M088016), at the lay-by where the road meets the coast.

This is one of the most interesting stops in the region. In a small area there is a wide range of landforms and habitats and in clear conditions it is a good vantage point for viewing the Aran Islands and the Burren.

Our first impression is of bare, grey limestone — some of it is ice-smoothed pavement, the rest angular, shattered blocks and boulders. However, on closer examination we will find within the grykes (the fissures in the pavement) a host of plants sheltering from the Atlantic wind and spray. Some are typically woodland plants that thrive in shady situations, like holly and hart's tongue fern. In early summer the delicate and rare maidenhair fern can, with diligent searching, be found in some of the dark, damp crevices.

Less obvious features, but significant in the evolution of the limestone surface and its vegetation, are the solution cups which etch the surface of the pavement. Ranging in size from a few centimetres across to several square metres, these depressions have been created by natural physical weathering and colonised by *cyanobacteria* (blue-green algae), mosses, sedges, rushes and grasses which gradually create a soil inhabitable by larger plants.

The short grassy swards are a delight from early May with colourful displays of spring gentians, early purple orchids, bird'sfoot trefoil, cat's foot (mountain everlasting), mountain avens, bloody cranesbill and the small, white-flowered Irish saxifrage, amongst many other species. The nearby hazel and hawthorn scrub is alive with small birds in the spring. Robins, blackbirds, wrens, dunnocks, whitethroats and the occasional yellowhammer generate a symphony of birdsong in the early morning sunshine, and in a quiet moment a pine marten or stoat may emerge momentarily from the craggy fastness.

On the seaward side of the road the broken ground leads us to the low vertical cliffs, sculptured by millenia of exposure to westerly winds and waves. In the tiny crevices at the top of the cliff there are small periwinkles (you will have to get down on your hands and knees to see them). These are marine snails, which, in their adult form can survive high on the shore where they are only occasionally wetted by sea spray.

At the foot of the cliff, when the tide is out, pools full of small brownish-green, spiny sea-urchins (*Paracentrotus*) can be seen fitted tightly into protective limestone pits which they have created for themselves. They belong to a southerly species and occur at the northern limit of their range in the west of Ireland. Beadlet anemones, barnacles, mussels and limpets occur on the more exposed rock surfaces. The mussels are tiny and never grow to full size in these exposed conditions.

To the south, the cliff drops away to a sloping platform and here, just below a crag, there is a pothole leading to an underground passage which runs southwards to another pothole and thence to the sea via a typical cave passage which is visible when the tide is low. This cave, which was probably formed before the last Ice Age when the sea-level was lower, gives us a good impression of what many of the caves in the Burren are like, without having to go underground. Further to the south there is an impressive storm-beach composed of large rounded boulders flung high on to the shore by an angry sea.

**Walk.**

A short walk northwards along the cliff tops and back along the road or across the ice-smoothed limestone pavement on the landward side of the road is both fascinating and exhilarating.

**Link** 6 miles/10 km.

About 1 mile/1.6 km north of Poulsallagh the road takes us past Ailladie, a smooth, vertical sea-cliff called Mirror Wall by the rock-climbing fraternity, some of whom display gravity-defying skills in their attempts to establish new and ever harder routes.

At Cloghanulk there is a track to the right which winds its way steeply up over limestone pastures, covered with mountain avens in spring, to the foot of the bog covered shales of Knockaunsmountain where it meets the 'green road'. It makes a superb walk for those who are sound in wind and limb and offers excellent views of Fanore strand, Black

Head, the Aran Islands and Connemara. The vegetation changes abruptly with the change in geology and the green of the pasture gives way to browns of the moorland. Pink lousewort, yellow tormentil and the tiny blue milkwort are amongst the flowers which adorn the damper slopes above the 'green road'.

The hills recede a little as we travel northwards making room for more pastures but soon close in again as we approach Fanore.

**Stop** Fanore (M148083), at the entrance to the beginning of the road leading to the strand car park.

Just to the north we find one of the few rivers which flow overground in the Burren. Although during the summer it will be dry, except for a few pools and little rivulets flowing beneath the boulders, in winter there will be a veritable torrent flowing seawards from the Caher Valley. The river rises high up the valley between Slieve Elva and Poulacapple in the east, first flowing intermittently above and below ground until it meets the impermeable glacial drift deposits at the bottom of the valley which have protected the underlying limestone from its erosive effects. The river has cut deeply into the glacial drift, as is evident from the steep cliffs on the north bank upstream of the youth hostel and church.

On the sea side of the road the main features of interest are the sand dunes. These, like most Irish sand dunes, are formed of glacial material deposited both on land and on the continental shelf during the dissolution of the last major ice sheet between 20,000 and 15,000 years ago. Although heavily eroded and further threatened by increasing recreational use, they harbour a variety of plants including sea sandwort, storksbill, sea holly, sea spurge and the occasional Portland spurge.

Meadow pipits, skylarks and flocks of finches frequent the dunes while choughs sometimes feed on the thin sward near the car park. Most of the common species of gulls can be seen on the beach along with waders such as curlew, oystercatcher and ringed plover. During spring and late summer whimbrel and terns often stop for a while on their migrations. Occasionally, in strong westerly winds, gannets and Manx shearwaters come close enough in to the shore to be easily recognisable, and at almost any time of the year small numbers of great northern divers might be seen and even the much less common red-throated and black-throated divers, too.

**Link** 8 miles/13 km.

A short journey northwards between stark, limestone pavements to seaward and craggy terraces brings us to the lighthouse at Black Head, named, it is reported, from the 'head' naturally etched into the limestone cliff beside the road several hundred metres to the east. Two small depressions form the eyes and a horizontal cleft below suggests a mouth from which, in wet weather, water flows into a marshy area below. See if you can find 'Black Head'.

The steeply shelving shore beside the road is popular with sea anglers and is also an excellent vantage point for observing passing harbour porpoises and common dolphins in late spring and summer. Great northern divers often feed close inshore here and large numbers have been recorded in winter and early spring.

The shallow waters confined by the spit leading out to Rine Point offer shelter for common seals throughout the year. Common seal pups are born in June or July. They have an adult-coloured coat at birth and swim out on the high tide following their birth on the beach. In contrast, grey seals give birth in the autumn and the white, furry pups cannot leave the land for the first three or four weeks. A wide range of ducks, geese and waders can be seen here in winter. Choughs sometimes feed on the short sward and snow buntings have been seen on spring migration at the spit.

**Walk.**

The energetic can climb Black Head to the Cathair Dhúin Irghuis perched on a flat shoulder overlooking both the open Atlantic and Galway Bay. A longer walk, however, starts at Cregg (M191099), near Gleninagh Castle and takes the track up the hill between Gleninagh and Cappanawalla to a coll which overlooks a wide amphitheatre of rocky terraces and floor of short cropped pasture. The track continues into the valley and joins the 'green road' at Feenagh.

**Link** 5 miles/8 km from Lisdoonvarna.

The R476 leads eastwards between rushy fields and forestry plantations to Kilfenora with its Burren Visitors' Centre, Cathedral and High Cross and then on towards Killinaboy (Kilnaboy), continuing via Leamaneh Castle. A left turn before the village takes us on our way to Carran. (However, it is worth going into Killinaboy (see page 191) to see the 11th–12th century parish church with the sheela-na-gig over the door and the other historical monuments in the village and then retrace your route to the Carran junction.) Following the road northwards 3 miles/5 km we reach Cahercommaun, signposted on the right. A short metalled road leads to a parking area. (An alternative route takes us through Corrofin and north-eastwards towards Gort; see later, pages 248, 249.)

**Stop** Cahercommaun (Cathair Chomáin) (R276958), in the area beside the two cottages.

Here we can follow the signposted track first to Cahercommaun, over the short-cropped pastures with limestone outcrops, through the hazel and hawthorn scrub and up on to the plateau. Typical Burren flowers abound and mossy saxifrage — a Burren speciality — occurs in abundance in and around the fort. The careful observer may also come across vernal sandwort, another species largely restricted to the Burren.

The fort is dramatically located on a cliff edge and commands a fine panoramic view of the surrounding countryside — limestone terraces and pavement, extensive hazel scrub and small, walled fields. Little is known about the history of the fort except that it was already in existence over 1,000 years ago. (See page 188.)

The sound of cuckoos fills the springtime air and, as elsewhere in the Burren where trees are so scarce, the sight of several cuckoos together is quite common. Often they are being pursued by the 'would-be' hosts of their eggs, meadow pipits. In a quiet moment, a herd of feral goats might appear on Glasgeivnagh Hill to the east, or a fox casually going about its business in broad daylight — such is the remoteness of this once inhabited place.

Returning to the fork in the track, the enthusiastic naturalist will find a walk towards the signposted cist (stone burial mound) and the seven streams inviting. The dense hawthorn and hazel scrub in the valley contrasts markedly with the barren plateau above. Song birds are common and, in spring, woodpigeons are numerous. No doubt, they are feeding on the large crop of ivy berries which the valley produces — a crop which is also exploited by the secretive pine martens whose telltale droppings (containing ivy seeds) may be seen on the tracks through the scrub. The pine marten is another link with the past because its remains were discovered, along with those of foxes, badgers, rabbits, red deer and ravens, during the 1934 archaeological excavations of the kitchen area of Cahercommaun.

A side track to the left, beneath the crag, follows stream beds up to a vertical mossy wall — an oasis in a desert of limestone, watered by a stream flowing from a spring on the hill slope above. In dry weather the seven streams are dry along much of their short overland course, though the presence of freshwater shrimps and mayfly nymphs in some of the pools indicates that they must be permanent. Any water soon disappears underground where it flows 3 miles/5 km south-eastwards to join the River Fergus to the east of Killinaboy.

**Link** 3 miles/5 km.

We follow the road northwards, turning left at Castletown and then right towards Carran and finally sharp left, just before the village, up a steep hill to the summit.

**Stop** Carran Turlough (R285985), beyond corner on the verge.

Looking back to the east we have a bird's-eye view of Carran Turlough, a large example of a uniquely Irish landscape feature, a turlough (tuarlach means 'a place which dries out' or 'a winterlake'). In dry weather the valley floor is waterless, except for some small pools and a short surface stream, but in wet weather water rises through swallow holes from the underground passages which honeycomb the limestone beneath and flood the valley up to the stone walls, many of which are covered with a characteristic dark moss, *Cinclodotus fontinaloides*. During dry weather the moss becomes dry, brittle and quiescent, but when it is submerged it springs back to life and with new growth turns a more typical mossy green. Its presence on walls and boulders is a sure indication of intermittent flooding and it is a good guide as to whether a 'dry' hollow is a turlough.

Turloughs are usually hollows in the limestone landscape which are lined with glacial drift, covered largely with terrestrial vegetation and used as pastures during the summer. The hollows date back to sometime during the last Ice Age, or earlier in some cases. They occur mainly in Counties Clare and Galway with outlying ones in Mayo, Roscommon, Longford, Sligo and Limerick. Turloughs do not occur anywhere else in the world and so this Irish name has been adopted in the geological nomenclature. Such uniquely Irish landscape features are clearly worthy of conservation.

**Link** 5 miles/8 km.

We can continue eastwards across the limestone plateau towards Poulnabrone (see page 187), or retrace our steps and turn left at the bottom of the hill into Carran Village and then right towards the turlough, continuing along this road, keeping to the western side of the valley and passing the signposted Tobernafiaghanta and penitential stones to the left. As the road rises, the valley to the right narrows and becomes cliff-bound. This enclosed valley is the most spectacular part of the Carran depression (of which Carran Turlough makes up only a part), one of the finest examples of such a feature in Ireland or Britain. Its formation is thought to have been initiated in Pliocene times (some three million years ago) by the coalescence of several smaller depressions (dolines) which had been formed by the collapse of the roofs of underground caverns.

To the left, and partly hidden by a hedgerow, we pass the Glen of Clab ('mouth'), a dry, enclosed valley with some (all too rare) natural woodland on its southern slopes. Beyond the coll the road passes through some nitrogen-green reclaimed pastures as it descends to the flower-rich limestone pavement of the Keelhilla National Nature Reserve.

**Stop** Keelhilla National Nature Reserve (M332033), at signposted gateway to the reserve.

The reserve, which was established in 1986, covers 323 acres/14.5 ha of typical karst (limestone) landscape with three distinct vegetation communities: limestone pavement, scrub grassland and woodland. Even at the side of the road there are spring gentians, early purple orchids, bloody cranesbill and other Burren specialities. Nearby, on the pavement, mountain avens grow in profusion on the thin peaty soil. Wood anemones grow in sheltered hollows close to the road and the burnet rose is common on the pavement. There are ant hills covered with thyme and, growing in a wet flush near the wall running across the middle of the pavement, are cuckoo flowers (lady's smock) and common butterworts — two species we might not expect in the middle of limestone pavement. Common frogs have also found this small oasis and breed here during the winter, and the small freshwater limpet *Ancylus* lives here in the spring, too. On warm, sunny days Ireland's only native reptile, the viviparous lizard, can sometimes be found 'warming up' on a prominent limestone knoll. Warm, sunny weather brings out the butterflies, too. Of the 30 or more species recorded in Ireland, most have been recorded in the Burren. The pearl-bordered fritillary, which flies at the end of May, appears to be confined entirely to the Burren where its larval food is the violet and its adult habitat hazel scrub. The brown

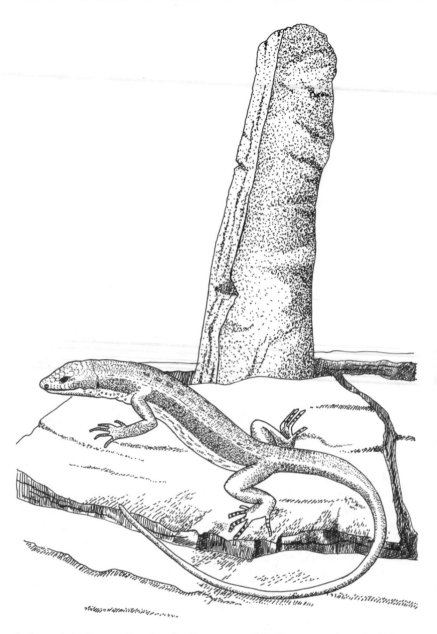

hairstreak is also confined to the limestone of the Burren and south Galway. It feeds on blackthorn and flies in August and September. Ravens nest on the crags above the hazel scrub and feral goats are sometimes visible as distinctive silhouettes against the skyline of Eagles Rock.

*Mullaghmore Mountain*

**Walk.**

For anyone with sturdy boots and strong ankles, a traverse of the pavement and hazel scrub to the foot of the crags will reveal, with a bit of searching, St MacDuach's Church and Well just beside a small, intermittent stream and a pleasant array of flowers around this well-chosen haven.

**Link** 6 miles/10 km.

We carry on northwards through the narrow cliff-lined valley to the crossroads at Cappaghmore and then continue straight on to join the Ballyvaghan–Kinvarra road just to the east of that village.

**Link** continuing from stop at Carran to Ballyvaghan 8 miles/13 km; or to Lisdoonvarna–Ballyvaghan road 8 miles/13 km.

The route continues across the limestone plateau, through the valley of the Meggagh depression (steep descent and ascent; cyclists beware!) to the crossroads. A right turn will take us past Caherconnell (Cathair Chonaill) to the left, Poulnabrone to the right and several other archaeological monuments on the way to Aillwee Cave and Ballyvaghan.

If, instead, we continue westwards, across the crossroads, the first right fork will bring us into the Kilcorney closed depression, narrow, cliff-bound and peaceful — a route for walkers and cyclists. In the west-facing cliff behind the 10th–11th century Kilcorney parish church is the Cave of the Wild Horses. One legend suggests that, when the depression flooded, a fairy herd of white horses came out of the cave. Many attempts were made to capture them and eventually one was caught and put to stud with the local mares to produce the famous strain of Clare horses. Another legend is referred to in the account of the Cliffs of Moher, see page 232.

Continuing for about 1 mile/1.6 km to the T-junction we turn right to join the Lisdoonvarna–Ballyvaghan road after about 2 miles/3 km.

**Link** from Killinaboy 2.5 miles/4 km.

It is a short distance from Killinaboy to Corrofin along the valley of the River Fergus to Lough Inchiquin.

**Stop** Lough Inchiquin (R273896), at the car park on the south shore of the lake.

Lough Inchiquin is a limestone lake with two wooded islands and is fringed at the east end with reeds. It is a popular trout angling water and is important locally for its wildfowl, particularly in winter. Large numbers of mute swans gather on the lough in spring while several pairs also breed, along with small numbers of tufted ducks, coots and moorhens. Cormorants clearly find it profitable to fly in from the coast to feed on the abundant fish in the lough. The River Fergus, which drains much of the south-east of the Burren through underground channels, flows into the northern arm of the lough and out again through a picturesque valley to the south.

Clifden Hill, overlooking the lough from the west, is an isolated outcrop of Namurian sandstone and shales and well wooded with planted sycamore, beech and many native species. It is a shame that the holiday cottages on the side of the hill look so stark and sterile by comparison. The road running across the face of the hill is a fine walking or cycling route which offers frequent aerial views of the lough and Mullaghmore in the background. Tourist cars would be an unwelcome intrusion on such a delightful byway.

**Link** 10 miles/16 km.

Our route goes north-east towards Gort, passing, on the right, the low-lying closed depression occupied by Lough Atedaun, Lough Cullaun, and the Ballyeighter Loughs. These are important loughs for wintering ducks such as wigeon, mallard, teal, tufted duck and small numbers of pintail, shoveler and pochard. Greenland white-fronted geese visit the lakes in winter as do mute, whooper and Bewick's swans.

Mullaghmore, with its dipping, saucer-like terraces, comes into view across the limestone plain to the left. This is the focal point of the recently established Burren National Park. Lough Bunny, with its flower-rich shore, is also an interesting bird haunt with a large colony of black-headed gulls nesting on an island close to the north-west shore.

About 2.5 miles/4 km further on, a left turn takes us past Kilmacduagh with its round tower, cathedral and associated remains and northwards past Garryland Wood National Nature Reserve on the right. Garryland Wood and the nearby Coole National Nature Reserve, with their combination of deciduous woods, limestone reefs, loughs and turloughs, constitute one of the most interesting Irish floral and faunal complexes still in existence.

About 1.5 miles/2.5 km to the north, in a deep hollow to the left, is Caherglassaun turlough. It is of particular interest because its level fluctuates with the tides in Galway Bay. Its waters discharge underground beneath the ruined castle on the west shore and appear again 3 miles/5 km distant on the shore beside Dunguaire Castle at Kinvarra. A rising tide in Galway Bay causes the freshwater to back up the underground passages and create a small but obvious rise in the level of the turlough.

A left turn at the next crossroads leads back to Kinvarra.

Coole Park can be reached by continuing north-eastwards from Lough Bunny to Gort and then taking the N18 northwards about 2 miles/3 km to the signposted entrance on the left. The quiet, woodland atmosphere is a welcome change from the windy openness of the Burren. The park is an attractive and fascinating mosaic of woodland, plantation, river, lake and turlough interspersed with historical monuments and recreation areas, well signposted and described in a Wildlife Service Nature Trail booklet which is available at the car park.

### Galway Bay — City Coast.

**Link** 8 miles/13 km.

We take the Galway road out of Ballyvaghan. The car park at Bishop's Quarter (M250193) makes an interesting intermediate stop. Across the bridge there is a sandy beach leading eastwards to eroding sand hills which merge into low boulder clay cliffs. In winter brent geese commute between this small bay and the muddy inlet to the west, and in summer common terns nest on the island at the western end of the promontory.

At Bealaclugga (Bell Harbour) the pier at the road junction makes an ideal viewing place for this shallow, very muddy bay which is a popular winter haunt for teal, shelduck, redshank, curlew and black-headed gulls.

A right turn takes us past Corcomroe Abbey, signposted to the left. It is of particular archaeological and historical interest, especially to the naturalist, because on the inner pillars of its presbytery and adjoining chapels there are depictions of several plant species carved during the period 1205–10. The seed pods of the opium poppy are fairly clear. Can you recognise any others? The Abbey also boasts a resident pair of kestrels and a noisy population of jackdaws.

A further left turn takes us 3 miles/5 km through extensive reclaimed pastures to the beginning of the 'green road' which skirts the northern slopes of Abbey Hill.

**Stop** Abbey Hill (M310102), at the end of the 'green road'.

Here we can stroll westwards along the 'green road' between the robust limestone walls. To the left the bare terraces, sculptured firstly by ice, then by water, form a giant staircase to the summit of Abbey Hill. Beside the track there are in springtime, primroses, gentians and the diminutive white flowers of the rue-leaved saxifrage which somehow finds a living on the shattered limestone.

To the right the sheltered terraces and patchy pastures lead our eyes down to the large, 'improved', coast-hugging pastures, then across the fast-flowing waters of Aughinish Bay to Deer Island with its cormorant colony, over open water to the low coastal fringe of Connemara hemmed in by the rolling, boggy, infertile granite hills, in turn overshadowed by the rugged quartzite peaks of the Maumturks and The Twelve Bens.

With the sun at our backs the ribbon of houses stretching from Galway westwards will sparkle a reminder of the impact of insensitive development on a sensitive environment. Sparkling, too, will be the boulder clay cliffs near Silver Strand, the last stop on the ecotour.

When the tide is low, the narrow, intertidal fringe of brown seaweeds forms a clear boundary between land and sea; but the common species, mentioned at the next stop, represent just a fraction of the 336 species of seaweed recorded in Galway Bay. No other area in Ireland displays such a diversity of seaweeds, which appears to be directly related to the wide range of habitats available and the moderate climate. The flora and fauna are particularly rich on the south shore of the bay which is washed by nutrient-enriched waters entering the bay from an upwelling south of Black Head.

**Walk.**

Abbey Hill offers a brief but challenging walk with spectacular panoramas, a colourful array of typical Burren flowers in summer and a bird's eye view of Corcomroe Abbey. The 'green road' continues for 2 miles/3 km around the flanks of Abbey Hill and provides easy walking and ever changing views of Galway Bay and the Burren.

**Link** 4.5 miles/7 km.

After a steep descent, we join the main road to Galway, pass the saltmarsh-fringed Corranroo Bay and enter the Burren lowlands of neat, stone-walled pastures, hazel scrub and turloughs.

**Stop** Kinvarra Pier (M373102), at the pier.

Nestled at the head of a shallow, sheltered bay, Kinvarra (or Kinvara as it is also spelt) is a popular destination for sailors, particularly those enthusiasts who sail traditional Galway Hookers — wooden boats with bulbous black hulls and brown sails.

Teal, wigeon, lapwing, redshank and black-headed gulls are the most common waterbirds wintering in the bay, though curlews and oyster-catchers are often seen lurking in the seaweeds, and an uncommon winter visitor to the region, the spotted redshank, has been seen occasionally near Dunguaire Castle. Swifts are notable summer visitors to the castle.

At low tide, carpets of brown seaweeds appear along the shoreline and, as elsewhere in Galway Bay, these include a number of common species which show typical zonation down the shore. At the top there is

the small, tufty, channel wrack followed in descending order (though not as strictly as might be assumed from the term zonation!) bladder wrack, knotted or egg wrack and serrated wrack with their associated species of periwinkles, dog whelks, barnacles and rock-hugging limpets. When the tide is low, patches of green alga become visible on the shore just to the west of Dunguaire Castle. These mark the 'Kinvarra Rising', the emergence from the the rocks of freshwater which has travelled underground from Caherglassaun Turlough about 3 miles/5 km to the south-east. Scurvy-grass and thrift, plants which can also be seen at the Cliffs of Moher, grow here along the shore just above the high-tide line.

**Link** 7.5 miles/12 km.

The road to Galway takes us past Lough Fingall through intensively grazed sheep country to the main Limerick–Galway road. After turning towards Galway, we take the second left turn, over the Dunkellin River, left again and follow the north shore of the estuary to the pleasant hamlet by the water.

**Stop** Moran's Oyster Cottage, The Weir (M407181). At car park.

Famous for its Clarinbridge oysters, Moran's is the natural place for us to consider the life of these most interesting and sought-after shellfish. Spawned in July, the oyster larvae, each no bigger than a pin head, drift with the tides for about three weeks until they are ready to settle and attach themselves permanently to a hard surface on the seabed. Of the one million or so larvae which a large female oyster can produce, perhaps only one will survive the five to seven years it takes to reach commercial size. Once oysters have spawned they change sex and, in exceptionally warm summers, can breed as both males and females!

In Galway Bay, oyster fishing takes place mainly in December and usually involves scraping the seabed with a special dredge hauled behind a small boat operated by one or two fishermen. Oysters occur in most suitable bays between Galway and Ballyvaghan and, though many

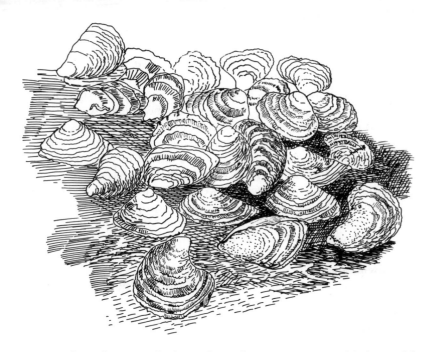

attempts have been made throughout this century to establish a viable oyster industry, the potential of Galway Bay for producing clean, high quality oysters has yet to be achieved.

In early summer, draft-net fishermen are busy setting and hauling their nets across the narrow estuary to catch salmon — more in hope than in certainty these days as salmon numbers decline, largely as a result of excessive drift-net fishing on the open sea.

There are long-standing plans to drain the Dunkellin catchment area in order to improve some of the marginal agricultural land upstream of the Weir. The proposed scheme is causing concern amongst oyster fishermen and naturalists because of its possible adverse effects on the oyster fishery and the wildlife of the area, especially at Rahasane Turlough which is a waterbird haunt of international importance and about 3.75 miles/6 km upstream from Moran's. Serious naturalists should visit Rahasane Turlough, particularly from September through to April when it is possible to see species such as Greenland white-fronted geese, whooper swans and Bewick's swans as well as ruffs on autumn passage (September) and black-tailed godwits on spring passage (April).

**Walk.**

As we walk downstream, past the grassy pier, the estuary passes between high banks of glacial drift eventually opening out into Dunbulcaun Bay where the Clarinbridge oysters grow.

**Link** 11.25 miles/18 km.

Retracing the route to the main road turn left and travel through Clarin-bridge and onwards to Oranmore. Turning left at the first roundabout and right at the edge of the village, we come face to face with Oranmore Bay. This shallow, island-studded bay is important for wildlife, particularly in the winter, but the thundering traffic on an increasingly busy road generates little enthusiasm to stop and stare. In quieter moments a wide range of ducks and waders can be seen quite close to the road and common seals are usually visible in profile, hauled out on the seaweed-topped islets.

We turn left at the first roundabout in Galway City and take the first left fork along the northern shore of Lough Atalia where Galway Corporation has recently provided two lay-bys and erected a colourful bird sign near the railway bridge — facilities greatly appreciated by local birdwatchers. Red-breasted mergansers occur throughout the year and great-crested grebes, little grebes and scaup, the latter being uncommon birds in the region, are the main attractions here in winter.

Following the water's edge around the docks and across the Wolfe Tone Bridge to the western side of the Claddagh and on to Nimmo's Pier, we pass through the historic centre of Galway.

**Stop** Nimmo's Pier (M300248), at the entrance to the pier.

It is heartening to find in Galway City a place such as Nimmo's Pier where we can get close to the wildlife — and in the middle of winter view up to 20 species of waterbirds. The mud, sand and shingle around the pier are important haunts for oystercatchers, redshanks, dunlin, bar-tailed godwits and turnstones. They can be seen in spring catching elvers (young eels) as these start their ascent of the River Corrib. Common seals and otters also take advantage of the fish shoals passing up and down the river.

Gulls are common throughout the year, especially black-headed ones which feed at the effluent discharge points around the dock area. Un-common gull species can be seen here fairly regularly and these include little, ring-billed, Iceland, glaucous and, on several occasions in recent years, a single Ross's gull.

Cormorants feed in the estuary and roost on the rocks to the east where ranks of herons also perch between meals; but the major ornitho-logical spectacle here is the build up of the mute swan flock from a low in December to a pre-moulting peak of up to 300 in early August.

A new sewage treatment plant to be located on Mutton Island will remove a large proportion of the nutrients which currently fertilise the waters around Nimmo's Pier, and it remains to be seen how the loss of this rich source of 'food' will affect the birdlife.

**Link** 3.75 miles/6 km.

The road continues westwards along the shore, through Salthill, joining the Spiddle road at 'Knocknacarra Cross'. After 2.5 miles/4 km we turn left to Silver Strand.

**Stop** Silver Strand (M254230), at car park by the beach.

At low tide this aptly named expanse of ripple-marked sand forms a sparkling gap in the narrow brown border of seaweed-covered boulders which are so typical of the north Galway Bay shore. To the east, across a natural barrier of large boulders, the sand gives way to a hard wave-cut platform of boulder clay (also called drift or till) strewn with rounded, water-worn boulders. Here there once stood a drumlin, the remains of which forms the overshadowing cliff. This is composed of a matrix of rock flour and often angular rocks of pink, white and black granite, fossil-bearing limestone and many other colourful rocks which were picked up and later deposited by an ancient glacier. The cliff is still being naturally eroded so we should heed the warning signs and beware of falling rocks!

To the west of Silver Strand, the observant beachcomber will find thin layers of peat amongst the boulders on the upper shore. These date back about 4,000 years to a time when Galway Bay was much lower than it is today.

To the north of the car park, just across the wall, is Loc Ruisin (or Lough Rusheen), a shallow lagoon connected to the sea by a narrow channel to the east of the boulder clay cliff. At low tide the lagoon provides shelter and rich feeding for a variety of waterbirds, especially during the autumn and winter. Teal, wigeon, and red-breasted mergansers are amongst the ducks which can be seen regularly in the winter, while oystercatchers, ringed plover, curlew, bar-tailed godwits, redshank and dunlin are common for all but the summer months. The greenshank, a fairly uncommon visitor to Ireland, occurs regularly in flocks of up to 24 when on southward passage from July through to October. In August, Loc Ruisin is used as a roost by large parties of sandwich terns as they too move southwards to their wintering grounds. Herons nest in the wood on the west side of Loc Ruisin. The birds using Loc Ruisin are protected by a No Shooting order but neither they nor this important habitat have any legal protection against the increasing agricultural, urban and recreational activities in the area.

**Walk.**

On the opposite side of the main road is Barna Beechwood, an amenity recently developed by Galway Corporation, and a welcome contrast to the seashore habitats which we have been visiting around Galway Bay. Pleasant, easy-going walks are laid out amongst the trees.

# GLOSSARY OF FLORA AND FAUNA

**ANIMALS**

| | |
|---|---|
| Badger | *Meles meles* |
| Barnacle | *Chthamalus stellatus* |
| Barnacle goose | *Branta leucopsis* |
| Bar-tailed godwit | *Limosa lapponica* |
| Beadlet anemone | *Actinia equina* |
| Bewick's swan | *Cygnus columbianus* |
| Blackbird | *Turdus merula* |
| Black guillemot | *Cepphus grylle* |
| Black-headed gull | *Larus ridibundus* |
| Black-tailed godwit | *Limosa limosa* |
| Bream | *Abramis brama* |
| Brent goose | *Branta bernicla hrota* |
| Brown hairstreak | *Thecla betulae* |
| Brown trout | *Salmo trutta* |
| Charr | *Salvelinus alpinus* |
| Chough | *Pyrrhocorax pyrrhocorax* |
| Common dolphin | *Delphinus delphis* |
| Common frog | *Rana temporaria* |
| Common gull | *Larus canus* |
| Common limpet | *Patella vulgata* |
| Common mussel | *Mytilus edulis* |
| Common rat | *Rattus norvegicus* |
| Common seal | *Phoca vitulina* |
| Common tern | *Sterna hirundo* |
| Coot | *Fulica atra* |
| Cormorant | *Phalacrocorax carbo* |
| Corn bunting | *Miliaria calandra* |
| Corncrake | *Crex crex* |
| Cuckoo | *Cuculus canorus* |
| Curlew | *Numenius arquata* |
| Dipper | *Cinclus cinclus hibernicus* |
| Dog whelk | *Nucella lapillus* |
| Dublin Bay prawn | *Nephrops norvegicus* |
| Dunlin | *Calidris alpina* |
| Dunnock | *Prunella modularis* |
| Edible periwinkle | *Littorina littorea* |

256

| | |
|---|---|
| Eel | *Anguilla anguilla* |
| Feral goat | *Capra hircus* |
| Field mouse | *Apodemus sylvaticus* |
| Fox | *Vulpes vulpes* |
| Freshwater limpet | *Ancylus fluviatilis* |
| Fulmar | *Fulmarus glacialis* |
| Gannet | *Morus bassanus (Sula bassana)* |
| Glaucous gull | *Larus hyperboreus* |
| Golden plover | *Pluvialis apricaria* |
| Grasshopper warbler | *Locustella naevia* |
| Grayling | *Hipparchia semele* |
| Great black-backed gull | *Larus marinus* |
| Great crested grebe | *Podiceps cristatus* |
| Great northern diver | *Gavia immer* |
| Greenland white-fronted goose | *Anser albifrons flavirostris* |
| Greenshank | *Tringa nebularia* |
| Grey wagtail | *Motacilla cinerea* |
| Guillemot | *Uria aalge* |
| Harbour porpoise | *Phocoena phocoena* |
| Hen harrier | *Circus cyaneus* |
| Heron | *Ardea cinerea* |
| Herring | *Clupea harengus* |
| Hooded crow | *Corvus corone cornix* |
| House martin | *Delichon urbica* |
| House mouse | *Mus musculus* |
| Iceland gull | *Larus glaucoides* |
| Irish hare | *Lepus timidus hibernicus* |
| Jackdaw | *Corvus monedula* |
| June chafer | *Phyllopertha horticola* |
| Kestrel | *Falco tinnunculus* |
| Kingfisher | *Alcedo atthis* |
| Kittiwake | *Rissa tridactyla* |
| Kumlien's gull | *Larus glaucoides Kumlieni* |
| Lapwing | *Vanellus vanellus* |
| Lesser black-backed gull | *Larus fuscus* |
| Limpet | *Patella vulgata* |
| Little grebe | *Tachybaptus ruficollis* |
| Little gull | *Larus minutus* |
| Little tern | *Sterna albifrons* |
| Mackerel | *Scomber scombrus* |
| Mallard | *Anas platyrhynchos* |
| Manx shearwater | *Puffinus puffinus* |
| Meadow brown | *Maniola jurtina* |
| Meadow pipit | *Anthus pratensis* |
| Merlin | *Falco columbarius* |
| Minnow | *Phoxinus phoxinus* |
| Moorhen | *Gallinula chloropus* |
| Orange tip | *Anthocaris cardamines* |
| Otter | *Lutra lutra* |
| Oyster | *Ostrea edulis* |
| Oystercatcher | *Haematopus ostralegus* |
| Peacock butterfly | *Inachis io* |
| Pearl-bordered fritillary | *Clossiana (Boloria) euphrosyne* |
| Perch | *Perca fluviatilis* |
| Peregrine | *Falco peregrinus* |

| | |
|---|---|
| Pike | *Esox lucius* |
| Pine marten | *Martes martes* |
| Pintail | *Anas acuta* |
| Pochard | *Aythya ferina* |
| Puffin | *Fratercula arctica* |
| Purple sandpiper | *Calidris maritima* |
| Pygmy shrew | *Sorex minutus* |
| Rabbit | *Oryctolagus cuniculus* |
| Raven | *Corvus corax* |
| Razorbill | *Alca torda* |
| Red-breasted merganser | *Mergus serrator* |
| Red deer | *Cervus elaphus* |
| Red grouse | *Lagopus lagopus* |
| Redshank | *Tringa totanus* |
| Red squirrel | *Sciurus vulgaris* |
| Ring-billed gull | *Larus delawarensis* |
| Ringed plover | *Charadrius hiaticula* |
| Ringlet | *Aphantopus hyperantus* |
| Roach | *Rutilus rutilus* |
| Robin | *Erithacus rubecula* |
| Rock dove | *Columbia livia* |
| Rock pipit | *Anthus spinoletta* |
| Rook | *Corvus frugilegus* |
| Ross's gull | *Rhodostethia rosea* |
| Rudd | *Scardinius erythrophthalmus* |
| Ruff | *Philomachus pugnax* |
| Salmon | *Salmo salar* |
| Sanderling | *Calidris alba* |
| Sand martin | *Riparia riparia* |
| Sandwich tern | *Sterna sandvicensis* |
| Sea lamprey | *Petromyzon marinus* |
| Sea trout | *Salmo trutta* |
| Scallop | *Pecten maximus* |
| Scaup | *Aythya marila* |
| Shag | *Phalacrocorax aristotelis* |
| Shelduck | *Tadorna tadorna* |
| Shore crab | *Carcinus maenus* |
| Shoveler | *Anas clypeata* |
| Skylark | *Alauda arvensis* |
| Small blue | *Cupido minimus* |
| Small heath | *Coenonympha pamphilus* |
| Small periwinkle | *Littorina neritoides* |
| Snipe | *Gallinago gallinago* |
| Snow bunting | *Plectrophenax nivalis* |
| Sooty shearwater | *Puffinus griseus* |
| Speckled wood | *Parage aegeria* |
| Spotted redshank | *Tringa erythropus* |
| Stoat | *Mustela erminea hibernica* |
| Stonechat | *Saxicola torquata* |
| Storm petrel | *Hydrobates pelagicus* |
| Teal | *Anas crecca* |
| Thayer's gull | *Larus thayeri* |
| Tree sparrow | *Passer montanus* |
| Tufted duck | *Aythya fuligula* |
| Turnstone | *Arenaria interpres* |

| | |
|---|---|
| Viviparous lizard | *Lacerta vivipara* |
| Water rail | *Rallus aquaticus* |
| Wheatear | *Oenanthe oenanthe* |
| Whimbrel | *Numenius phaeopus* |
| Whitethroat | *Sylvia communis* |
| Whooper swan | *Cygnus cygnus* |
| Wigeon | *Anas penelope* |
| Woodcock | *Scolopax rusticola* |
| Woodpigeon | *Columba palumbus* |
| Wren | *Troglodytes troglodytes* |
| Yellowhammer | *Emberiza citrinella* |

**PLANTS**

| | |
|---|---|
| Alder | *Alnus glutinosa* |
| Beech | *Fagus sylvatica* |
| Bell-heather | *Erica cinerea* |
| Bird's foot trefoil | *Lotus corniculatus* |
| Bladder wrack | *Fucus vesiculosus* |
| Bloody cranesbill | *Geranium sanguineum* |
| Bog asphodel | *Narthecium ossifragum* |
| Bog bean | *Menyanthes trifoliata* |
| Bog cotton | *Eriophorum spp.* |
| Bog pimpernel | *Anagallis tenella* |
| Bulrush | *Schoenoplectus lacustris* |
| Burnet rose | *Rose pimpinellifolia* |
| Cat's foot | *Antennaria dioica* |
| Channel wrack | *Pelvetia canaliculata* |
| Common butterwort | *Pinguicula vulgaris* |
| Cross-leaved heath | *Erica tetralix* |
| Cuckoo flower (Lady's smock) | *Cardamine pratensis* |
| Cuckoo Pint (Lords and Ladies) | *Arum maculatum* |
| Early purple orchid | *Orchis mascula* |
| Fragrant orchid | *Gymnadenia conopsea* |
| Fuchsia | *Fuchsia magellanica* |
| Gorse (furze or whin) | *Ulex europaeus* |
| Harebell | *Campanula rotundifolia* |
| Hart's-tongue fern | *Asplenium scolopendrium* |
| Hawthorn | *Crataegus monogyna* |
| Hazel | *Corylus avellana* |
| Heather/Ling | *Calluna vulgaris* |
| Holly | *Ilex aquifolium* |
| Horse-chestnut | *Aesculus hippocastanum* |
| Irish saxifrage | *Saxifraga rosacea* |
| Knotted pearlwort | *Sagina nodosa* |
| Knotted wrack | *Ascophyllum nodosum* |
| Lousewort | *Pedicularis sylvatica* |
| Maidenhair fern | *Adiantum capillus-veneris* |
| Marram grass | *Ammophila arenaria* |
| Milkwort | *Polygala vulgaris* |
| Mossy saxifrage | *Saxifraga hypnoides* |
| Mountain avens | *Dryas octopetala* |
| Opium poppy | *Papaver somniferum* |
| Pignut | *Conopodium majus* |
| Pipewort | *Eriocaulon aquaticum* |
| Pondweed | *Potamogeton spp.* |

| | |
|---|---|
| Portland spurge | *Euphorbia portlandica* |
| Primrose | *Primula vulgaris* |
| Purple moor grass | *Molinia caerulea* |
| Reed | *Phragmites australis* |
| Reedmace | *Typha latifolia* |
| Roseroot | *Sedum rosea* |
| Rhododendron | *Rhododendron ponticum* |
| Rue-leaved saxifrage | *Saxifraga tridactylites* |
| Rush | *Schoenoplectus lacustris* |
| Scots pine | *Pinus sylvestris* |
| Scurvy-grass | *Cochlearia officinalis* |
| Sea campion | *Silene vulgaris maritima* |
| Sea holly | *Eryngium maritimum* |
| Sea milkwort | *Glaux maritima* |
| Sea pink (thrift) | *Armeria maritima* |
| Sea sandwort | *Honkenya peploides* |
| Sea spurge | *Euphorbia paralias* |
| Serrated wrack | *Fucus serratus* |
| Sessile oak | *Quercus petraea* |
| Spring gentian | *Gentiana verna* |
| St Dabeoc's heath | *Daboecia cantabrica* |
| St Patrick's cabbage | *Saxifraga spathularis* |
| Storksbill | *Erodium cicutarium* |
| Sundew | *Drosera spp.* |
| Thyme | *Thymus praecox* |
| Tormentil | *Potentilla erecta* |
| Vernal sandwort | *Minuartia verna* |
| Water lobelia | *Lobelia dortmanna* |
| Western gorse | *Ulex gallii* |
| White-beaked sedge | *Rhynchospora alba* |
| Willow | *Salix spp.* |

# GEOLOGICAL TIME SCALE

| ERA | PERIOD | EPOCH | AGES (millions of years before present) |
|---|---|---|---|
| CENOZOIC | QUATERNARY | Holocene | 0.01 |
| | | Pleistocene | 2 |
| | TERTIARY | Pliocene | 13 |
| | | Miocene | 25 |
| | | Oligocene | 36 |
| | | Eocene | 58 |
| | | Palaeocene | 70 |
| MESOZOIC | CRETACEOUS | | 135 |
| | JURASSIC | | 180 |
| | TRIASSIC | | 225 |
| PALAEOZOIC | PERMIAN | | 270 |
| | CARBONIFEROUS | | 350 |
| | DEVONIAN | | 400 |
| | SILURIAN | | 430 |
| | ORDOVICIAN | | 500 |
| | CAMBRIAN | | 600 |
| PRECAMBRIAN | | | |

# SUGGESTIONS FOR FUTURE EDITIONS

We have tried to provide visitors to the region with the most comprehensive possible information. Inevitably, we have left gaps and we would welcome any suggestions or comments that readers may have. It was only when we began to gather the vast amount of information required for the book that we realised the inevitability of errors, omissions and inaccuracies. We hope that there are relatively few but, in the nature of things, some will undoubtedly exist.

Readers who wish to offer comments and suggestions should do so addressed to:
>   The Authors
>   Insider's Guide to Connemara, Galway and the Burren
>   c/o Editorial Department
>   Gill and Macmillan
>   Goldenbridge
>   Inchicore
>   Dublin 8

# INDEX